Believe Me

STORIES ABOUT MENTAL HEALTH & ADDICTION

IMAGINED · LIVED · ANALYZED

Believe Me

STORIES ABOUT MENTAL HEALTH & ADDICTION
IMAGINED · LIVED · ANALYZED

Isabella Mori

THREE OCEAN PRESS

Library and Archives Canada Cataloguing in Publication

Title: Believe me : stories about mental health & addiction : imagined, lived, analyzed / Isabella Mori, M. Ed.
Names: Mori, Isabella, 1955- author
Description: Includes bibliographical references.
Identifiers: Canadiana (print) 20250161346 | Canadiana (ebook) 20250161737 | ISBN 9781988915548 (softcover) | ISBN 9781988915555 (EPUB)
Subjects: LCSH: Mentally ill. | LCSH: Psychotherapy patients. | LCSH: Mental illness. | LCSH: Mental health. | LCSH: Patients' writings.
Classification: LCC RA790.5 .M67 2025 | DDC 616.89—dc23

"Noodle Oracle" was first published in *isabella mori's teatable book* (Alphaglyph Publications, 2006).
An earlier version of "Purgatory" was published in *Signs of Life* (2021).
"When the Doorbell Rings" was first published in *Prachya Review* (2019).
"Bicycle Creatures" was first published in *English Bay Review* (2020).

Editor: Kyle Hawke
Proofreader: Carol Hamshaw
Book Designers: PJ Perdue & Kyle Hawke
Cover Designer: PJ Perdue
Author Photo: Caroline Low

Three Ocean Press
Vancouver, BC
778.321.0636
info@threeoceanpress.com
www.threeoceanpress.com

First publication, April 2025

Praise for *Believe Me*

Isabella Mori has written a rare, deeply human, and well-researched book. They do a masterful job of integrating the language of both art and science, including the latest psychological science on various mental health problems. Mori compassionately takes the reader through individual stories of human suffering and healing. Their personal and professional experience with mental health offers a realistic hope for better understanding and mitigating the impact of mental health problems. *Believe Me* is a must read for all persons, including mental health practitioners, as no one is immune to sufferings of the mind.

INGRID SÖCHTING, PhD
Clinical Psychologist and Clinical Professor, Department of Psychiatry,
University of British Columbia

The author and story-evoker has created a unique piece of writing that leads with the individuals' experience through their own voice, then brings in research and integrates the two. Magnificent! Every chapter is a page turner. A unique approach and refreshing read, at times personally evoking many feelings, given my own life experiences.

PAUL W. GALLANT, CHE
Strategic Consultant, BC Centre for Disease Control, retired

Combining creative writing, interviews of people with lived experience and thorough research, Isabella Mori's *Believe Me* is an illuminating examination of the intricacies of mental illness and substance use. With powerful quotes from interviewees ("I want to be so full of hope that there is no room for doubt"), this is a decidedly welcome addition to the array of books exploring the facets of mental illness and substance use.

VICTORIA MAXWELL
Mental Health Speaker, Performer, and Strategic Advisor
for British Columbia Mental Health and Substance Use Services

As a therapist with many years' experience, and as an established writer and poet, Isabella Mori is perfectly placed to write about poetry, prose, and science.

Each chapter of this book begins with a piece of their own writing, followed by an interview with a reader's interpretation of the poem/prose, then concludes with research which links to the complex mental health themes that emerge.

Despite the darkness of many of the topics — depression, suicidality, addiction, stigma, intimate partner violence — Mori's light and tender touch is felt on each page, linking the authentic and subjective 'true self' with the relative objectivity of research and flowing seamlessly from one realm to the next.

This is only made possible by the author's skillful use of metaphor, together with her own erudite scope of knowledge (Latin etymology, Virgil, Perceval, Bateson, and Alice Cooper all make an appearance) enabling the language of autobiography, poetry, myth, and metaphor to intricately intertwine with the firm and clear language of science throughout the book.

This book will be of interest to anyone with an interest in mental health and personal and relational narratives.

"The deeper we go, the more we learn" and readers who delve into this magical book will emerge from it wiser and more reflective.

DR. ANNIE HICKOX
Clinical Psychologist/Clinical Neuropsychologist
dranniehickox.co.uk

A personal reflection on *Believe Me*

I identified with so much of what what is discussed in this book. My daughter experienced obesity, alcoholism, and rape. The section that talks about how best to communicate and motivate without judgement was a comforting checklist to refer to. This quote describes part of what I struggled with and was a powerful reminder there's always hope: "Stressed relationships make communication difficult for families. The solution that offers itself so easily is to fix things. However, that rarely works — negativity abounds, wounds deepen, connections become more and more frayed."

G.M.
(full name withheld to protect anonymity)

*This book is dedicated
to the millions of
people all over the
world who live with
a mental health
challenge or addiction.
May your suffering
subside, and may you
live with ease.*

Acknowledgements

With much gratitude, I want to acknowledge all the people with lived experience of mental illness or addiction who made this book possible: The contributors who generously gave of their time and experience for the interviews and the thousands who were participants in the studies quoted here. Without them, this book and the hundreds of studies mentioned would not have happened.

Many thanks go to the Historic Joy Kogawa House. The two-month residency in this beautiful place, imbued with famed Canadian writer Joy Kogawa's spirit and that of so many writers before, gave me just the right framework for a thorough edit of *Believe Me*.

Much of the inspiration for this book came from the Family Support and Involvement Team at Vancouver Coastal Health's Mental Health and Substance Use Services, where I worked for over ten years. Co-editing and contributing to our newsletter *Family Connections* (originally the brainchild of Jessica Wilkins) helped me flex my muscles for this project.

Another person who inspired me was Curtis Neil, to whom I had somewhat casually mentioned the idea for this book and who replied, "If you've been thinking about this for a while, it means you should do it!"

My beta readers, all of them writers, were extremely helpful. Jennifer Ashton, Karen Poirier, Margo Lamont, and Stella Harvey were always there to support and inspire me and to read many a confusing draft.

A thousand thanks go to Kyle Hawke, editor and publisher. I am so grateful for his insight, wisdom, and skill.

I'm not sure that this project would have gotten legs without Simon Fraser University's The Writer's Studio, whose influence continues to far exceed the ten-month course I took there.

I also think of the many researchers whose studies I quote; I know the majority of them get paid very little for the important work they do. Thank you for your tireless dedication.

Last, but absolutely not least, I want to thank my daughters Mindemoya and Tova, who along with my husband Glenn, offered enthusiastic and absolutely indispensable support and advice for my writing endeavours. I appreciate you so much!

CONTENTS

Chapter 11

INTRODUCTION

believe that i
cry
believe that i
lie
in my tears and
cannot swim.

believe that
while you can't believe the
pain.

believe that i bleed
believe me
mother
believe me
i beg you on my knees that
kneel here on the ground
with no skin left
no meat
just bare bones and
blood

This is the beginning of the poem at the start of Chapter 2. What do you feel and think as you read this poem? Does it remind you of something or someone? How common are the sentiments expressed in the poem? What would a psychologist think of it?

These questions help illustrate the process followed in this book, combining short stories or poems with interviews and research on the topics of mental health and addiction.[1] The process started with presenting a person with a short story or poem I had written (a 'text'). If the person resonated with the

1   By 'mental health', I refer to the wider area of mental health, not only mental illness. Clearly, issues such as autism and loneliness are not illnesses, but they have an impact on a person's mental health. The term 'addiction' is not used much in clinical circles these days, mostly because it often carries stigmatizing connotations. However, it is still the most widely used umbrella term for a wide variety of dependencies, which is why I often use this term interchangeably with 'substance use'.

text, I interviewed them about their impressions and reactions to it. Did the text tell a story that made sense? Is it grounded not just in my experience and imagination but also in theirs? In each interview, some themes emerged. The interviewee and I agreed on a central theme, after which I looked at and summarized some of the research on that theme and pointed out any similarities with the text and the interview.

Three Points of View

Poetry and stories, interviews, research — each point of view contributes significantly to understanding the human condition in general and, as illustrated in this book, experiences such as depression, domestic violence, or addiction. Writers from Plato to Shakespeare to Murakami have explored and explained the human psyche; through drama, poetry, and storytelling, they penetrate into layers of understanding that may be hard to reach in entirely rational ways.

Research, on the other hand, is a precision tool that helps understanding on a different level: What precisely is meant by a particular experience such as, say, depression? What are the facts? How do these facts relate to each other?

Most importantly, experiences are located in individuals. The term 'depression' may be a construct used abstractly by researchers, but it is a real phenomenon in a person's life. This is what I investigated in the interviews. I was curious whether the poems and stories struck a chord, one that connected to that flesh-blood-heart experience.

An Example

As an example, "Believe Me" is a poem, or text, about someone begging their mother to hear and believe that they are in pain. A participant read the poem, saying she resonated with it. Subsequently, I interviewed her about her impressions, memories, reactions, etc. Eventually, we agreed that I would look into something that came up for her during the interview — how her difficult upbringing made sibling and other relationships extremely challenging for her, even after many decades. I then delved into the research on that topic and summarized it. In the end, these three parts make up a chapter in the book: the text, the interview, and the summary of the research on the agreed-on topic. Each chapter can be imagined as a Venn diagram like the one below, using Chapter 1 on sibling relationships as an example. Each part of the chapter has a number of themes; some overlap, some don't.

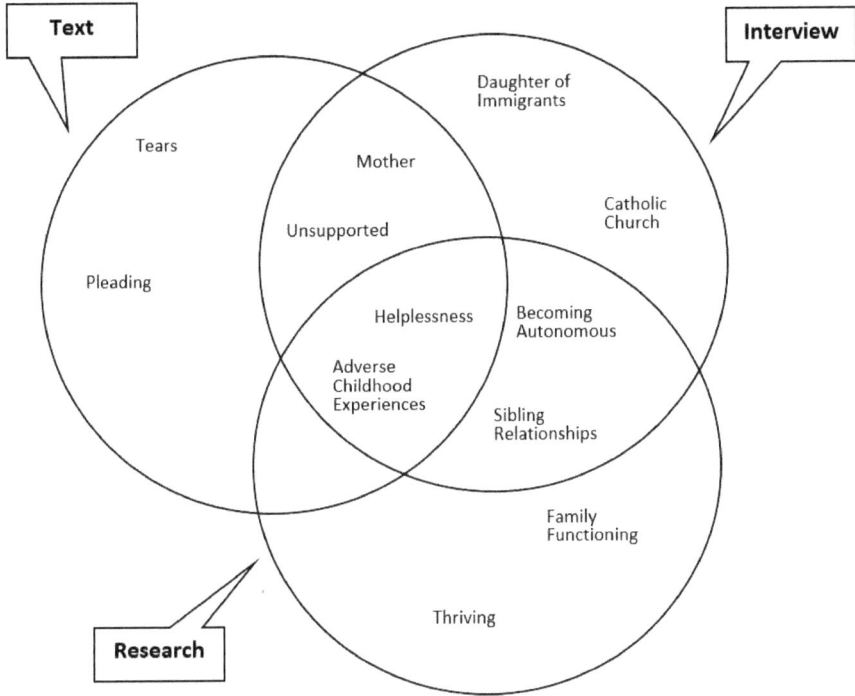

Text

Interview

Daughter of Immigrants

Tears

Mother

Catholic Church

Unsupported

Pleading

Helplessness

Becoming Autonomous

Adverse Childhood Experiences

Sibling Relationships

Family Functioning

Thriving

Research

The Stories and Poems

The texts are part of a portfolio of writing that spans the several decades I have spent writing in English (born in Munich, I first started writing in German, then in Spanish when I lived in South America). They were not written with the view of illustrating a certain theme like, for example, the domestic violence portrayed in Chapter 9. Rather, as for many writers, the text sprang spontaneously from that mysterious well of creativity that is fed by a myriad of sources: personal history, glimpses of observations, falling in love with a specific word, a vague need to deal with hurt, joy, confusion…

I wanted to take that approach because it is the one that most mirrors the kind of literature and poetry that helps us understand the human condition, from Dostoevsky working through his personal experience with addiction in *The Gambler* to Mary Oliver shining light on what war does to soldiers in "Death at Wind River" to Alice Walker exploring the vagaries of relationships both racial and personal in *The Temple of My Familiar*. None of them set out to lecture on these topics; they just sat down and wrote what they needed to write.

A commentary on each text can be found in the Appendix.

The Interviews

A fascinating part of this project was to see what aspects of the text interviewees were interested in and where else they wanted to go. I would have never guessed that someone would talk about sibling relationships after reading the poem "Believe Me." Others stuck very close to the text's theme (for example, Chapter 8, on loneliness). One person disagreed with the premise of the text (Chapter 7, on yoga and substance use).

Eight of the question-and-answer style interviews were done over the telephone; three were conducted in person. The interviews are reproduced as verbatim as possible while ensuring a smooth reading experience. They were all vetted by the interviewee before I used them. All interviewees signed a waiver that discussed matters such as consent, confidentiality, etc.

I let interviewees meander as much as they liked as long as they stuck generally with the text; that way, I hoped to get their most genuine reaction. Even though I am a counsellor by trade and the topics touch on sensitive issues, the participants and I agreed that the interviews were not counselling sessions. Having said that, I made every effort to leave the participant — and the reader — in a positive and hopeful frame of mind; these are heavy topics. None of the interviewees were past or present clients. In selecting interviewees, it was very important to me to find those who would find the experience affirming and illuminating; I consciously did not choose individuals who I thought could be retraumatized.

The Research

"What's really going on here? Why? How? Show me proof!" That attitude has been with me since I can remember. It complements the mysteriousness out of which grow stories and poems. Some would say it is the opposite, but I like what theologian Michael Dowd offers about 'night' and 'day' language (perhaps harking back to Ursula K. Le Guin's essay "The Child and the Shadow"). "Night language is the realm of poetry, myth, symbol, metaphor and traditional religious language. It's the language that inspires; it touches the heart, moves the soul, brings us to tears and calls us to awe." Day language, on the other hand, is the language of science, of what can be measured, what we can agree on as reality. Just like we need night and day, we need those two languages.

The authors whose work I quote are people trained in the day language of the sciences, most of them psychologists, but also nurse researchers, epidemiologists, psychiatrists, neuroscientists, sociologists, and the like. Paraphrasing philosopher of science Edwin Hung, science has two aims: to search for truth and to find explanations. In the search for truth, scientists generate hypotheses and theories, such as sociologist Robert Weiss's theory of loneliness (Chapter 8). Evaluating and justifying hypotheses constitutes the bulk of scientific work and accounts for many of the articles quoted in this book.

The systematic discovery, collection, and interpretation of facts is another task of science. Interviews done by the authors of the research articles are part of that, and the reader will find many examples of them here, for instance in the moving words of a nursing student describing her experience of sitting with a woman who had just birthed a stillborn baby (Chapter 4). The interviews offered by the authors of the research articles also represent a coming together of all three aspects of this book: they are real-life examples gathered by a researcher and are often spoken in the type of night language that we find in the stories and poems.

As to the quality of the research papers, I took pains to ensure that most of them adhered to certain standards of quality. In some areas, there was very little research, so I took what I could find in the academic literature. In some cases, as for example with the harm reduction approach to supporting families of people who use drugs proposed by Patt Denning (Chapter 10), the paper was not a research paper in a strict sense but was highly relevant and its content very loosely based on a more systematic approach. It was also cited over fifty times, which gave me some comfort. How often an article is cited can be a measure of quality, but that is not always the case. For example, more recent articles or master's and PhD theses may very well be of high quality but don't typically have many citations.

The number of citations could be interpreted as a form of after-the-fact peer review; in-depth reviews and critique by other researchers well-versed in the topic at hand before publication is, of course, much more important. Other indications of at least some reliability of the findings include a large number of research participants (or 'subjects' as they used to be called), a good theoretical base of the study, measurements that are adequate for the research question, a good connection between the research question and the conclusions, a robust section on the limitations of the research, a cautious interpretation of the results, etc. There are, in fact, methods for evaluating the quality of a research article, such as the *Cochrane Reviews* in healthcare, but I did not use such a method. The research articles chosen should be taken as a careful but discretionary selection of what has been written on any given topic. Systematic reviews collate and evaluate numerous research articles on a specific topic, often combing through thousands of available references. I did try to reference systematic reviews, meta-analyses, and the like wherever possible.

Finally, it's important to point out that much research looks at trends, not at individual cases or absolute truths. In the social sciences, research results are typically so varied that even weak trends are interpreted as meaningful.

The following image (a "scatterplot") is an illustration of the (imaginary) relationship between a person's income and how much pocket change they carry around. The greater the income, the smaller the amount of change, and/or the other way round: this type of statistics — a correlation — does not explain what causes what. Looking at the image, Jo and Eve have a strong correlation between the two variables. (If there was a perfect correlation, the line would be at a 45-degree angle and all the points would lie exactly on one straight diagonal line.) But what about Vic and Ed, who are at the same income level but Ed carries more change, or MJ and Raj, who carry a similar amount of change but are at a different income level? Therefore, we can only talk about a trend in terms of a relationship between income and change carried on a person.

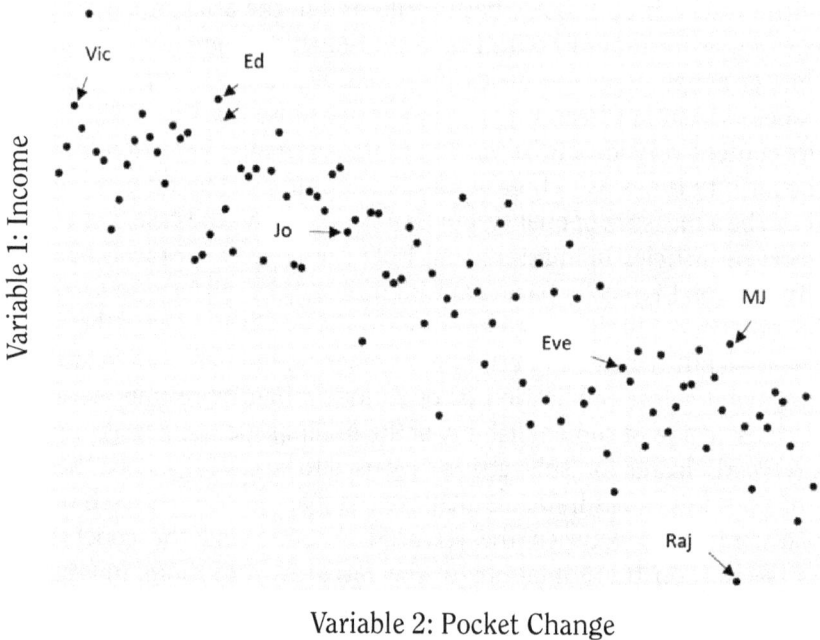

Variable 2: Pocket Change

IMAGE SOURCE: https://commons.wikimedia.org/wiki/File:Ggplot2_scatter_plot.svg
(with modifications made to the x and y axis, and names inserted)

An Origin Story

How did this all come about? Some years ago, in the process of deciding whether and, if so, where I should do my PhD, I realized a number of things. One was that I would not be a good candidate for a regular psychology PhD;

I have spent too many decades thinking outside the box. This made me turn to interdisciplinary studies and also helped me realize how much I enjoyed mixing genres. I wrote my second book, *A bagful of haiku: 87 imperfections*, which just like my first, mixed poetry with prose, but this time with a more scholarly bent, examining some of the history of haiku; I found that thoroughly enjoyable. The idea germinated that if I were to do my PhD, I would like to do it in narrative psychiatry, another genre-bender.

Narrative psychiatry is a branch of narrative medicine. Narrative medicine "fortifies clinical practice with the narrative competence to recognize, absorb, metabolize, interpret, and be moved by the stories of illness," says Rita Charon, one of the founders of narrative medicine.

One part of narrative medicine is reflective and creative writing. Charon states that narrative medicine is based on the principles of attention, representation, and affiliation. This intrigued me. As a counsellor, I pay attention. As a writer, I represent. As someone deeply committed to equality and equity, I try my best to affiliate — ally — with the person with lived experience of mental health or addiction. And as someone with a strong belief in science, I affiliate with research.

In the end, I did not study narrative psychiatry, but was inspired by it. I began to home in on the project before you when I decided to focus on writing instead of working on a PhD and got a certificate in Creative Writing from Simon Fraser University's The Writer's Studio.

But we could go back further than that. Growing up in post-Nazi, post-Holocaust Germany, I was raised in an artistic family that was a difficult, beautiful, and chaotic jumble of literature, poverty, art, disability, philosophy, sexual liberation, theology, music — the list goes on. My father, a painter, had bipolar disorder, and used every substance imaginable. He was also a wise, caring, and generous man with a highly disciplined intellect and very, very funny. His friends were fellow artists, bohemians, and of course, people who thoroughly enjoyed alcohol and drugs. (It was often my job to go out and buy wine and spirits on tab, as young as nine years old.) Enough of our friends and family died by suicide for me to think for the longest time that that was quite a normal way for a person's life to end. It was my mother's job to hold it all together. A genius painter husband who was rarely healthy enough to earn any money or otherwise contribute to the household, my mother's own stressful life, my deaf sister, our enormous old apartment, and somewhere, there was me.

And while I was fascinated by my father applying gold leaf to his paintings or collecting broken watches (because "I can always use it in a collage") and admired my mother spending many of her evenings in beautiful textile art, I was drawn to the word. My first 'job' at six years old was typing up envelopes for one of my father's gallery openings. What did I do with the money? I bought a fountain pen. At nine, a friend and I decided to publish a handwritten newsletter for school; at eleven, I tried my hand at a romance novel, on an ancient 1930s typewriter; at thirteen, I wrote my first love poem; and at twenty-two, I had my first job that had writing as an important element.

Until I was in my thirties, I mostly worked in positions that helped people but it wasn't until a dramatic breakup that I felt free to pursue working in social services. I soon realized that I really enjoyed listening to people's stories. Where others felt that their clients were venting too much or got impatient with what seemed interminable narration, I was intrigued by their worlds and their words, the little details ("that was my dad's old 1972 Ford"), the intonations, the gestures. This is the stuff of people's lives; everything is important.

This book before you naturally draws it all together — the poems and stories that rise from the fertile mix of others' and my experience, listening to individuals talk about what's important to them, and paying attention to the details that are so crucial in research.

BIBLIOGRAPHY: INTRODUCTION

Charon, R. (2011, November 4). Honoring the stories of illness. [TEDx Atlanta video] YouTube. https://www.youtube.com/watch?v=24kHX2HtU3o

Charon, R. (2005). Narrative medicine: Attention, representation, affiliation. *Narrative, 13*(3), 261–70.

Dostoevsky, F. (1957). *The Gambler and Other Stories*. C. Garnett (trans.). William Heinemann (Original work published 1866).

Dowd, M. (2008). *Thank God for Evolution: How the Marriage of Science and Religion Will Transform Your Life and Our World*. Penguin.

Hung, E. (1997). *The Nature of Science: Problems and Perspectives*. Wadsworth.

Le Guin, U.K. (2024). *The Language of the Night* (rev. ed.). Scribner.

Mori, I. (2017). *A bagful of haiku — 87 imperfections*. Self-published.

Oliver, M. (1986). "Death at Wind River". In J. Parisi (ed.), *Poetry, 1986*, 330.

Walker, A. (1990). *The Temple of My Familiar*. Penguin.

CHAPTER ONE

"Believe Me"

FRACTURED RELATIONSHIPS

In the poem "Believe Me," a child pleads with her mother to acknowledge the harm done to her.

This resonated with Gina, brought up in a strict Italian Canadian family. Not long before she was born, her father suffered through the Italian Canadian internment during World War II. Gina was raised with four biological siblings and one brother who was adopted after a promise made to God. The adopted brother never really integrated into the family; the parents had great difficulty connecting emotionally with their children. Physical abuse was commonplace in the Catholic school Gina attended and mostly disregarded by her family. These harsh childhood experiences, described by Gina as "a complete sense of hopelessness, drowning, lack of power" led to fragmented relationships between Gina and her adult siblings.

The research portion explores families touched by trauma and the troublesome adult sibling relationships that can result. It also touches on how other women who have experienced childhood trauma have learned to triumph over it.

THE POEM

Believe Me

believe that i
cry
believe that i
lie
in my tears and
cannot swim.

believe that
while you can't believe the
pain.

believe that i bleed
believe me
mother
believe me
i beg you on my knees that
kneel here on the ground
with no skin left
no meat
just bare bones and
blood

believe what you
see
mother
believe me, whatever you
do
believe me

believe that i
cry
believe that i
lie
in my tears and
cannot swim.

Isabella Mori

THE INTERVIEW

Gina

To prepare for the interview, Gina settled herself into "a completely different chair" in front of the fireplace, nice and comfortable. It felt a door was opened for something new. Then she read the poem out loud.

What comes up for you as you read this poem?
"believe that / while you can't believe the / pain."
  I believe my mother could believe the pain but didn't know how to deal with it. When I was in grade school, I was often beaten by this nun who was bloody crazy. I had her as a teacher in grades 7 and 8. She would make us kneel on our knees and hit us with the black strap. I would get hit a lot because I was never one to conform. At one point, we were cheerleaders and went into the cloakroom and were practising. The nun got very, very angry when she saw us. We were on our knees and she was beating me with the black strap. She lost it and hit me on my neck and head, and I was bleeding. Finally, my mother believed me and took action and phoned the school board.

"in my tears and / cannot swim"
  There is a complete sense of hopelessness, drowning, lack of power. I can relate that to my life now. In many ways, I feel powerless in many situations. This week, there was someone who had put a lot of trust in me and was sharing a story concerning the internment. I had asked that she send the story to me. She is a professor at a university who is writing about the internment. She sent me the write-up and said I could share it with my siblings, but not online. I have a very terrible older brother. When I shared it, I said not to put it online but he said he would. He is very anti-anyone who is educated and feels they never truly honour those who were interned. I had a meltdown, almost like a nervous breakdown. I called my aunt and even my cousin who is a bishop and asked them to keep him from doing that. Thank God they convinced him.
  There was that sense of powerlessness again that I was feeling and that I was jeopardizing someone. It comes from my childhood and a family that was very Catholic and would never believe that any Catholic priest or nun would harm anyone — and yet their daughter was battered every day. Even though I told them. Only when I was bleeding, they had to accept it. Or maybe they always thought it was my fault.

What the poem also brought up was when I was smashed across the head by a priest in grade 9 so hard that I flew across the classroom. My sister witnessed this and I still remember her saying "Don't cry, Gina."

Where it says kneeling and bleeding and feeling like you're drowning because nobody will believe you — my intentions as a human were always good. I never thought what I was doing was wrong, but in the family where I was brought up, it was hard to tell on your own what was right or wrong. You were never given the opportunity to think for yourself. Right and wrong existed only according to the church, so there was no inner development of what a human is.

And now, I think I had no autonomy. Presently, I have a great lack of a feeling in belonging. And also feel a lot of rejection. It is almost like I put myself in situations where I will continue this feeling of not belonging. This month, I am finally seeing a therapist about this.

I remember trying to be very good and went to church to confession every Saturday, as we were told. Once, I went to the priest and told him I was very good that week and had not screamed at my mother or done anything else — basically, I felt I was free from sin. He just screamed at me "Who do you think you are?!" Same as my mother, she said that all the time too. So you could never be who you were because if you did, you were smacked back into the wall. You didn't want to be better than others, you just wanted to be yourself. But in the end, you feel *less* than others.

There was a lot of smothering of who you are, right from the beginning of childhood. I don't know if others were brought up like that. There was nothing that helped me to become a person. No lessons in life. No books. No children's books. We never knew any of them, never read any of them. No examples of life through fairy tales or through anything because we were never read to.

The poem reminds me of that. First when I read it, it made me think of the beating with the black strap and the bleeding, but if I go deeper, that was just a symbol of my childhood, of being beaten into the ground at any moment. I don't really remember a happy moment of my childhood. Not one. My parents were busy, they were trying to live the best they could, but I guess they had no clue. And now the family is a disaster.

We were never beaten by our parents, except for once by my father, with a belt. My mother told him to and when he started, she screamed at him to stop. He did. That was my sister and I. We had run away from home.

There was no character development encouraged at all. We could only be whatever they wanted us to be and that was forced. One was playing instruments — the piano or the violin — the other, the church. My mother was a music teacher, but didn't teach us.

At one point, they tried to teach us Italian, but by then we were so wild it didn't work. I think the internment had something to do with it. In the story the professor sent me, it talks not only of the Italians being interned but also what happened afterwards. Graffiti, fights broke out — the Italians suffered a lot of discrimination. My dad was six months in the internment camp until they proved he was not a threat and not a follower of Mussolini and had no association with any anti-Canada activities, but the damage was done and the fear was there. We never had Italian spoken in the house. It was not until high school that they started even to acknowledge anything about being Italian. That's why I'm trying to regain my identity now by learning Italian.

What from this experience carries on?
What is it that carries on? What is it? The lack of development? Feeling powerless, not knowing what I'm doing, going around like a lost soul.

The fact that my mother never believed me has developed into a feeling of often being unsupported.

Last night, a friend called me, wanted to see me. I was so happy. Someone acknowledges that Gina needs input, needs attention. We were always taught to have output. Now I'm trying to regain myself and wait for input. Not always output, output, output into relationships that don't work. And my dearest friend has found a new partner and now I'm not invited as much by them anymore and often feel left out. I do not have the heart to tell them.

We were never allowed to relate to each other. My mother brought an adopted child into the family but would not allow us to talk to him one-on-one. He was disturbed and is still disturbed to this day. I send him things and another brother pays attention to him, the rest won't talk to him at all. Into a scene that was awful anyway, my mother created yet another situation that was awful. Without consulting any of us… just one day we had a new brother… apparently a promise she made to God. If God saved the life of my oldest brother (the terrible one). Making deals with God.

The idea that we were never allowed to relate to each other stays with me. We all tried to swim and we all drowned, every single one of us. The relationship with this family — that's what carried forward. My aunt always says forget, forget, don't engage, but it's hard for me because I want relationship. And I am trying to create a relationship that was never there.

What carries on, for me — the idea that I had no power and I feel often incapable of anything. For example, I'm part of a writing group but, when it comes to writing, I don't feel capable of writing.

There was this lack of development of character, lack of my family understanding that a person needs development, needs to self-ize. That just wasn't in our story and I think, because of that, I think I don't have a sense of self, a warm, thick self — I just don't have it. For that to develop, one needs to have opportunity and the support.

What is something hopeful and affirming that we can take from this conversation?
The deeper we go, the more we learn.

The beauty that comes from sharing our suffering. It is like compost — you throw out all the things that are gross and rotten, and it turns into beautiful soil.
Yes, like the lotus that grows from the mud. And we carry on!

But I'm not sure this expression really goes deep enough for me… because somehow I haven't thrown out all that is rotten. It is still here. But I do compost!

What is a positive message in all of this?
[Referring to a comment from me in an earlier conversation] I like that you suggested I go out and notice where people support me. I did that and felt good about this. But still, one friend brought me a gift last evening and all I could think of how much trouble she went to to get it and whether I am really worthy of all that.

THE RESEARCH

Interviewing Gina felt like following her down a winding staircase. We hardly spent time at the surface and quickly went deeper and deeper. Let us retrace those steps.

By settling into a "completely different chair," Gina decides to do something new — decides, perhaps, to walk down those stairs. She starts with the constant beatings at school. Eventually her mother believed her pain, but didn't know how to deal with it. Quickly, though, Gina goes deeper, into hopelessness, drowning, a feeling of powerlessness, things that stay with her still, after over fifty years. She connects this with her strictly Catholic family that hardly even had room for crying when she was violently assaulted.

This relates to Gina's next steps, further into the depths of her childhood memories: "It was hard to tell on your own what was right or wrong." The connection with reality suffers and, with it, sensing what's right or wrong. Natural reactions are suppressed, such as crying after an assault. Only the church's abstract, external sense of right and wrong was allowed and so "there was no inner development of what a human is," no autonomy, and a lingering feeling of rejection where ideally there would have been one of belonging.

Constantly hearing "Who do you think you are?!" meant Gina could never be who she was. She saw herself as less than others and felt smothered. Added to this was a lack of stimulation: "No lessons in life. No books... No examples of life through fairy tales..." The black strap she thought of when she first read the poem becomes a symbol of her childhood, "of being beaten into the ground."

Finally, Gina arrives at the topic she is most concerned with for the research part of this chapter: "We were never allowed to relate to each other. My mother brought an adopted child into the family but would not allow us to talk to him one-on-one... The idea that we were never allowed to relate to each other stays with me. We all tried to swim and we all drowned, every single one of us."

Hearing these experiences brings up a lot of sadness. At the same time, they are a rich tapestry. Gina's Italian background conjures up the wealth of images in Dante's *Inferno*.

When asked what to focus on in the research part, Gina talked about "not knowing how to develop relationships ... no existence of relationship with siblings... this is important to me."

This importance follows us throughout our lives.

The Adverse Childhood Experience Studies (ACE)

One of the most impactful investigations in the social sciences in the 1990s was preventive medicine researchers Vincent Felitti and Robert Anda's study on the far-reaching health effects of adverse childhood experiences, now commonly referred to as ACEs. Related research on trauma (e.g., by Judith Herman with her widely read *Trauma and Recovery*) shows that immediate responses to trauma are feelings of shock, fear, and helplessness. Helplessness is one of the experiences Gina talks about. And because these experiences are so shocking, they leave an indelible trace that can still be found in the immune, endocrine (hormonal), and nervous systems of the now-adult person. For example, individuals who have experienced ACEs tend to have a smaller prefrontal cortex than those without ACEs.

ACE and Sibling Relationships

Ben Donagh is a researcher specializing in topics relating to children and youth. Together with colleagues, he carried out a review of 148 research articles on ACEs related to siblings. 19% of those articles were about adult siblings. Donagh mentions no findings specific to adult siblings. Generally, however, it was noticed in some studies that when one child experienced abuse, there was a higher likelihood for other siblings to experience it as well, particularly when it came to maltreatment and neglect, as appears to have happened in Gina's family. Also, simply having more than one child in the family in and of itself increased the risk of ACEs. Donagh also points out that sibling relationships are understudied, even though they tend to be the longest-lasting relationship for most individuals.

Family therapist Kelly Strick used the ACE questionnaire (now widely available online) to investigate the impact of ACEs on sibling relationships. The questionnaire has ten sections with twenty-three specific questions which inquire about adverse physical, emotional, and sexual experiences, as well as topics such as mental illness or divorce in the family. The higher the ACE score, the more health problems a person tends to have in later life. Judging from Gina's interview, she might score a three out of ten — she was put down, she was hit, and the siblings did not have much chance to be close to each other.[2]

Felitti's study, and the many ACE studies that followed, mostly investigated direct impacts on physical health (e.g., diabetes, chronic pulmonary disease, alcoholism, suicide). Strick is one of the few who specifically researched

2 To show an example of the impact of a 3 on the ACE score, in Felitti's study, 9.4% of persons who scored 3/10 had made one or more suicide attempts and those who scored 0 only 1.2%. That is an almost eightfold difference.

psychosocial impacts and, to my knowledge at the time of this writing, offers the only study about adult sibling relations and ACE.

To evaluate sibling relationships, Strick used psychologist Heidi Riggio's Lifespan Sibling Relationships Scale which looks at feelings, behaviours, and thoughts about present and past relationships with a sibling. It presents research participants with statements such as "I enjoy my relationship with my sibling," "my sibling frequently makes me very angry," "I remember feeling very close to my sibling when we were children," and "my sibling and I did not spend a lot of time together when we were children."

Family Functioning

Strick was also interested in a related topic, family functioning. For this, she used the McMaster Model of family functioning. This model consists of six dimensions of family functioning: problem-solving, communication, family roles, behaviour control, and how family members deal with emotions ('affective responsiveness' and 'affective involvement'). Like many other family models, it sees a family as a system within wider systems (e.g., the system of a church congregation) and a system with subsystems (e.g., the sibling subsystem).

The family system is concerned with life tasks such as meeting basic needs from and with others in the family, helping individuals move through life stages, etc. It is also a sort of laboratory where children can learn social, psychological, and other skills. And of course, this laboratory takes place in ever-larger circles of other environments, from church congregation to the church at large to a nation's culture, etc. They all influence each other.

From Gina's interview, it seems that neither she nor her family fared well in many of the areas just mentioned. Family functioning was measured with the Family Assessment Device, which is based on the McMaster Model. Developed by psychiatrist Nathan Epstein and colleagues in 1983, this questionnaire is still widely used. It asks for the degree to which people agree or disagree with statements such as "we cannot talk to each other about the sadness we feel," "individuals are accepted for what they are," "we don't get along well together," and "in times of crisis, we can turn to each other for support." Gina would most probably score the functioning of her family of origin extremely low.

Emotional Involvement and Responsiveness

To delve deeper into the concept of family functioning, we can take the dimensions of affective (emotional) involvement and responsiveness. They are at the centre of the poem: "i beg you on my knees that / kneel here on

23

the ground / with no skin left / no meat / just bare bones and / blood / believe what you see." This plea to the mother to get emotionally involved and acknowledge what is going on right in front of her with her child resonated with Gina, who wanted her mother to acknowledge what was happening at school.

Since there was little communication going on between the siblings, it is probably safe to assume that there was also little affective involvement on the part of the siblings. In addition, implied in the poem is a plea for an emotional (affective) response from the mother — loving words, a gentle touch, a protective gesture. Gina did not experience that, neither with her mother nor her sister, who simply told her not to cry.

The outcome of Strick's study was that while high ACE scores were related to low relationship scores, it was impossible to tell why and how exactly. However, Strick did find that family functioning predicted sibling relations — the higher the family functioning, the better the sibling relations. She says this makes sense since "families are considered a laboratory for development, therefore, the laboratory environment of the family system would influence the sibling subsystem." Also, researchers such as psychologist Avidan Milevsky and colleagues have suggested the spillover effect hypothesis, an idea which is easy to understand intuitively: parenting approaches "spill over" into, or model, sibling relationships and, from what Gina tells us, it appears that parenting skills in Gina's family were low.

Are we then to condemn Gina's parents and her siblings? Of course not. Gina's father was declared an enemy alien and interned at the beginning of WWII. Her parents suffered from the animosity and discrimination inflicted on them as did so many other Italians Canadian families in her town. Gina's parents were no doubt traumatized themselves, possibly also by the strictness of the Catholic Church, just as Gina was. Because of the connection with the church and because of general practices at the time, one can imagine that Gina was affected by intergenerational parenting and schooling practices that left traces of trauma on all concerned.

Overcoming Difficult Childhood Experiences

How do women like Gina overcome adverse childhood experiences? Despite difficult aftereffects, there are those who thrive and have remarkable achievements in work and education. Nursing researchers Sandra Thomas and Joanne Hall conducted a series of in-depth interviews with twenty-seven women aged seventeen to over sixty. Participants' early trajectories had this shape:

- Many start off with traumatic experiences in "houses of horror." For Gina, that was church and school.
- "Becoming resolute." One girl climbed a tree, stayed there for half a day, and escaped abuse for at least that one time. Others formulated goals for the future. At age nine, one research participant decided to be the first in her family to go to college. Perhaps Gina telling the priest she had nothing to confess falls into this category.
- "The school years." School was a safe place for participants, although to varying degrees. While we don't know everything about Gina's school experiences, it certainly was anything but the "welcome refuge" that some of the participants in Hall's study had in school.
- "The escape." In order to move towards an autonomous, healthy self, it was essential to leave home. One woman went so far as to create a new birth certificate for herself, explaining that it was now safe to let her "pure, innocent, untouched, perfect self shine bright for all the world to see." Would it help Gina to create a new birth certificate for herself?

The trajectory then continued with early adult years and, for some women, therapy. In the next phase, participants used self-strengthening metaphors such as "climbing the mountain," "climbing out of a deep pit," and "learning to sail my ship" to describe the hard work of overcoming their past. A later stage was described as generativity, sometimes through community service or choosing human service professions (e.g., child abuse prevention program, mental health advocacy). Some of Gina's story falls into this category: she became a teacher and particularly liked a job that supported newcomers to Canada.

Finally, as astonishing as it sounds, survivors often used words such as "lucky," "blessed," "fortunate," and "grateful" to describe their lives.

As Gina put it, they are "like the lotus that grows from the mud."

BIBLIOGRAPHY: CHAPTER ONE

Danese, A. & McEwen, B. (2012). Adverse childhood experiences, allostasis, allostatic load, and age-related disease. *Physiology & Behavior, 106*, 29–39.

Donagh, B., Taylor, J., Al Mushaikhi, M. & Bradbury-Jones, C. (2022). Sibling experiences of adverse childhood experiences: A scoping review. *Trauma, Violence, & Abuse, 24*(5), 3513–3527.

Epstein, N.B., Bishop, D.S. & Levin, S. (1978). The McMaster model of family functioning. *Journal of Marriage and Family Counseling, 4*(4), 19–31.

Epstein, N.B., Baldwin, L.M. & Bishop, D.S. (1983). The McMaster Family Assessment Device. *Journal of Marital and Family Therapy, 9*(2), 171–180.

Felitti, V.J., Anda, R.F., Nordenberg, D., Williamson, D.F., Spitz, A.M., Edwards, V., Koss, M.P. & Marks, J.S. (1998). Relationship of childhood abuse and household dysfunction to many of the leading causes of death in adults: The adverse childhood experiences (ACE) study. *American Journal of Preventive Medicine, 14*(4), 245–258.

Herman, J.L. (1992). *Trauma and recovery*. Basic Books.

Milevsky, A., Schlechter, M.J. & Machlev, M. (2011). Effects of parenting style and involvement in sibling conflict on adolescent sibling relationships. *Journal of Social and Personal Relationships, 28*(8), 1130–1148.

Riggio, H.R. (2000). Measuring attitudes toward adult sibling relationships: The Lifespan Sibling Relationship Scale. *Journal of Social and Personal Relationships, 17*(6), 707–728.

Simons, R.L., Whitbeck, L.B., Conger, R.D. & Wu, C.-i. (1991). Intergenerational transmission of harsh parenting. *Developmental Psychology, 27*(1), 159–171.

Strick, K. (2017). *The Impact of Adverse Childhood Experiences on Adult Sibling Relationships* (Doctoral dissertation, Purdue University).

Thomas, S. & Hall, J. (2008). Life trajectories of female child abuse survivors thriving in adulthood. *Qualitative Health Research, 18*(2), 149–166.

CHAPTER TWO

SLURPING: FOOD, ADDICTION, AND AUTHENTICITY

The poem "Noodle Oracle" is a conversation between the narrator and a bowl of ramen. She is not ready yet to give up the noodles but knows that, eventually, she'll have to confront what it is that she really wants.

Gabrielle, a music teacher, improvises over this poem with musings about her own problems with food, how they were accompanied by "pretending," and how that played out in her relationships. We conducted the interview as she was vacationing at her mother's place, bringing back memories of how her relationships with food and people were formed: "Creative, smart, loudmouthed people were not really valued very much and I got mixed messages about whether who I was was okay." Gabrielle has personal experience with bipolar disorder and is currently in recovery from a food addiction. She is in her fifties, married, and a mother. She loves poetry and is passionate about teaching music to children.

Gabrielle is interested in the relationship between addiction and authenticity. The research portion investigates authenticity as a concept, its connection with addiction and problematic eating, and the related topics of self-silencing and reinventing oneself through self-narration.

THE POEM

Noodle Oracle

read the soup last night
12 midnight
was good
good hot soup in the fall
few days before new moon

read the soup and the soup said
"i'm your noodle oracle —
mamma mamma,
hear you cry mamma,"
the noodle soople oracle said to me
"mamma mamma,
hear you cry mamma"
and i nodded to the noodles —
reluctantly, i dare say,
but i noddled, yes,
covered in lavender sports coat over beige lady outfit
cause it was starting to get cold
12 midnight
a few days into fall —
but the soup was good and hot.

a few days before new moon
the noodle pasta ooracle said
furthermore
— as i slurped —
"listen, between those wafts
of monosodium glutamate fogs
rising up from my steaming body,
listen, i can feel
you
the eater of my noodle essence
longing for more warmth
than my hot liquid can ever give you.
i can see you yearn
for softer softness

than my white dough even though
it caresses, traverses, mushingly, over your lips and tongue —
and no one noodle, gliding down inner throat into
the depths of your sad, weeping stomach
can fathom the ravine of your soul
— needing more, needing more —"

there i stopped.
i stop now.
do i want to hear more, noodle oracle?
do i want?
do i?

and yes
the moreness of my hungry, driven soul
lifts its arms and says
"give me, soup, more of your nasty, disturbing
words
give me
more
as more is that which i always
want."

so the soup says,
"see —
there's more of me…
in other forms and other words…
i hear you cry mamma
pasta mamma pasta mamma
but mamma is gone
yet
there is more of me…
in other forms and other words…"

and i pretend
not to stand

not to under-stand
words
pasta oracle noodle words
i pretend
to be hungry for food…

until i can't stand
i can't stand
it no more.

THE INTERVIEW

Gabrielle

What were your first impressions after you read this poem?
Sensuous! The slurping, it had sexual overtones. I loved that. I loved the sound effects. That line with the word "mushingly" … contrasting that with what I read as a little bit of pain and longing in the child for comfort from the mom who maybe didn't know how to give it any other way than with food. There is sadness and confusion and anger. A longing for some other solution, for some other sort of understanding, some other sort of love.

It's interesting. The latest food path that I'm exploring is intuitive eating. I'm on my second stay at home with my mom with that concept. It's difficult to come to this world at home where the food issues originated and to have to face that.

Reading that other lady's story [Chapter 1], part of me felt that I have nothing to complain about. But if I look at some of the things that are/were difficult for me — I was a creative, smart, loudmouthed person in a family where creative, smart, loudmouthed people were not really valued very much and I got mixed messages about whether who I was was okay. To this day I wonder, had I had a family that was more familiar with the performing arts, would I have pursued that dream? At core, I am a performer. To this day, I feel judged by my siblings.

I have to tell my mom all the time "I'm not manic, I'm just me" and explain to her what the signs are when I'm truly manic — but cheerfully joining in to a conversation or sitting down at a piano and writing a song or getting excited about anything — that's not manic, it's just me.

It's taken me a long time to realize that that judgment of who I am is not right. It's a bunch of bullshit. It's hurtful on a very core level and some of the mental health bumps I've run into — I look back at them and wonder how much of those labels of bipolar were comfortable labels for people who didn't really get or accept who I was. That said, I am currently not medicating for bipolar, with my doctor's and psychiatrist's permission. I am calmly coming more into myself and have stopped apologizing and realize at fifty that I don't have to be anybody but myself. If people don't like that, that's okay. There are lots of people in the world who are perfectly happy with who I am.

I just watched a movie called *The Other Side*. It was tagged as teen romance. A young lesbian relationship, a love triangle, with a really, really lovely main character who resonated for me in a way that I didn't expect her to. It's kind of a Cyrano[3] thing with Cyrano being the young gay confused lady.

That girl was not interested in boys. I look back at myself as a teenager — I didn't get boys and it makes me wonder, makes me question what would be had I had relationships with girls. "To yearn for softer softness" — a very sexual phrase in the poem.

The idea of the food talking to me — in this process where I eat intuitively, one of the things is to enjoy the sensual more, to slow down, make eating more than inhaling calories. I feel like I am colouring some of my answers with food addiction and some with sexual confusion.

I have siblings that have unconditional love for me and three I don't talk to. I've come to the point where I have decided that family is better chosen than just accepted. Just because sisters and brothers are related doesn't mean they're friends or good for me or like me. It's painful because there is this fantasy of the family unit.

You are talking quite a bit about siblings. Why is that?
The interview with your other friend where she talks about not feeling seen. I felt seen but rejected. I was pretty hard to miss because I was quite full of myself as a teenager, always kind of riding that edge of 'too much' for everybody in my family.

How does it feel to be talking about this right now?
I feel sad about the memory of my relationship with one sister that has gone so far to pot. My memories of us as kids is that we were quite close. She was my pusher of candy.

The worst for me about having fights with people and siblings is I'm never quite sure what I've done wrong. That question comes up for me in my collegial relationships as well. If someone takes a dislike of me, I don't know what to do. I can't pinpoint "that's the thing that made her/him hate me." I'm trying to learn to let it be. My work relationships have gotten worse and worse and worse over the years and my fear of being hurt is a big part of that.

I related to the other lady saying it's difficult to make friends. My idea of what a friend is feels like it's not the way people do things anymore. I read an article on 'scruffy hospitality' once and loved the idea. Hey, potluck at my place tonight, just bring whatever you have in the fridge, and it's about getting

3 Referring to the 1897 play *Cyrano de Bergerac* by Edmond Rostand. Cyrano is a French nobleman and soldier, gifted with words, music, and the art of duelling. Because of his large nose, he sees himself as ugly. In ways both tragic and comedic, that makes it very difficult for him from to declare his love for the beautiful Roxane.

together, not showing off your place or fancy food or whatever. Relationships can be so surface-y.

How does the word 'surface-y' fit with the poem?
I want the noodles to be more. I want them to be protein-packed and lasting and I want them to make my heart happy. I want them in some ways, and in some ways I don't want them. I want more than noodles. I want pork and I want dumplings and I want wontons and carrots and ginger and I want soup that isn't so salty and I want deeper friendships. I want people who talk about real things and not run away from real conversations.

I don't want ever to talk about diet or exercise again. I want my mother never to mention those words again ever and yet they come up every day. Then she takes it [that] I don't want to eat and we skip meals. It's a control battle here. But this is the least out of control I ever felt here. That's a good step forward.

 One of the things that my family is very crappy about is talking about things when things go wrong. We are very good at pretending that things are going right when they really aren't. My mom and I just had a blow-up. She works in subtleties. She is not happy with me, so she phoned one of my siblings who don't like me so much and said nasty things about my child and made sure I could overhear her. I felt hurt.

My new communication skills tell me to say I felt hurt when you said he is a klutz and broke something, but I don't care, *ha ha ha*. And yet I feel that if I attempt to have that conversation, she'll deny she meant it, deny that it was hurtful, she'll tell me I'm overreacting. So I'm stuck in my emotions. But I've talked to my husband about it and to others. That's the joy of recovery: we find the best way forward with help.

I think my first bipolar breakdown came from an inability to admit something was wrong. That I was in the wrong field, in the wrong school, didn't know where I should be, didn't know how to tell anybody I felt lost. All that built up into not sleeping for a month and I ended up in a psych ward. Not such a healthy way to deal with problems.

"The moreness of my hungry, driven soul." The moreness hungry for love, not dismissal and embarrassment. I was on a church call with my mom earlier this week. Halfway through, I realized she was embarrassed because I was talking too much and I said, "Am I talking too much?" She said yes and they all laughed. There was moreness in my talking.

"The moreness of my hungry, driven soul." This intuitive eating thing says eat when you're hungry. I don't think I ever let myself get hungry, didn't know what actual physical hunger felt like. Every night of my life in this house, sneaking down to get more food.

I pretend not to understand the words. I pretend a lot. I pretend all the time.

I've just started answering honestly when people ask "How are you doing?" We all have a thin veneer of 'fine'. Some of the veneers are thicker than others, but most of us are not that fine. Our inability to be honest will kill us, never mind the pesky pasta.

THE RESEARCH

Gabrielle was interested in "the topic of authenticity and how all addictions act as a mask to it." Let's first explore the concept of authenticity.

In 2019, the journal *Review of General Psychology* devoted a whole issue to this topic. In the summary, authenticity is presented as "a valued, yet elusive concept." There are some commonalities in the definitions, e.g., that feeling authentic both produces and is produced by psychological well-being, and that most people believe that persons, organizations, things, and experiences have a certain essence. Staying true to that essence shows authenticity. But there are many things researchers disagree on, and those include a conclusive definition of authenticity.

Authenticity — What Is It?

But what are some of these definitions, even though they are not agreed on? In 2006, psychologists Michael Kernis and Brian Goldman wrote a widely cited chapter in which they referred to authenticity as "the unobstructed operation of one's true, or core, self." They proposed that authenticity has four components:

- a desire to be aware of one's beliefs, feelings, and goals
- self-honesty
- acting in accordance with one's values, needs, and desires
- an openness that allows others to see the real self (something that Gabrielle is working on right now).

All this requires a certain amount of autonomy where, as psychologists William and Richard Ryan point out, the person willingly endorses, carries out, and owns their actions. It's also interesting to note that Buddhist therapist Ken Bradford refers to authenticity as "unfabricated authentic presence," and that Abraham Maslow (of hierarchy of needs fame) supposedly called it "the reduction of phoniness toward the zero point."

But these are all expert definitions. What do ordinary people think of when they talk about authenticity? Balazs Kovács, a management researcher, asked 257 U.S. participants to think of words associated with authenticity in five areas: brands, organizations, persons, restaurants, and paintings. Participants came up with a wide variety of words, but the one word that showed up the most (137 times) was 'honest' in regard to people. 'Real' and 'genuine' were also frequently used words.

Inauthenticity

In this context, it's useful to also look at inauthenticity, reported by Ryan and Ryan as "deceptive, defensive, false, or conveying only a pretense" or by Kernis and Goldman as "acting merely to please others or to attain rewards or avoid punishments." Inauthenticity is associated with anxiety, depression, and other problems. Here, we hear echoes of Gabrielle as well as the poem, where both speak of pretense. Gabrielle points out how she pretended, exactly to please others such as her mother and how this pretense is ultimately connected to her hospitalization.

The descriptions reported by Ryan, Kernis, and Goldman feel quite harsh, especially since it is difficult to behave authentically in an unsupportive environment. Ryan and Ryan, social psychologists both, looked at the challenges around authenticity experienced by lesbian, gay, and bisexual persons, showing that when their authenticity is diminished, it is not just for personal reasons but also because the environment — from personal relationships to culture in general — often is not open to how they wish to express their authenticity.

Another take on lack of authenticity is *self-ambiguity*, put forward by philosophers Doug McConnell and Anna Golova. Self-ambiguity refers to: a) uncertainty about one's characteristics such as sexual preferences; b) uncertainty about how to shape one's life or self — e.g. which career to pursue or which appearance to portray ("Are nose rings really me?") — which involves developing a sense for one's true priorities so that the inevitable clash of choices can be resolved; and c) uncertainty about whether one's self-narrative (what stories one tells others and, more importantly, themselves about themselves) truly represents who one is. The place of self-narrative in addiction will be further discussed below.

Addiction, Food Addiction, and Eating Disorders

'Addiction' is also a very general term. According to Eliza Gordon, a health and psychology researcher, food addiction falls into the general category of substance-use disorders, for which the *Diagnostic and Statistical Manual*, 5th edition (DSM-5) has the following criteria:

1. Impaired control, e.g., consuming large amounts, having cravings, etc. (In the interview, Gabrielle talks about "every night of my life in this house sneaking down to get more food" and the poem about "needing more, needing more.")

2. Social difficulties, e.g., preferring the company of food over the company of people
3. Risky use, e.g., continuing to eat large amounts of sweets despite being diabetic
4. Drug effects, e.g., withdrawal symptoms.

The community of Overeaters Anonymous (OA) usually refers to this addictive phenomenon as 'compulsive overeating'. However, classifying compulsive overeating as a food addiction is quite controversial. Psychologist Adrian Meule tells us that the concept of addiction in connection with food was already used in the late 1800s, and around the 1950s, 'food addiction' was frequently referred to both by scientists and laypersons. Currently, the term is rarely used by researchers. However, many people themselves still identify as having food addictions. Many psychiatrists, such as Denise Wilfley, see the problem as an eating disorder and refer to it as Binge Eating Disorder. Similarities can be observed between Binge Eating Disorder, anorexia, and bulimia, such as a preoccupation with weight and negative body image.

It also bears mention that while the interview was with a woman, men experience similar challenges, which is often overlooked. According to the US-based National Eating Disorders Association, over six million men experience disordered eating at some point in their lives: "rates for eating disorders in males are increasing at a faster rate than for females ... many men have misconceived notions about their weight and physique, particularly the importance of muscularity."

In the following sections, we will see how authenticity is discussed in the context of eating disorders and addiction in general. No direct reference was found regarding food addiction and authenticity.

Honesty and Shame Among Overeaters Anonymous Members

As we saw earlier, 'honesty' was the most frequently used word when laypersons described authenticity. It did not show up much in the research on authenticity and addiction, but therapist Michael Grubb does provide an example in his dissertation on Overeaters Anonymous members who also received psychotherapy. In the interviews he conducted, four themes emerged, two of them shame and honesty. Grubb suggests that the dishonesty he observed in his participants was a type of dissociation.

For example, they hid their eating from their sponsors and other OA members but also talked about it in such a way that it essentially hid their undesired behaviours from themselves. That is, they were not able to have the self-knowledge so important for authenticity. (In the poem, we see how the speaker actively bars this type of knowledge.) The hiding leads to shame — and shame always leads to more hiding. The twelve-step declaration "I'm only as sick as my secrets" applies here. The self-shaming also interacts with the other-shaming that often occurs when a person weighs more than what is expected by society.

Eventually, many of Grubb's participants were able to emerge into honesty and "not merely a factual, logical correspondence of truth ... but rather ... a vital, shared, affective, interpersonal experience that serves to regulate behavior." This honesty, suggests Grubb, dissolves dissociation, so much so that one participant explained "recovery has given me this ability to see who I really am, past what the disease [of compulsive overeating] tells me I am."

Self-Silencing

In 1982, feminist, ethicist, and psychologist Carol Gilligan published the book *In a Different Voice,* in which she criticized male-dominated psychology. According to Harvard University Press, the book "started a revolution, making women's voices heard, in their own right and with their own integrity, for virtually the first time in social scientific theorizing about women."

Inspired by a lecture by Gilligan, psychologist Dana Jack then introduced the concept of 'self-silencing' of feelings, desires, and needs by girls and women. Self-silencing occurs because from early on, females are taught (and some, including Gilligan, say they inherently want) to maintain relationships at all costs. For societal and other reasons, this results in heightened self-consciousness, careful monitoring of thoughts and emotions, and a great vulnerability to the opinions of others. This forces women to cope with a variety of negative feelings, it disempowers them, decreases their social support, diminishes self-esteem, and distorts their relationship with their bodies. The result is a wide gap between the woman's outwardly portrayed self and her true self.

Self-Silencing and Eating Disorders

In Gabrielle's words:

> I think my first bipolar breakdown came from an inability to admit something was wrong. That I was in the wrong field, in the wrong school, didn't know where I should be, didn't know how to tell anybody I felt lost.

Dana Jack talks about self-silencing and dieting as female rituals expected by society and about an expectation for women to tone themselves down. Women 'lobotomize' parts of themselves in order to conform with societal ideas about what women *should* do. From that perspective, Gabrielle's 'loudmouthing' is not acceptable!

Clinical psychologist Ruth Striegel-Moore and colleagues suggest that the constant scrutiny of the female body often results in insecurity and hyperfocus on physical appearance, which frequently leads to a negative body image. External evaluations of physical appearance are easily internalized; the woman becomes as critical of herself as, for example, the media or classmates are. Striegel-Moore and colleagues found a relationship between this hyperfocus on physical appearance (which is common among people experiencing disordered eating) and the ability "to construct an adequate social self." The result is a self preoccupied with public acceptance, not grounded in an internal 'true self'. In Striegel-Moore's study, women with high scores on an eating disorders scale tended to also score high on the Perceived Fraudulence Scale. This scale measures the degree to which a person is afraid of being exposed as a fraud even in areas in which they are successful. Therefore, they are constantly engaged in their own image management — all of this signs of a struggle with authenticity.

Gabrielle finally comes to grip with this:

> I was a creative, smart, loudmouthed person in a family where creative, smart, loudmouthed people were not really valued very much and I got mixed messages about whether who I was was okay. ... It's taken me a long time to realize that that judgment of who I am is not right. It's a bunch of bullshit. ...

Nurturing and Mothers

Psychologist Lucia Farinon cites researchers Katrina Brown and Karin Jasper who suggest that when we eat, it is often a metaphor for more general nurturing, and that people who eat emotionally are not entirely aware of what it is that they need. This is one of the themes of the poem ("you / the eater of my noodle essence / longing for more warmth / than my hot liquid can ever give you. / i can see you yearn / for softer softness / than my white dough"). It is not a big step to the relationship with mother, the first nurturer. In the poem, we hear the protagonist "cry mamma" which right away becomes "pasta mamma," a mother intricately linked to food.

Gabrielle talks about "at home where the food issues originated" and has compassion for the "pain and longing in the child for comfort from the mom who maybe didn't know how to give it any other way than with food." Gabrielle also locates some of the beginning of her own inauthenticity in her upbringing, a family used to "pretending that things are going right when they really aren't." She is exasperated with her mother who lets off steam at Gabrielle by making sure she overhears disparaging remarks about her son in a phone call to another daughter.

So what about the mother?

> The mother-daughter relationship is inevitably an ambivalent one, for the mother, who herself lives a life circumscribed in patriarchy, has the unenviable task of directing her daughter to take up the very same position that she has occupied. Explicitly as well as unconsciously, she psychologically prepares her daughter to accept the strictures that await her in womanhood. She needs to do this so her daughter is not a misfit.

This from psychotherapist Susie Orbach's 1985 book *Fat Is a Feminist Issue* (updated in 2006 because fat is still a feminist issue).

Anorexia and Authenticity

With so many similarities between eating disorders, and hence similarities between anorexia and overeating, we should also look at how authenticity relates to anorexia. In a series of interviews with women with anorexia, psychiatrist and ethicist Jacinta Tan noted that questions of authenticity were so important to the interviewees that they arose spontaneously, without prompting. They typically spoke of it in connection with inner conflict, for example:

> When [the anorexia] takes control, particularly when I'm at a very low weight, its voice if you like is loud, very, very loud, and I can't, the real me can't battle against it … At a higher weight the real me is more able to challenge the anorexic me.

Tan and colleagues see potential in this conflict because it can lead to change, and they propose some ways in which this could happen. For example, it gives the person space to grow towards the self they desire: "discovering one's authentic self sometimes involves a search for understanding one's motivation; and reflecting on authenticity can lead to overall self-development and self-knowledge."

Authenticity, Addictive Behaviour, and "Feeling Good"

While many, including Gabrielle, assume that the 'real self' is good from a moral/philosophical point of view, there is also the self that is experienced as authentic simply because it feels good. This applies particularly to 'state authenticity', i.e., moments in which a person feels authentic (as opposed to 'trait authenticity', which is more stable and enduring). Psychologist Constantine Sedikides and colleagues asked research participants to write about times when they felt "most me." They found that those moments were accompanied by success, familiarity, spending time with friends and loved ones, helping others, creativity, and fun.

This fun can become problematic: When a person feels authentic while they're having fun gambling (i.e., playing because it enhances their mood), they are dealing with "a dangerous cocktail," explain social work professor Jamey Lister and colleagues. People who said things like "I feel very comfortable when I bet on sports" and "when I am betting on sports, I feel like my true self" tended to gamble more often and have more of a rollercoaster ride with large wins and losses.

These findings have some similarities with an extremely thorough series of nine studies by researcher Michail Kokkoris and colleagues, who, among other things, asked research participants to state what they would do after being presented with the following scenario:

> Imagine that on a weekday after work, you go to the mall to buy a pair of socks. As you are on a diet to lose some extra pounds you've recently put on, you want to avoid fat and sweet food. However, walking through the mall, you pass your favorite deli in the food court. As you are looking through the display, you see a mouth-watering tray of strawberry cheesecake, your favorite dessert. You feel a strong craving for it immediately. You don't go often to this mall, as it is a bit far from your place, and it is rather unlikely that you will happen to bump into this deli again soon.

Those who said they would buy the cheesecake felt more authentic when they put less restraint on themselves. Self-control can be perceived as an 'inner dictatorship' where intrinsic needs and desires are ignored and external rules dominate. Losing self-control and being spontaneous can feel very authentic.

Authenticity and Internet Addiction

However, more often it looks like Gabrielle's experience — the combination of addictive behaviour and inauthenticity does not feel good. The only researcher I could find who explicitly linked addiction and authenticity was the psychologist Gazanfer Anli. Various researchers have already proposed that internet addiction is related to depression, hostility, and anxiety, as well as that anxiety is related to self-alienation. Anli went on to measure authenticity (i.e., the opposite of self-alienation) among 420 grade 12 high school students, particularly those who scored high on internet addiction, and found that internet addiction and self-alienation were significantly and highly correlated. As well, those with internet addiction scored high on accepting external influences and low on 'authentic living', with low scores on these statements: "I think it is better to be yourself than to be popular," "I am true to myself in most situations," or "I live in accordance with my values and beliefs."

Addiction and the Story of Identity

Some researchers, such as health behaviour scientist Adams Sibley and colleagues, look at addiction as a story of losing one identity and forming another. A woman might go from
thinking of herself as a lawyer to thinking of herself as a heroin user. The reverse can also be true: if this woman holds on to her identity as a lawyer despite her heroin use, she may well be more successful in treatment.

Addiction, then, is at least in part a question of 'self-narrative change'. In the poem, the change has not happened yet but is anticipated: eventually, the woman "in beige lady outfit" plans to listen to that inner voice. Gabrielle's interview, for its part, can be taken as a new self-narration, for example when she talks about starting the practice of intuitive eating — a quintessentially authentic act — or when she asserts "I don't ever want to talk about diet or exercise again."

Philosophers Doug McConnell and Anke Snoek conducted 145 interviews with sixty-nine individuals in treatment for substance dependence. They asked them to tell the story of their lives, both before they started using and up to the present, and prompted them to talk about their past and current hopes, dreams, and values, as well as how they imagined their future. In this study, McConnell and Snoek's aim was not to establish any cause and effect, but simply to describe how self-narratives relate to a person's path towards recovery. They found that for some, addiction self-narratives became deeply entrenched. For example:

> You're a drug addict person. People look to you in a different way ... they judge you, they're scared of you ... Different from normal people. ... You're really low, you're just like nobody.

This can be reinforced by others:

> The other addicts ... don't want to see someone get on with their life ... they're comfortable. I don't know, it's kind of like misery loves company.

When these narratives are told over and over again by the person themselves and then reinforced by others, they become a self-fulfilling prophecy which is hard to escape: "I'm an addict, this is what I do, this is who I am."

As time went on, though, some people questioned the addicted identity:

> "[Ice][4] did [help], yeah, it really did. But obviously only short term. ... I think it made my mental health worse. ... I think it made me confident but in the wrong way, you know. You can't learn to be confident through ice, that's for sure...

Slowly, new plans can be made and new stories told:

> See, my problem is I don't have many hobbies and I don't have many things that interest me but something that does interest me is anatomy and, you know, all that sort of medical stuff... I didn't really realize how much I enjoyed it until I went back to uni.

However, letting go of old stories is hard work; indeed, in counselling, telling and retelling old and new stories is often referred to as 'narrative work'.

4 Crystal methamphetamine

The stories that humans tell about themselves and others tend to follow certain patterns. One story pattern is a 'redemption script', in which the narrator turns a difficult passage in their lives into the beginning of a life she or he feels happy with and proud of.

In the interview, Gabrielle is starting to accept and celebrate her life as it is, not as she pretends: "Hey, potluck at my place tonight, just bring whatever you have in the fridge, and it's about getting together, not showing off your place or fancy food or whatever."

BIBLIOGRAPHY: CHAPTER TWO

Anli, G. (2018). Examining the predictive role of authenticity on internet addiction in Turkish high school students. *Universal Journal of Educational Research*, *6*(7), 1497–1503.

Bradford, K. (2019). Radical authenticity. *Existential Analysis: Journal of the Society for Existential Analysis*, *30*(1), 115–127.

Brown, C. & Jasper, K. (1993). *Consuming Passions*. Second Story Press.

Farinon, L. (1998). *The Relationship of Anger, Self-Silencing and Feminist Consciousness to Disordered Eating Symptomatology in Women* (Doctoral dissertation, University of Toronto).

Gilligan, C. (1982). *In a Different Voice: Psychological Theory and Women's Development*. Harvard University Press.

Gordon, E.L., Ariel-Donges, A.H., Bauman, V. & Merlo, L.J. (2018). What is the evidence for "food addiction?" A systematic review. *Nutrients*, *10*.

Grubb, M.L. (2016). *Concurrent Psychotherapy and Twelve-Step Recovery for Compulsive Overeating: An Interpretative Phenomenological Analysis* (Doctoral dissertation, Pacifica Graduate Institute).

Hicks J.A., Schlegel R.J. & Newman G.E. (2019). Introduction to the special issue: Authenticity: Novel insights into a valued, yet elusive, concept. *Review of General Psychology*, *23*(1), 3–7.

Jack, D.C. (1991). *Silencing the Self: Women and Depression*. Harper Perennial.

Jack, D.C. (2011). Reflections on the silencing the self scale and its origins. *Psychology of Women Quarterly*, *35*(3), 523–529.

Johnson, P. (2013). 'You think you're a rebel on a big bottle': Teenage drinking, peers and performance authenticity. *Journal of Youth Studies*, *(16)*6, 747–758.

Kernis, M.H. & Goldman, B.M. (2006). A multicomponent conceptualization of authenticity: Theory and research. *Advances in Experimental Social Psychology, 38*, 283–357.

Kokkoris, M.D., Hoelzl, E. & Alós-Ferrer, C. (2019). True to which self? Lay rationalism and decision satisfaction in self-control conflicts. *Journal of Personality and Social Psychology, 117*(2), 417–447.

Kovács, B. (2019). Authenticity is in the eye of the beholder: The exploration of audiences' lay associations to authenticity across five domains. *Review of General Psychology, 23*, 32–59.

Lister, J.J., Wohl, M.J.A. & Davis, G.C. (2015). The dark side of authenticity: Feeling "real" while gambling interacts with enhancement motives to predict problematic gambling behavior. *Journal of Gambling Studies, 31*(3), 995–1003.

McConnell, D. & Golova, A. (2023). Narrative, addiction, and three aspects of self-ambiguity. *Philosophical Explorations, 26*(1), 66–85.

McConnell, D. & Snoek, A. (2018). The importance of self-narration in recovery from addiction. *Philosophy, Psychiatry, & Psychology, 25*(3), E31–E44.

Maslow, A.H. (1971). *The Farther Reaches of Human Nature*. Viking.

Meule A. (2015). Back by popular demand: A narrative review on the history of food addiction research. *Yale Journal of Biology and Medicine, 88*, 295–302.

National Eating Disorders Association (2024, September 11). *Eating Disorders in Men and Boys*. https://www.nationaleatingdisorders.org/eating-disorders-in-men-and-boys/

Overeaters Anonymous. (2018). *The Twelve Steps and Twelve Traditions of Overeaters Anonymous* (2nd ed.). Overeaters Anonymous, Inc.

Piran, N. & Cormier, H.C. (2005). The social construction of women and disordered eating patterns. *Journal of Counseling Psychology, 52*, 549–558.

Rostand, E. (2012). *Cyrano de Bergerac*. L. Blair (trans.). Signet Classics. (Original work published 1897.)

Ryan, W.S. & Ryan, R.M. (2019). Toward a social psychology of authenticity: Exploring within-person variation in autonomy, congruence, and genuineness using self-determination theory. *Review of General Psychology*, *23*(1), 99–112.

Sedikides, C., Lenton, A.P., Slabu, L. & Thomaes, S. (2018). Sketching the contours of state authenticity. *Review of General Psychology*, *23*(1), 73–88.

Sibley, A.L., Schalkoff, C.A., Richard, E.L., Piscalko, H.M., Brook, D.L., Lancaster, K.E., Miller, W.C. & Go, V.F. (2020). "I was raised in addiction": Constructions of the self and the other in discourses of addiction and recovery. *Qualitative Health Research*, *30*(14), 2278–2290.

Striegel-Moore, R.H., Silberstein, L.R. & Rodin, J. (1993). The social self in bulimia nervosa: Public self-consciousness, social anxiety, and perceived fraudulence. *Journal of Abnormal Psychology*, *102*, 297–303.

Tan, J.O.A., Hope, T. & Stewart, A. (2003). Anorexia nervosa and personal identity: The accounts of patients and their parents. *International Journal of Law and Psychiatry*, *26*(5), 533–548.

Wilfley, D.E., Schwartz, M.B., Spurell, E.B. & Fairburn, C.G. (2000). Using the Eating Disorder Examination to identify the specific psychopathology of binge eating disorder. *International Journal of Eating Disorders*, *27*, 259–269.

Wood, A., Linley, P., Maltby, J., Baliousis, M.J. & Joseph, S. (2008). The authentic personality: A theoretical and empirical conceptualization and the development of the authenticity scale. *Journal of Counseling Psychology*, *55*(3), 385–399.

CHAPTER THREE

"Depressed"

"But You Don't Burst": What Keeps a Person from Suicide?

The story "Depressed," in the lyrical Japanese form of haibun, which combines prose with haiku, traces the thoughts and concrete experiences of a person with depression.

Lucinda is in her twenties and has battled anxiety and depression since she was a child. She takes the story as a springboard to talk about how suicidal ideation accompanies her depression and how she has kept from acting on these ideas. She is often on "the teetering line between I don't want to live and the part that wants to live, feel joy."

The research part focuses on a theory that illuminates what might lead people from suicidal thoughts to attempts. Having some hope and feeling connected are suggested as two elements that prevent people from carrying out suicide attempts.

THE STORY

Depressed

It cannot be done. The blanket is too heavy, the legs too tired. "The fog —" you want to add… but you need to rest. You close your eyes. You cannot think long sentences.

The fog too thick.

Like cotton. Not fluffy-cloud cotton; dusty cotton stuffed in your mouth. You can hardly breathe. How can you lift a blanket?

The alarm goes again. You are, indeed, alarmed. Alarmed at the cotton. Alarmed that you can feel nothing, at the tiredness, and at your heartbeat with dread all at the same time. This is when you can think long sentences: when they are about that never-ending, boring ugliness.

You hear yourself, though distantly, explain to yourself and to a world that does not care how your limp hair will repel anyone mistaken enough to feel attracted to you; how you know that the letters on your laptop will dance in front of your eyes again, utterly unwilling to reveal any meaning; how you will buy a cinnamon bun and it will just taste bland and your response will be to buy more with money you don't have and stuff your pimply face until you burst.

But you will not burst. Even that cannot be done.

> endless landscape
> an icy wind blows dust
> across the tundra

Thirty minutes later, you find yourself out the door. Somehow you ended up in clothes; you even thought to put on rubber boots and bring an umbrella. You look up. The rain has stopped. For now.

> beetle crawls
> over the dung heap
> a rainbow brightens its carapace

THE INTERVIEW

Lucinda

What were your reactions to reading this story?
It's about a person struggling to get up in the morning because what's the point? You'd rather be hiding under the blanket or somewhere safe.

"You hear yourself, though distantly, explain to yourself and a to world that does not care, how your limp hair will repel anyone mistaken enough to feel attracted to you" — There's no way I can be attractive enough, I won't be able to focus. There's stress eating — at some point eating was enjoyable, but not anymore. Enjoying is a difficult concept for this person. That's relatable.

"Even that cannot be done" — As much as you want to kill yourself, it's not possible, as much as that seems nice or stress-relieving.

Then the part about somehow managing to get up, to be prepared... The intensity is over but not totally gone, the wanting to escape is not totally gone.

The last poem — there's some semblance of possibility with the rainbow. The person feels insignificant, disgusting, trying to get through life, but it's hard to feel. The person is still focused on the dung heap.

The poems come out of nowhere. The rest is very relatable. But from fog to cotton to snow in the tundra to beetle to dung — it's too much. It takes away from what's going on.

What would you say is the main theme?
Being stuck between the part of you that wants to do something, to be happy, be productive, and the "I don't want to be here, don't want to deal with anything" — but you don't burst. The inner struggle between wanting something positive and to just to live... the teetering line between I don't want to live and the part that wants to live, feel joy.

What's a positive message?
"But you will not burst" — there is a glimmer of hope. It has promise.

The amount of times I've thought about totally ending it. There is a part that stops myself. Or when I tell someone, can you please take this knife away from me? There is some sort of internal break or barrier. I always find ways to tell myself, no, you don't want to jump into traffic, no, you don't want to hurt someone else by killing yourself. As much as it sounds so much easier and pleasant, there is this obstacle, there is possibility for happiness or less stress.

How do you feel talking about this?

I've gone to the point where it's something I'm talking about quite a bit, but it doesn't mean it's not going to affect me. There are parts of me that want to cry. I'll probably feel tired after this. It's hard feeling vulnerable and weak, especially if you have expectations of yourself. All the years I've forced myself to tell people and to talk about it… sometimes it hurts more to put what you feel into words, hoping someone will understand what you're going through.

What do you need right now?

A self-soothing coping mechanism. Originally, I was going to do some homework. But now I am going to watch some Netflix, have some tea, so that I feel more with it, less tired, more in the present rather than sitting in a whole bunch of negative emotions.

What's a positive thought we can end with?

Something I've been trying to work on — my mental health is not who I am. It doesn't completely define me, although it's helped shape me. I'm not just someone who's depressed or going through a lot of anxiety — that's not who I am completely. Hard to teach myself that, but I'm not totally defined by this negative, gross thing.

The Research

> "But you will not burst" — there is a glimmer of hope. It has promise.
>
>   The amount of times I've thought about totally ending it. There is a part that stops myself. Or when I tell someone, can you please take this knife away from me? There is some sort of internal break or barrier. I always find ways to tell myself, no, you don't want to jump into traffic, no, you don't want to hurt someone else by killing yourself. As much as it sounds so much easier and pleasant, there is this obstacle, there is possibility for happiness or less stress.

What is this barrier that Lucinda talks about? To understand it, we can look at the path that leads from thinking about suicide to making an attempt. This is the topic that Lucinda suggested I pursue.

Statistics

According to the World Health Organization, about 800,000 people die of suicide each year; it is the fifteenth-leading cause of death worldwide. Rates vary widely by country, in Organisation for Economic Co-operation and Development (OECD) countries for example, from 4 deaths per 100,000 individuals in Greece to over 24.6 per 100,000 in Korea. Psychologist Matthew Nock estimates that about 9% of the population experiences ideation at one or more points in their life and that close to 3% will make an attempt. An attempt is a predictor for subsequent attempts; however, the vast majority of individuals — about 93% — who make an attempt do not die of suicide.

The Path from Ideation to Attempt

One of the newer theories about how ideation (thinking about suicide) may lead to an actual attempt has been developed by psychologist David Klonsky and colleagues in their Three-Step Theory. It revolves around the amount of emotional or physical pain a person experiences, how much hope they have (step 1), how connected they are to those around them (step 2), and whether they have the ability and disposition — the capacity — to carry out an attempt (step 3).

What leads to thoughts about suicide to begin with? In this theory, it is the combination of pain and hopelessness. Of course, this does not mean that everyone who feels pain and hopelessness will start thinking about ending their life.

Pain — Physical and Emotional

Pain can show up in different ways. Chronic physical pain was present in 9% of suicides in a large study by epidemiologist Emiko Petrosky and colleagues. However, for most, it is emotional pain, or 'psychache', that leads to ideation. Emotional pain has many faces: grief, a feeling of defeat or of being trapped, or self-hate and other negative self-perceptions. Social isolation, a lack of a sense of belonging, or perceiving that one is a burden to others can cause great suffering as well. According to psychiatrists Ilya Baryshnikov and Erkki Isometsä, this pain needs to reach a certain level for someone to engage in suicidal behaviour; unfortunately, there are few reliable ways to measure that, which weakens the Three-Step Theory somewhat.

Hope and Hopelessness

Klonsky and colleagues add that "if someone in pain has hope that his situation can improve and that the pain can be diminished, the individual will strive to achieve a future with diminished pain rather than consider suicide." This could make sense of the fact that ideation tends to be higher both in adolescents and seniors. Adolescents often just do not have enough experience to know that their painfully negative view of themselves could eventually transform, which makes it more difficult for them to have hope. At the other end of the spectrum, some older people may have diminished hope because they do not feel they have much to live for anymore.

What can we say about hope? Psychologist Rick Snyder and colleagues define hope as "a positive motivational state that is based on an interactively derived sense of successful (a) agency (goal-directed energy) and (b) pathways (planning to meet goals)." In other words, according to this theory, hope consists of a combination of "I can" and "I see a way." Snyder worked in positive psychology, which investigates how people's strengths help them thrive.

However, when trying to understand hopefulness in people who experience depression, it may be more useful to measure how they are not entirely without hope rather than how 'big' their hope is. A person who is not depressed may often have thoughts like "sure, I can do this" or "I'm just going to figure out a way to get to XYZ." Those types of thoughts are often miles away for a person with depression. In such a person, even the slightest glimmer of hope counts. "Sure, I can do this" may feel unattainable, but "I guess it's possible that one day I find a way to do some of it" can still seem like quite the victory.

Measuring Hope

How does a researcher tell whether someone is hopeless or hopeful? According to psychologist Aaron Beck's Hopelessness Scale, people who feel hopeless may agree with statements such as:

- My future seems dark to me.
- I never get what I want, so it is foolish to want anything.
- I might as well give up, because I can't make things better for myself.

On the other hand, they may have problems agreeing with statements like:

- When I look ahead to the future, I expect I will be happier than I am now.
- I have enough time to accomplish the things I most want to do.
- My past experiences have prepared me well for the future.

Lucinda phrases a lack of hope as "It's about a person struggling to get up in the morning because what's the point?" She is also quite ambiguous: "Being stuck between the part of you that wants to do something, to be happy, be productive, and the 'I don't want to be here, don't want to deal with anything' — but you don't burst." Then there is a tentative improvement, albeit still phrased in a somewhat pessimistic way with "The wanting to escape is not totally gone," and a glimmer of real hope: "There's some semblance of possibility with the rainbow."

Connectedness

Klonsky and colleagues' Three-Step Theory proposes that ideation escalates when pain is greater than connectedness. A paper by Klonsky and one of those colleagues, Alexis May, stresses that connectedness does not only refer to feeling connected to people. It can also "refer to one's attachment to a job, project, role, interest, or any sense of perceived purpose or meaning that keeps one invested in living."

"No, you don't want to hurt someone else by killing yourself." Lucinda is connected enough to be aware of how important she is in the lives of those around her. (In contrast, feeling a burden and that others might be better off if the person ended their life is seen as a major factor in many theories of suicide.)

Seizing on the ideas of role and meaning, we note that Lucinda sees herself as "not just someone who's depressed or going through a lot of anxiety — that's not who I am completely." More precisely, this is a question of identity; something that Klonsky and May could have included in their list of connectedness. Connectedness is also where the research on hope (as opposed to hopelessness) could come in. As mentioned above, one of the hallmarks of hope is being oriented towards goals — being connected to goals, one could say. Lucinda does express some goals, even though she does not use that terminology. One of her goals is to finish her studies, otherwise she would have stopped going to university. She also says there is a part in her "that wants to live, feel joy." She seems to like the "possibility for happiness or less stress." Readers may wonder where depression factors in. Of course, experiences such as self-hate, isolation, and feeling defeated are often significant in depression. May and Klonsky note that while depression is a strong predictor for the first step — pain and hopelessness leading to ideation — a diagnosis of depression does not seem to predict a move from ideation to attempt; they theorize that it is a lack of connectedness that predicts that move.

Capacity

If ideation is strong, the last important fact is whether the person has the capacity to carry out an attempt. Can or will the person act on suicidal thoughts? Klonsky and colleagues suggest that the answer to that depends on three elements: a) disposition, b) acquired capacity, and c) practical factors. One example of disposition is simply lower pain sensitivity, which has a strong genetic component. An instance of acquired capacity is habituation to — becoming used to — pain, injury, fear, or death. This may partially explain the higher-than-average suicide rates in prisons, where repetitive self-harm is not unusual and many have lost some sensitivity to fear and pain.

Of great importance is the practical element — does the person have the means? Indeed, one of the most frequent recommendations for suicide prevention is restricting the means by which a person could harm themselves. Population-wide, public health researcher Marie-Claire Ishimo and colleagues surveyed one hundred studies and found that universal prevention strategies, particularly erecting barriers on frequently used places to jump, were quite effective, especially with regard to preventing the death of men. Restricting access to commonly used means of harm — e.g., firearms in the U.S., pesticides in rural China — also seems to have good results.

Other Theories About Pathways from Ideation to Attempt

According to the frequently cited Interpersonal Theory of Suicide, developed by psychologist Kimberley Van Orden and colleagues, an active desire to end one's life occurs when a person's fundamental need to belong is unmet and the person feels they are a burden to important people in their life. When this coincides with the capacity for suicide, a person may progress to an attempt.

Health psychologist Rory O'Connor developed the Integrated Motivational–Volitional model. It begins with a motivational phase, which provides the 'why'. Feelings such as defeat or humiliation in the face of adverse life circumstances combine with poor coping skills, which leads to a feeling of being trapped. This in turn can bring the person to see suicide as the only solution, which may lead to suicidal intent. In the following phase, the volitional or action phase, factors such as impulsivity and access to lethal means can make an attempt more likely.

Protective Factors: Problem-Solving Skills and Positive Reframing

Aside from connectedness and restricted means, what could be other protective factors? Effective problem-solving skills are mentioned in a paper by psychiatrist Mark Sinyor and colleagues that studied global trends in suicide. That study also tentatively proposes religion, with the caution that the protective effects of religion may be limited to certain cultures and age groups. One would assume that there are also many overlaps between religion and connectedness, for example in terms of human connection and life purpose.

Psychologist Adam Horwitz mentions positive reframing, which is shifting one's perspective on an issue, literally giving it a different, more positive frame (e.g., "I try to see things in a different light."). Psychology researcher Andre Mason and colleagues analyzed messages on Reddit, one of the oldest social media sites, to understand what users who were contemplating suicide said about not following through. Most of the themes that held them back tracked with Klonsky's theory, e.g., friends, family and pets, having a purpose, and fear of pain.

Protective Factors in People Who Have Lived with Ideation for a Long Time

Of interest is also the experience of people who have lived with, and survived, ideation for many years. Psychologist Cheryl Hunter facilitated a series of interviews, workshops, and other events with people who had lived with ideation and/or attempts for some time. Sharing their own experiences and advocating in the mental health field was meaningful, including offering "reasonable hope" to each other, a theme also occurring in intimate partner violence (Chapter 9). Living with the shame and stigma associated with suicide was hard for many of them. For some, this was counteracted by experiences with people who valued and accepted them:

> I started to have more nourishing relationships with people [...] an accumulation of thousands of little acts of consideration, kind acts, small acts that don't bubble over the surface, they just keep under the surface, little acts of kindness, consideration, people wanting to celebrate my birthday, people doing me a kindness, people helping me with an essay ...
>
> The person felt like these kind acts gathered in them ... like beads, coming to sort of critical mass [...] I was around my fifties when the beads had gathered enough for it to be a tipping point [...] that took me away from constantly walking on the edge of a cliff, of which one side was definitely suicide and the other side was safety.

The Reasons for Living Scale

An approach that has helped Lucinda is Dialectical Behaviour Therapy, or DBT. It was first developed for people diagnosed with Borderline Personality Disorder, the diagnosis with the highest rate of suicidality of all mental illnesses. Based on cognitive behaviour therapy and using both group settings and individual coaching, DBT incorporates mindfulness and helps individuals learn healthy coping strategies, deal with emotional ups and downs, and improve relationships. DBT has also been shown to be effective in helping people affected by suicidality in general. One of the tools used in DBT is the Reasons for Living Scale. Psychiatrist Camélia Laglaoui Bakhiyi found that two subscales specifically predicted a tendency for lower suicidality: the Moral Objections to Suicide subscale and the Survival and Coping Beliefs subscale. They contain statements such as "My religion forbids [suicide]," "I consider [suicide] morally wrong," "I have the courage to face life," and "I have hope that things will improve and the future will be happier."

"But You Don't Burst"

The part in the story "Depressed" that stood out the most for Lucinda was what she interpreted as an allusion to suicide: "But you don't burst." It is interesting that, while she took that part in a more negative direction than I had originally imagined, she also drew some hope from the story. Would she have seen that hope in her darker moments, when she was deep in her suicidal ideation? We don't know. But for now, she has hope and connectedness, moving her away from both attempts and ideation.

BIBLIOGRAPHY: CHAPTER THREE

Baryshnikov, I. & Isometsä, E. (2022). Psychological pain and suicidal behavior: A review. *Frontiers in Psychiatry*, *13*, 981353.

Beck, A., Weissman, A., Lester, D. & Trexler, L. (1974). The measurement of pessimism: The Hopelessness Scale. *Journal of Consulting and Clinical Psychology*, *42*, 861–865.

Broadbear, J., Dwyer, J., Bugeja, L. & Rao, S. (2020). Coroners' investigations of suicide in Australia: The hidden toll of borderline personality disorder. *Journal of Psychiatric Research, Vol. 129*, 241–249.

Crosby, A., Ortega, L. & Melanson, C. (2011). *Self-Directed Violence Surveillance: Uniform Definitions and Recommended Data Elements, Version 1.0*. National Center for Injury Prevention and Control, Centers for Disease Control and Prevention (CDC).

DeCou, C., Comtois, K. & Landes, S. (2018). Dialectical behavior therapy is effective for the treatment of suicidal behavior: A meta-analysis. *Behavior Therapy*, *50*(1), 60–72.

Fazel, S., Ramesh, T. & Hawton, K. (2017). Suicide in prisons: An international study of prevalence and contributory factors. *The Lancet Psychiatry, Vol. 4*(12).

Gunnell, D. & Eddleston, M. (2003). Suicide by intentional ingestion of pesticides: A continuing tragedy in developing countries. *International Journal of Epidemiology*, *32*, 902–909.

Horwitz, A.G., Czyz, E.K., Berona, J. & King, C.A. (2018). Prospective associations of coping styles with depression and suicide risk among psychiatric emergency patients. *Behavior Therapy*, *49*(2), 225–236.

Hunter, C. (2020). *Living With Suicide: Collective Narrative Practice With People Experiencing Ongoing Suicidality* (Doctoral dissertation, University of East London School of Psychology).

Ishimo, M.C., Sampasa-Kanyinga, H., Olibris, B., Chawla, M., Berfeld, N., Prince, S.A.,... & Lang, J.J. (2021). Universal interventions for suicide prevention in high-income Organisation for Economic Co-operation and Development (OECD) member countries: A systematic review. *Injury Prevention, 27*(2), 184–193.

Joiner, T. (2005). *Why People Die by Suicide*. Harvard University Press.

Klonsky, D. & May, A. (2015). The Three-Step Theory (3ST): A new theory of suicide rooted in the "ideation-to-action" framework. *International Journal of Cognitive Therapy, 8*(2), 114–129.

Klonsky, D. & May, A. (2016). What distinguishes suicide attempters from suicide ideators? A meta-analysis of potential factors. *Clinical Psychology: Science and Practice, 23*(1), 1–16.

Klonsky, D., May, A. & Saffer, B. (2016). Suicide, suicide attempts, and suicidal ideation. *Annual Review of Clinical Psychology, 12*, 307–330.

Klonsky, D., May, A., Saffer, B. & Bryan C. (2018). Ideation-to-action theories of suicide: A conceptual and empirical update. *Current Opinion in Psychology, 22*, 38–43.

Mason, A., Jang, K., Morley, K., Scarf, D., Collings, S.C. & Riordan, B.C. (2021). A content analysis of Reddit users' perspectives on reasons for not following through with a suicide attempt. *Cyberpsychology, Behavior, and Social Networking, 24*(10), 642–647.

O'Connor, R. (2011). Towards an integrated motivational-volitional model of suicidal behaviour. In R. O'Connor, S. Platt & J. Gordon (eds.), *International Handbook of Suicide Prevention: Research, Policy and Practice, 1*, 181–198.

Parra-Uribe, I., Blasco-Fontecilla, H., Garcia-Parés, G., Martínez-Naval, L., Valero-Coppin, L., Cebrià-Meca, A., Oquendo, M.A. & Palao-Vidal, D. (2017). Risk of re-attempts and suicide death after a suicide attempt: A survival analysis. *BMC Psychiatry, 17*(1).

Petrosky, E., Harpaz, R., Fowler, K., Bohm, M., Helmick, C., Yan, K. & Betz, C. (2018). Chronic pain among suicide decedents, 2003 to 2014: Findings from the national violent death reporting system. *Annals of Internal Medicine*, *169*(7), 448–455.

Sinyor, M., Tse, R. & Pirkis, J. (2017). Global trends in suicide epidemiology. *Current Opinion in Psychiatry*, *30*, 1–6.

Snyder, C., Irving, L. & Anderson, J. (1991). Hope and health: Measuring the will and the ways. In C.R. Snyder & D.R. Forsyth (eds.), *Handbook of Social and Clinical Psychology: The Health Perspective*, 285–305. Pergamon Press.

Van Orden, K., Witte, T., Cukrowicz, K., Braithwaite, S., Selby, E. & Joiner Jr., T. (2010). The interpersonal theory of suicide. *Psychological Review*, *117*, 575–600.

World Health Organization (2023, August 28). *Suicide*. https://www.who.int/news-room/fact-sheets/detail/suicide

CHAPTER FOUR

"Balloons"

SIDE-BY-SIDE: APHASIA AND PERSON-CENTRED CARE

Eva has had a stroke and cannot communicate well anymore. And yet, in the story "Balloons," she is the one who shows her friend and ex-therapist the way.

The interview is with Julie, a university professor of nursing. One of her specialties is the care experience of people with cognitive challenges in institutional settings. She says, "There is no black and white. It isn't linear, not like in a lab. When you care for someone like Eva, every day will be very different. And there is togetherness. Sometimes the words don't seem to matter. It's about being attuned to the person."

Her interest in walking alongside the patient and person-centred care is the central theme explored in the research section.

THE STORY

Balloons

"There's too many… too many… tinsel in my head."

The woman's face is all scrunched up. It's from the effort to find the words, Barbara thinks. They are probably there, but old Eva just can't reach or see them. Maybe it's like being on the ferry back home to Hornby Island — she knows the island is there, but in the dense fog, she can't see it and it disorients her. It's a familiar disorientation though, softened by the knowledge that eventually she'll arrive.

Facing the retirement home's garden beyond the big French windows, Barbara sits in the rocking chair. Relaxed as always, she holds Finny on her lap, the most comfortable cat imaginable. All the residents love him. He jumps up on you when you're good and ready, stays soft and still there — none of that frantic kneading that other cats like to get into — and hardly ever holds it against you when you get up.

Barbara sits and listens. Today, she has time to visit. Only two clients scheduled for today and both of them cancelled.

Eva's face lights up. "No, not tinsel! Thoughts! Too many thoughts! They all bump into each other and I can't tell which is which and then I… then I…"

"It gets a bit chaotic in there, doesn't it?" Barbara strokes Finny. "Maybe it feels more chaotic than it used to, but don't forget, there's chaos in everyone's head. Lots of it."

Eva's smile is still so sweet, so delightful — maybe more so now after the stroke. Something exquisite and shiny crept into her that night when she just keeled over in the middle of the dinner party.

"It's not the stroke, it's not that she can't talk so well anymore," Barbara told her stepson Len a few weeks ago, "or that her face looks a little, how should I say? Well, you know, with her eyebrow drooping — no, it's not that!" She had tried to explain it all to him a number of times, but he didn't seem to understand. Sitting here with Eva, the memory of that frustration stirs in her stomach.

Barbara looks down at the cat. She won't tell Eva about that conversation with Len. But:

"There's lots of chaos in my head too, I can tell you that. Should I take this teaching gig in the summer or not? What if I do? How will Len react?"

Eva's smile rests on Barbara. Like the cat on her lap. He's there, soft and kind. Receptive.

"And what about the book? I only have one more chapter to write — can you believe it? — and I haven't touched it for six months. What's that all about? Then there's Len's wheelchair. It needs fixing — he says I don't need to worry about it, I'm not his caretaker — but still.

"I wish I was like Finny." Barbara sighs.

Finny doesn't seem to mind. He is probably used to humans getting all tied up in knots. To him it's just like the weather, nothing to fret over.

Eva opens her mouth. "Balloons!"

Barbara looks at her, her head a little to the side. "Balloons...?"

Eva nods.

"Hmmm.... Balloons..." Barbara tries: "Oh! You're saying all these thoughts, they're balloons?"

Eva laughs. "Yes! It's just the word that came out of my mouth, but yes, that's it! Just let them be balloons, going up in the, in the... you know?"

She manages a sentence or two, then the words disappear again. But her smile is still there, a big grin now.

Suddenly, tears run down Barbara's face. Here she is, Barbara, the brilliant therapist, all about being a good listener, doing the sitting-relaxed-in-the-chair thing, showing herself off as the woman who has her life together — here she is, across from Eva, her client (or her ex-client?, she wonders), who is probably never going to fully recover from her stroke — and Eva is the one who shows her the way.

Balloons!

Ah, maybe it could all be so easy, like floating balloons — maybe ...

But then there is Len, who came into her life only three years ago, after he reconnected with Fred, his father, Barbara's second husband. Fred died only six months later, a merciful death after a short battle with cancer. Barbara offered that Len could stay with her in the big house, then somehow she'd slid into becoming his mother.

That was strange and often trying enough, but then it turned out that Len was buddy-buddy with Eva's favourite niece, Clara. Eva had been Barbara's client, off and on, for twenty years. Now, after the stroke, somehow Barbara's relationship with Len had become entangled with her professional — was it still professional? — relationship with Eva. She'd visit Eva and bump into Clara as they'd come out of Eva's little apartment in the extended care home, or she'd overhear Len and Clara talking about what to get Eva for her birthday.

What was she thinking, talking with Len about Eva? Barbara opens her eyes wide at this huge faux pas. She sits up in the chair.

Eva leans forward. "What — what's on the ladder?"

"What's the matter? I just remembered something. I should — I shouldn't..."

Eva smiles.

Barbara can tell. She just knows that Eva understands. She understands what it's like not to know the words — or wait, that's not it. That's not Barbara's problem. She knows the words but doesn't want to say them, doesn't want to, should not tell Eva that she'd been talking with Len about her. No.

Chaos in her head. Or wait — does Eva understand more? More than that Barbara doesn't seem to be able to find the words?

"It's different now, you know?" she hears Eva saying.

What's different?

Briefly, Barbara finds her way out of the jungle of thoughts. She looks at Eva.

* * *

For a while, they don't say anything. Their eyes meet in a soft place and they feel a connection, a band of weightless appreciation that carries them both as they walk together, side by side, through a small yet infinite measure of time. The hummingbirds outside the French windows whirr, a breeze lifts a few bamboo branches out of their droopy sleep and makes them swish, and little shadows from the poplars dance on the roof of the garden pagoda, framed so lovely by the big old gilded windows. Far, far away, the sound of nursing students chatting — only a few metres down the hallway, but yes, far away.

Slowly, Eva leans forward and pats Barbara's hand.

"The... the man.... the man in the, the coach..."

Barbara looks at her. "The coach? You mean...?"

"Yes!"

"Len?"

"Yes!" That smile again. A big, open, friendly, reassuring grin now. "Don't worry about him. It's all different now. We can't be, we can't be, we can't be — strangers? Strangers anymore? You and I. Don't worry. It's all easy now."

Barbara slides back into the jungle.

Strangers? They are not strangers! Years and years of therapy together —

And back out of the jungle again. Held by the weightless band.

Together. Oh. They are doing therapy together? Not therapist and client, but therapy together?

Barbara smiles too, now. Together. Side by side. No one guides the other. Side by side. Indeed, they are together now.

The bamboo leaves keep swishing. Finny gets up and stretches. Eva and Barbara sit there, without words, smiling together.

THE INTERVIEW

Julie

What was your first impression after reading this story?
Folks I work with come to mind. I used to work in a special care unit. There were many people like Eva — they might have a language difficulty. The relationship between people and their caregivers. The grace. How people live with confusion and you go along with it.

There are people with different kinds of personality. Some fight it [an experience like a stroke or not being able to speak properly] and get very frustrated, but some people go along with it. There is chaos, they fumble with words, and some don't find it. Eventually, the words will come. I see many people like that and I see how Barbara just goes along.

"No one guides the other," they are "side by side"; it's important to walk alongside with the person, just to be there.

If you have a therapist or a caregiver trying to demand a person think in a certain way, it doesn't work very well. It's very much about meeting the person where they're at.

People with a lot of experience working with people with frailty and language difficulties — care aides, nurses — would resonate with what you wrote. That's how they carry out their work, it's part of their care practice.

Ah, that's part of their care practice.
Care practice is interesting. I'm thinking about myself, I wear many hats — professor, nurse, educator. But still, the actual care work is walking alongside the person, to be there, to be present, to play along, to go along. The care itself is about being attuned with the person and their reality, meeting their needs. If you don't understand what they are going through, if you are not in their reality, you can't do a good job of caring for them.

There is no black and white. It isn't linear, not like in a lab. When you care for someone like Eva, every day will be very different. And there is togetherness.

Sometimes the words don't seem to matter. It's about being attuned to the person. Like the slow smile at the end.

There is a bit of a role reversal in the story; Eva seems to be teaching Barbara. What do you think of that?
Yes, it's reciprocal. They're doing therapy together. I don't know about the care aides, they may not identify with that, they wouldn't call it a role

reversal, but they might resonate with learning from that person. Making adjustments, that's good care, every time learning a little more about the person. Tinkering. Definitely learning from each other.

There is a lot of learning that they need to do. What works, what doesn't work. If I talk too fast, that may confuse them. Or some phrases make them laugh. Or if you hum, maybe they like that, then you use it again. Constantly learning from the person.

In therapeutic interactions, there is often talk about 'use of self'. It doesn't sound like caregivers do that a lot, then.
That takes a lot of confidence. It's not something a new grad would do. They are too nervous. They see feeding as a skill and learn all these techniques. They are not ready to use the self. It's another level and then, yes, we improvise.

Do caregivers see similarities between their own lives and that of their patients?
Depends. In a traditional care setting, I think people tend to see themselves as caregivers. They may not use a lot of themselves, especially not in institutions. People may not bring a lot of their own lives into the work. They feel this is paid work, they are here to provide care work. Maybe some exceptional people with a lot of confidence would do that.

Sometimes you can observe the caregivers talk down to patients or drag them a little as they walk somewhere with them. That is not side by side.

Side by side, equal, mutual, a lot of adjustment, that's important. For example, slow down so that they can be side by side.

This side-by-side thing resonates with me. It's important for the person being cared for and also for the caregiver.

Why is it important for the caregiver?
Good care requires that you be really there. If you are willing to walk alongside, it might be different each time, working with someone rather than doing something for them or to them. It's in contrast with the other scenario, dragging the person: "eat your meal, time for a bath, brush your teeth."

When we work with the person and it's about relationship and it's about supporting that person, it's not about finishing a task so that you can go home.

Can you say something about aphasia — in this case, difficulty finding words?
Eva seems to be comfortable with that. I see that in many people. But some folks really struggle with that, they get so frustrated with that. Eva is quite

comfortable with that. As caregivers, we don't get to choose people like Eva. If all were like Eva, work would be so much easier.

High achievers have done a lot of things in their life and they are much more particular about how they present themselves and things they are not able to do. They tend to get more frustrated. Makes me think how the very skillful caregivers are able to work with all sorts of people. Good care is understanding each person is unique, then you have to make some adjustment.

Do less experienced caregivers get frustrated when there are language struggles like that?
A person with less experience tends to go by more concrete steps. "I follow steps one, two, three." But then you need to feel comfortable when a person behaves differently. Over time, you get experience with that. You back up a little bit, use things in your toolbox, what works for that particular person. You won't be so nervous that you have to make adjustments. That's person-centred care. Not doing steps one, two, three exactly as described. Always make the adjustment, respond in the best way. That can be hard when you talk about evidence-based practice, but in reality, people always have to make adjustments. You use evidence but you customize it to the person's needs if, for example, the person has a bad day, maybe there's pain or a difficult visit. A memory can come to them and they get stuck in it.

This reminds me of a story. A person was having trouble eating and the care aide almost gave up. "Look at her, she's doing it again!" she said. The person had taken their teeth out and the care aide got very upset and tried to force the dentures back in. I sat down with the person and listened to her and she was deep in the memory of a time with her dad. It had nothing to do with teeth or breakfast, she was just stuck in the space of thinking about Dad. We had a conversation, then she put the dentures in her mouth and ate the breakfast. I knew she could do it, I had seen her eat chicken wings without a problem. It wasn't about the dentures. It's about the caregiver understanding where the person is at, being with the person side by side, joining in her reality.

THE RESEARCH

Julie immediately resonated with the words "side by side" and wanted to focus on that as a topic. "'No one guides the other,' they are 'side by side,'" she says in the interview, "it's important to walk alongside with the person, just to be there."

I will start with some research articles that directly address these terms. Even though the articles are not written in the context of people like Eva, who has speech difficulties and lives in a long-term care home, it is interesting to see how 'side by side' and 'alongside' are interpreted by the authors.

'Side by Side'

There were very few papers that mentioned those specific words in connection with our topic; for example, searching Google Scholar for "side by side with the patient" in 2020 nets only 159 search results, and 7 more in 2023. Only a few were at least somewhat relevant to this chapter. (As a comparison, searching for the opposite, "guiding the patient," brought almost twenty times as many results.) I found even fewer results using the similar word 'alongside'.

Only one article I found was specific to interactions with older adults like Eva, who live in a long-term care facility. Together with colleagues, Janet Reed, like Julie a university nursing instructor, conducted a study about the use of artificial intelligence–generated images in nursing education with a specific interest in how such images could encourage self-reflective practice among nursing students. Said one student:

> I liked the picture of the nurse walking side by side
> with her arm around an old woman using a walker
> the most. The nurse is not physically supporting the
> patient at all, rather they appear to be walking as
> an allied front. Participating in this activity helped
> me reflect on myself as a person, and I think it is
> the first time I sat down and wrote down my honest
> reason for choosing the nursing profession.

Nursing instructor Malin Karlberg Traav says "most RNs [Registered Nurses], including me, also have a desire to work evidence-based in the daily clinical work side by side with the patient, more as a 'skilled companion' rather than someone who tells the patient what to do or how to live."

However, she does not elaborate what this working side by side is or how it relates to evidence-based practice. The desire she speaks of almost sounds like a fleeting dream.

Witnessing and the 'We' Relationship

The majority of the articles that talked about 'side by side' or 'alongside' were about caring for cancer and/or palliative patients. Nursing faculty Mir Aghaei found "being alongside the patient" to be one of three important characteristics in palliative care practitioners forming bonds with cancer patients. The care team does not only accompany the patient for treatments but also on their psychological journey. Physical presence is an important aspect of this: one nurse spoke about holding the patient's hands to help her feel calmer, while a patient mentioned how important it was for them that someone would come when called.

Lesley Wilkes, a professor of nursing, traced the development of nursing students and described being side by side with the patient as a 'we' relationship. She shared an example of a student caring for someone who had given birth to a stillborn baby, where it shows how important the word 'with' is in a 'we' relationship:

> I let her talk — um — let her cry, I cried with her. There were times when I just went in and sat with her, she just wanted someone to sit there, not to do anything — um — I think that was important.

In addition to being *with* the patient, what is also implied here is witnessing. In her master's thesis on caring for clinically deteriorating patients, Kate Hinvest points to this explicitly, as well as to a sense of co-experiencing: "The nurse is also there alongside the patient, having their own experience of the same moment." This is reminiscent of the 'togetherness' Julie mentions in the interview.

Every day, nurses witness human suffering and loss, but also love and generosity. Said Ben, a nurse, about working with a dying patient and her family:

> I can still remember the doctor having the conversation with her family about all the things we could try and do. I was right next to her, holding her hand. She turned to me and said, "I just want to go to sleep, I don't want any heroics."

Ben stood up for her and then:

> …we turned the page from thinking about how to keep fighting to thinking about how we could make this good for her. She ended up passing away with her daughter holding one hand, her granddaughter holding the other, and her sister stroking her forehead.

Coming Alongside in Advocacy

This stance of advocacy brings us to the only article that mentions the word 'alongside' in the title — *Coming Alongside a Patient Throughout Their Cancer Journey*, Kristina Vimy's master's thesis in nursing. It is not directly about patient care but about patient navigation, something quite similar to advocacy. Healthcare systems are complex and difficult to understand even for people who work in them, so healthcare navigators can be extremely helpful in guiding people to access timely and appropriate healthcare services. For Vimy, "coming alongside" as a navigator is patient-driven and a "basic social process consisting of providing support, preparing patients, and bridging gaps for them as they go through their cancer experience" or, as one navigator describes it, "whatever the patient … needs, whenever they need it in their journey." Vimy notes the meaning of 'alongside': parallel, to the side of, together in cooperation with. This implies a mutual coming together, quite close to the spirit of Julie's interview.

Person-Centred Care for Older Adults

The vast majority of the research pertinent to Eva's and Barbara's story and Julie's interest can be found under the topic of person-centred care. A great amount has been written about the concept. Social work researcher Mark Wilberforce and colleagues note that ideas about person-centredness pull in various directions and are sometimes only vaguely applied, for example when it is just about "giving people what they ask for."

Wilberforce traces some of the origins of person-centred care back to people such as psychologist Carl Rogers and his "unconditional positive regard" for patients, and to Michael and Enid Balint, who introduced psychoanalytic approaches into the work of family physicians. Another important influence was the rise of the biopsychosocial model of care, which opened purely medical approaches of care to psychological and social dimensions.

The Balints called the purely medical approach "unnatural" and stressed the importance of meaningful communication between doctor and patient. They referred to this process as 'two-person medicine', where patient and doctor constantly influence each other. This encapsulates perfectly the relationship between Eva and Barbara.

Wilberforce also discusses the influence of the disability movement on person-centred care, as well as the influence of client-centred approaches in occupational therapy and Tom Kitwood's research on dementia care (which we will look at more closely below). Pulling all of this together, Wilberforce sees three themes: 1) understanding the person, 2) engagement in decision-making, and 3) promoting the care relationship. Sub-themes include honouring a) patients' values and preferences, b) their capabilities and roles, and c) their uniqueness, despite the fact that they may have similar challenges — for example in Eva's case, communication difficulties following a stroke.

The Person in Person-Centred Care: A Social Being

Tom Kitwood was a psycho-gerontologist (i.e., someone who works in the psychology of older people) whose theory of dementia care also contributed significantly to person-centred care for older people generally. Kitwood's core idea is that we need to move away from the person purely as an individual and put more emphasis on the person as a social being. As infants and toddlers, we slowly become persons through interactions with others; this process needs to be redone or strengthened when personhood is radically changed through developments such as psychosis, dementia, or other interruptions of 'normal' ways of interacting with the world.

When healthcare providers perceive such a person as "neurologically impaired, damaged, derailed, deficient" and themselves as "basically sound, undamaged, competent," there is an "Us vs. Them" situation where the problem is squarely in 'them'. This does not lead to building real relationships and leaves the person as someone with "challenging behaviours" rather than just a fellow human being. Kitwood suggests that the problem of dementia care actually stems from *everyone*, not just the patient, being "damaged, derailed, deficient," with one party being neurologically impaired and the other party being "frozen" in a "pathology of normality," protecting themselves with denial about their own flaws and their fears of aging, decline, and mortality.

Unfreezing themselves from this 'pathology' can lead to the real relationships so important for any person. These in turn lead to signs of well-being that are not overly dependent on the cognitive faculties that are neurologically impaired. These signs are:

- assertion of desire or will
- ability to experience and express a range of emotions
- initiation of social contact
- affectional warmth
- social sensitivity
- self-respect
- acceptance of others with similar challenges
- humour
- creativity and self-expression
- showing pleasure
- helpfulness
- relaxation.

Therapeutic Alliances

Kitwood offers an example of social sensitivity:

> [Nurse] C is feeling low in spirits … [Patient] Mrs. D comes close to her, looks her in the face, and says, "You're not so good today, dear, are you?" C squeezes her hand, and says, "I'm feeling a bit sad, Mrs. D., but I'm here." Mrs D. smiles and squeezes C's hands. Somehow Mrs. D. seems to understand.

This reminds one of the relationship between Eva and Barbara, where, just like in this example, it is the supposedly 'impaired' person who offers empathy and understanding.

Also interesting is that Barbara is a therapist, whose very job it is to build good relationships. As Kitwood, Wilberforce, and others such as speech and language pathologist Michelle Lawton and colleagues point out, notions of relationship building, including the idea of a therapeutic alliance originate in psychotherapy.

Some elements of effective alliances are:

- mutual agreement on the patient's goals
- collaboration between therapist/healthcare provider and patient
- an "interpersonal bond," which includes the therapist's/healthcare provider's attunement to the patient
- "use of self" (defined by nurse researcher Asifa Jamil and colleagues as "the intentional use of personal qualities,

emotional intelligence, and interpersonal skills to promote healing and improve patient outcomes")
• creating and increasing hope
• fostering motivation
• boosting confidence — a patient: "Talking was absolutely, you say you're going backwards, but if you talk and talk and talk, and the therapist does help, the whole thing is bolstered."

Relationship-Centred Care and Working Conditions

Person-centred care remains a much-used term to this day, but in 2004, Mike Nolan, a professor of gerontological nursing, found that it is "not the panacea it is held up to be." Part of his misgiving is that, in an effort to counterbalance the notion of impairment or deficit in older people, a 'heroic' model of aging arose, in which aging is almost entirely positive. But neither of these two models — heroic or deficit — do the situation justice; individualism and independence don't reflect the reality of older people receiving care. In order for this care to be of the quality the person deserves, three things need to be in place:

1. *Respecting personhood.* This is similar to Kitwood's idea — the person must be seen not only as an individual but also as a relational being.
2. *Interdependence.* "The best relationships are reciprocal," says Nolan. With that, he means reciprocity and mutuality on all levels: reciprocity between patient and healthcare providers (like we saw in the example above) but also with and within the whole network, of which the patient is part. Nolan points out that the problems that older people in healthcare facilities encounter often stem from healthcare providers themselves not feeling that their opinions and values matter to their colleagues. Their personhood needs to be respected just like the patient's. If they don't feel comfortable, it is hard to create the right atmosphere for a patient.
3. *Investment in caregiving as a choice.* Gerontology and long-term care work are not highly respected areas like, say, surgery, and does not typically attract healthcare professionals who are interested in advancing their careers. Nurses who start in or move to jobs in long-term care often think — erroneously — that it will be easy.

They also often think that they will not be able to make much of a difference, only finding that the differences they can make may be just as big, just on a more subtle level. The working conditions in long-term care are also often not ideal. Nolan argues that all of this can contribute to healthcare staff not being as passionately engaged in the quality of care they give as they could be. He asks for building the sorts of supportive social conditions that encourage staff to more intentionally and enthusiastically choose gerontology and long-term care.

One certainly does not get the impression that Julie lacks passion or enthusiasm. However, what has been discussed for a long time sharply came to light during the Covid-19 epidemic: working conditions in many long-term care homes (which are the majority of facilities for older people unable to live at home), or LTCs, are indeed substandard. For example, an Ontario Ministry of Long-Term Care staffing study suggests, among other things, that staffing in LTCs and funding for it needs to increase, workload needs to decrease, LTCs need to be modernized, and the culture in LTCs needs to change. This change includes a more respectful team environment, leadership accountability, better oversight, and recognition of and career opportunities for non- or semi-professional personnel.

Nurses' Competence — "It's the Whole Body Now"

Julie also suggests that some staff, often the more experienced ones, are more able to be relationship-based. In her nursing master's thesis, Emily MacDonald quotes a nurse frustrated with some of her colleagues:

> They really need to be thinking broader ... They need to be thinking case management. They need to be thinking you know why is this person like this today? So if all of a sudden somebody has had 3 falls, WHY? It's not just a matter of filling out that falls investigation form, tick-tick-tick, and putting it aside.

This "tick-tick-tick" is what Julie referred to when she said "A person with less experience tends to go by more concrete steps. 'I follow steps one, two, three.'" In the same vein, critical care nurse Annette Mollerup quotes nurse-researcher Bente Høy, who contrasts formal competence, where nurses have the requisite qualifications and can perform specific duties, with "real competence," which includes the ability to "demonstrate attitudes appropriate to the specific situation." MacDonald also points out that most nurses are trained in and for acute care whereas nursing in long-term care takes a more holistic approach. Said one nurse:

> You know when at the hospital, somebody had chest pain you consulted cardiology … you know you just broke apart the body. You dealt with the part of the body that was surgery, that they had surgery on, and the body was broken into pieces.

In long-term care, she adds, it is different: "It's the whole person now."

Relating to a person as comprised of body parts is reminiscent of the 'unnatural' character of the biomedical approach that Balint abhors. Balint was influenced by theologian Martin Buber, who famously coined the term 'I and Thou', a whole-person, mutual relationship between two people. This is contrasted with an 'I–It' relationship, characterized above by breaking the body into pieces. (Interestingly, philosopher Patricia Meindl points out that Buber explicitly went beyond a "side-by-side" relationship and towards a "with-one-another.")

Are experienced nurses better than novice nurses at creating and fostering these relationships? Two studies I looked at saw no or little difference. One, by Dan Lecocq, a lecturer in public health sciences, found that both professional and student nurses were good at "comforting care" and "humanistic care" (e.g., considering patients as complete individuals) but were not particularly good at "relational care" (e.g., the nurse "helps me to explore what is important in my life").

The other study, a doctoral thesis in nursing by Edtrina Moss, found that the more competent nurses were, the more caring behaviours they showed, but nurses' years of experience did not play a role. Both studies, however, used self-rated questionnaires; this is different from observations made by a supervisor or instructor like Julie. A third person — perhaps such as a supervisor or mentor — might indeed be useful in fostering or deepening the I–Thou relationship between nurse and patient. Nursing educator Kara Sealock studied empathic engagement with patients and families among fourth-year nursing students. A surprising observation was that nurses found more meaning in their exchanges with patients when a third person took part in debriefing of the experience.

Not Finding the Words — Aphasia

Eva is experiencing aphasia, a cognitive/language disorder which often, as in Eva's case, follows stroke. Aphasia literally means to be without ('a-') speech ('phasia'). It may come as a surprise that aphasia is more common than well-known conditions such as multiple sclerosis or Parkinson's disease. What we see most in Eva is paraphasia, a subtype of aphasia, which means substituting ('para') one word for another. In Eva's conversation with Barbara, this does not pose much of a problem; Barbara is patient and interested in what Eva has to say.

Not being rushed (something Julie also referred to) is helpful in interacting with people with aphasia. Speech-language pathologist Tyson Harmon interviewed people with aphasia about their experiences and found that impatience hampered their ability to communicate well. "It's quick, quick, quick; hurry, hurry, hurry," complained one person he interviewed. Another interviewee with similar complaints added that to her, impatience meant disinterest and made her feel ignored.

Some people also lost friends: "Friends long ago, it was like boom boom boom and then no one." It is no surprise, then, that aphasic individuals often suffer from depression, feel isolated, ignored, excluded, and sometimes unsafe.

Good Relationships Foster Good Communication

It is not unusual for healthcare providers to find communication with people who experience communication challenges after a stroke time-consuming, overly difficult, even unnecessary. Rehabilitation researcher and speech pathologist Felicity Bright and colleagues point out, not surprisingly, that building and maintaining a relationship is key. This means, for example, getting to know the person and active, intentional listening for meaning. Most of all, it means engaging in "relational work ... the cornerstone of therapy." Rote techniques for building rapport are rarely enough; providers should not take on the mantle of disconnected professionals or engage in "practitioner-centred monologue" but, rather, be there as a person and see the other as a legitimate, valued conversation partner.

Sharing harmless personal information is encouraged. For example, when a person with aphasia had trouble remembering a word and looked to his wife for help, a healthcare provider normalized the moment by saying that he does exactly the same thing when he can't remember something. (In the story, it worked the other way round as well. Eva, the person who was supposed to be the one with the problem, normalized confusion for Barbara, the supposed healthy person.)

When all these elements — a genuine relationship, listening, valuing the other — are in place, the person feels cared for.

Easing the Feeling of "Being in a Foreign Country"

Health psychologist Louise Clancy reports that people with aphasia can feel like they are in a foreign country, not able to speak the language and communicate effectively. This is particularly true for people living in facilities (like Eva). Especially in the beginning, right after the shock of the stroke, the unfamiliar, noisy, and fast-paced environment can be confusing and bring uncertainty.

Intellectually, the person in this 'foreign country' might be in good form, but the words just don't come out. This speech difficulty despite intellectual ability is often referred to as 'masked competence'. Fortunately, in addition to building good relationships, helpful techniques have been developed. In terms of verbal communication, the communication partner can, for example, repeat words, check understanding, speak slowly, and not give lots of information at once or ask complicated questions. Props can be useful too, such as word lists, images, and using large fonts. Writing or drawing are often helpful. Nonverbal attentiveness and cues are other important elements, such as eye contact, gestures, and showing through body language that there is no need to hurry.

Conversation Partner Training — The Disability Rights Perspective

A person widely cited in the literature on aphasia is Aura Kagan, who at the time of this writing was the executive director of the Aphasia Institute. One of her contributions is the development of a training program for conversation partners with people with aphasia. Some people, like Barbara in the story, come naturally by the ability to communicate well with people with aphasia; in most cases, it needs to be trained.

Kagan's training uses a social model, which has two aspects — communication related and societal. The societal aspect leans on the work of the disability movement, which "defines disability in terms of societal barriers and restrictions rather than in terms of an individual's inability to carry out normal activities." The person with aphasia should be treated not as 'other', but as an integral part of whatever social group(s) they are part of. In this connection, let's look at the Communication Bill of Rights, especially for individuals with severe disabilities. Put forth by speech language pathologist

Nancy Brady, it consists of fifteen points, including:

- the right to interact socially, maintain social closeness, and build relationships
- the right to make comments and share opinions
- the right to ask for and give information, including information about changes in routine and environment
- the right to have communication acts acknowledged and responded to even when the desired outcome cannot be realized.

A model that emphasizes the societal aspect is the Life Participation Approach to Aphasia (LPAA) discussed, among others, by speech pathology educator Roberta Chapey and colleagues. LPAA is driven by people with aphasia (as well as their supporters) who strive to achieve their life goals, however small or large, however short- or long-term. Julie's story comes to mind, where the person wouldn't eat until they could speak about a memory of her father — dealing with that memory was her personal goal at that moment, not the externally scheduled goal of eating when their caregiver wanted her to. LPAA focuses on creating and maintaining supportive environments and stresses that communication is not just a method for exchanging information but also crucial for maintaining social links.

Kagan aptly sums up the importance of the societal part of the training: "Conversation is central to life participation ... this is where the work of society gets done."

Conversation Partner Training — The Conversation Itself

The second aspect of Kagan's training is about conversation skills. Kagan observed that until her work in the 1990s, the focus was usually on how to overcome the deficit on the part of the person with aphasia. Healthcare providers, and speech-language pathologists specifically, were (and in many cases still are) 'fixers' of communication deficits. However, they are ultimately conversation partners and, as such, their own communication abilities and styles have just as important a role to play as the person with aphasia. Kagan's training gives potential conversation partners — healthcare providers, friends, family, etc. — skills to serve as a "communication ramp" for the person with aphasia. (This is reminiscent of Vimy's patient navigation work, where she comes alongside to bridge communication gaps.) Conversational competence encompasses:

- Ensuring comprehension on the part of both the aphasic partner and their conversation partner
- Ensuring that the person with aphasia can express their feelings and thoughts, which may include responses to the conversation partner.

The aim of the training is to create and increase opportunities for aphasic individuals to participate in daily life. An important aspect of it is to learn how to acknowledge and bring forth the aphasic person's communication-related competence. The training itself includes understanding the experience of persons with aphasia and increasingly sophisticated role play.

Images are used extensively. For example, the person is shown a menu of things they may want to have a conversation about — e.g., 'my children', 'money', 'the future' — each with a corresponding icon. The same method is used for the question "What might prevent you from doing an activity?" with menu options such as "understanding what others say" and "nervous about a new situation."

Kagan was a true pioneer in this field. Her conversation partner training, as well as something similar, communication partner training, took off since her initial work in the 1990s. For example, until 1997, Google Scholar shows one search result on communication partner training, and between 1998 and 2020, it shows almost nine hundred results for either conversation or communication partner training in aphasia.

"Conversation Is a Gift"

I would like to conclude with Dorothy Tinney whose PhD thesis investigated social interactions with residents in aged care. She states that, in addition to all the factors already mentioned, such as recognizing and accepting the person vs. ignoring them, an important factor is a willingness to demonstrate an interest in the person's ideas and history. Their story is worth hearing and telling. Even more so, such histories, ideas, and conversations are a gift in exchange for the care given by the healthcare provider.

BIBLIOGRAPHY: CHAPTER FOUR

Abramovitch, H. (2015). The influence of Martin Buber's philosophy of dialogue on psychotherapy: His lasting contribution. *Dialogue as a Trans-Disciplinary Concept*, 160–182.

Aghaei, M.H., Vanaki, Z. & Mohammadi, E. (2020). Emotional bond: The nature of relationship in palliative care for cancer patients. *Indian Journal of Palliative Care, 26*(1), 86–94.

Balint, E., Courtenay, M., Elder, A., Hull, S. & Julian, P. (1993). *The Doctor, the Patient and the Group — Balint Revisited*. Routledge.

Brady, N.C., Bruce, S., Goldman, A., Erickson, K., Mineo, B., Ogletree, B.T., Paul, D., Romski, M., Sevcik, R., Siegel, E., Schoonover, J., Snell, M., Sylvester, L. & Wilkinson, K. (2016). Communication services and supports for individuals with severe disabilities: Guidance for assessment and intervention. *American Journal on Intellectual and Developmental Disabilities, 121*(2), 121–138.

Bright, F., Kayes N., McPherson, K. & Worrall, L. (2018). Engaging people experiencing communication disability in stroke rehabilitation: A qualitative study. *International Journal of Language and Communication Disorders, 53*(5), 981–994.

Chapey, R., Duchan, J.F., Elman, R.J., Garcia, L.J., Kagan, A. & Lyon, J.G. (2001). Life participation approach to aphasia: A statement of values for the future. In R. Chapey (ed.), *Language Intervention Strategies in Aphasia and Related Neurogenic Communication Disorders* (4th ed.), 235–246. Lippincott, Williams & Wilkins.

Clancy, L., Povey, R. & Rodham, K. (2018). "Living in a foreign country": Experiences of staff-patient communication in inpatient stroke settings for people with post-stroke aphasia and those supporting them. *Disability and Rehabilitation, 42*(3), 324–334

Harmon, T. (2020). Everyday communication challenges in aphasia: Descriptions of experiences and coping strategies. *Aphasiology, 34*:10, 1270–1290.

Hinvest, K. (2020). *The Meaning of Nurses' Caring for Clinically Deteriorating Patients* (Master's thesis, Auckland University of Technology).

Jamil, A., Kamboh, G.M., Bibi, S. & Iltaf, S. (2024). The therapeutic use of self: A concept analysis. *Journal of Health and Rehabilitation Research, 4*(3).

Karlberg Traav, M. (2020). *Evidence-Based Nursing — Reflections from Different Perspectives* (Doctoral dissertation, Örebro University).

Lawton, M., Haddock, G., Conroy, P., Serrant, L. & Sage, K. (2018). People with aphasia's perception of the therapeutic alliance in aphasia rehabilitation post stroke: A thematic analysis. *Aphasiology, 32*(12), 1397–1417.

Lecocq, D., Delmas, P., Antonini, M., Lefebvre, H., Laloux, M., Beghuin, A., Van Custem, C., Bustillo, A. & Pirson, M. (2020). Comparing feeling of competence regarding humanistic caring in Belgian nurses and nursing students: A comparative cross-sectional study conducted in a French Belgian teaching hospital. *Nursing Open, 8*, 104–114.

Long-Term Care Staffing Study Advisory Group (2020). *Long-Term Care Staffing Study*. Ministry of Long-Term Care.

MacDonald, E. (2017). *An Institutional Ethnographic Exploration of the Transitional Experience of Registered Nurses Entering the Long-Term Care Environment* (Master's thesis, University of New Brunswick).

Meindl, P., Leon, F. & Zahavi, D. (2020). Buber, Levinas, and the I-Thou Relation. In M. Fagenblat & M. Erdur (eds.), *Second-Person Normativity and the Moral Life*, 80–100. Routledge.

Mollerup, A. & Skovby, P. (2004). Nurses' perceptions of their own level of competence. *Connect: The World of Critical Care Nursing, 3*, 70–73.

National Aphasia Association (2016). *Aphasia Statistics*. https://www.aphasia. org/aphasia-resources/aphasia-statistics/

National Joint Committee for the Communication Needs of Persons with Severe Disabilities. *See* Brady et al.

Reed, J., Alterio, B., Coblenz, H., O'Lear, T. & Metz, T. (2023). AI image-generation as a teaching strategy in nursing education. *Journal of Interactive Learning Research, 34*(2), 369–399.

Sealock, K. (2019). *Understanding Empathic Engagement of a Fourth-Year Nursing Student Through Narrative Inquiry* (Doctoral thesis, University of Calgary).

Tinney, D.J. (2006). *Still Me: Being Old and in Care: The Role of Social and Communicative Interactions in Maintaining Sense of Self and Well-Being in Residents in Aged Care* (Doctoral dissertation, Faculty of Medicine, Dentistry & Health Sciences, Population Health, The University of Melbourne).

Vimy, K. (2017). *Coming Alongside a Patient Throughout Their Cancer Journey: A Constructivist Grounded Theory of Cancer Patient Navigation From the Perspective of Registered Nurses in the Navigator Role* (Master's thesis, University of Calgary).

Wilberforce, M., Challis, D., Davies, L., Kelly, M., Roberts, C. & Clarkson, P. (2016). Person-centredness in the community care of older people: A literature-based concept synthesis. *International Journal of Social Welfare, 26*(1), 86–98.

Wilkes, L.M. & Wallis, M.C. (1998). A model of professional nurse caring: Nursing students' experience. *Journal of Advanced Nursing, 27*(3), 582–589.

CHAPTER FIVE

"To Smile at with a Nod"

FRIENDSHIP AND THE AUTISM SPECTRUM

In "To Smile at with a Nod," young Martin, who has an unusual way of relating to people and things — some call it autism — encounters a girl who might just become a new friend.

The interviewee, Olivia-Rose, is a woman in her forties. While at university, she was diagnosed with Asperger Syndrome, nowadays referred to as high-functioning autism. She works part-time in a non-profit agency and is a published author of poetry. Her faith is very important to her. Olivia-Rose lives with a relative, which is not always easy. Developing and maintaining friendships has been hard throughout her life. In her words, "It's hard for me to know that someone is my friend unless they tell me. Even if I've spent quite a bit of time with them, unless they say they're my friend, it's hard for me to tell."

Among other things, the research portion looks at the concept and experience of friendship. It also challenges the deficit assumptions common among some autism researchers.

THE STORY

To Smile at with a Nod

"Ellarina!" Or something like that. The voice wasn't far but he couldn't make out the words over the sound of the waves. Her voice was so excited, it squeaked.

Martin covered his ears. Loud, high-pitched sounds flipped a switch inside him worse than a fire alarm.

But looking out the window, he noticed the girl was pleasing to his eyes, that red dress waving in the breeze, one hand keeping a big straw hat from blowing off, stalking around the beach in brown cowboy boots.

"Ridiculous," Aunt Brenda snorted when she saw the girl.

That word gave Martin an itch in the stomach, dull bristles poking from inside. 'Ridiculous' meant something to laugh at, from the Latin *ridere*, to laugh. 'Ridiculous' was often accompanied by a snort and it was not a nice laugh. What Aunt Brenda was laughing at, he could not tell, only that it had something to do with the girl. There was nothing about the girl in the red dress that made him laugh in a not-nice way. *Adnuere* is what he wanted to do, 'to smile at with a nod'. Nodding is what you do when you say 'yes' and there was something about the girl that made him want to say 'yes'.

But how could he say yes when he had to cover his ears at the sound of her voice? Those were not two things you could do at the same time. It used to be that he did not know that there were things he could not do simultaneously, like scream and breathe deeply at the same time. Dr. Polt had taught him that. That was nice of Dr. Polt. Dr. Polt had done many nice things. Now he knew to say 'thank you' to him; something else he had learned from the doctor. When someone does something good for you, you thank them.

Lately, Martin had observed that people sometimes said things like 'Thanks a lot' when they didn't mean it. "That's called sarcasm," Dr. Polt had explained. Martin was still pretty fuzzy on that idea but what he did understand was that it had something to do with meaning one thing and saying the opposite, but for some reason it wasn't lying. Was it sarcasm that he had to cover his ears when the girl started squeaking but at the same time he wanted to … watch her more? Get closer? No, that was probably something different.

He felt confused. He was sure of that because confusion was always right there at the tip of his right anterior deltoid — there was a muscle fibre that twitched when his mind was muddled up, a fasciculation. It was good to know that it was confusion. Knowing was a feeling he liked. He could sense it all over his body, like a light, golden leaf covering him from head to toe. Feeling that, or even just thinking about it, calmed him, soothed him.

He peeked at the girl again. It looked like the squeaking had stopped — maybe. She was bending down now. Her long blond hair had fallen all over her face, front, and shoulders. Martin shook himself; the hair looked nice, but wouldn't it be awful to have it all over you? In your face of all places? He brushed that feeling away; it made him gag. Yet something else he had learned from Dr. Polt. You didn't have to stay in every feeling that happened, you could make it go away. That was neat, really neat. He liked that word, neat. *Scitum* was probably the best Latin word for it, but 'neat' felt better as you said it, with the 'n' starting it off, the tongue pressed against the front palate, the 'ea' coming off easily, all you had to do is take the tip of the tongue down, then back for the 't' with a bit of a spit.

The girl too, there was something 'neat' about her. It made Martin's legs and feet stand him up. Up, up. "He's so tall for his age," Aunt Brenda always said, with a sound that made him feel small and slippery like a slug. 'For his age' meant… he was not entirely sure because it involved math. A man once said to him that people who were good at Latin should also be good at math. Martin could remember the voice, dark and boomy — "maaath" — like he was talking into Aunt Brenda's big black pot, but he couldn't remember who it was. What that man said made no sense. Numbers were hard and jagged, Latin round and pliable. Martin did figure out that 'for' was f-o-r, not the number four, but that made it even more difficult to understand why 'for his age' had something to do with math. He also had not worked out yet why Aunt Brenda had that angry look on her face when he explained why it didn't make any sense, but maybe it was because she didn't like Latin. There were many people who didn't like Latin or talking about the difference between the sartorius and quadriceps muscles. The thought that Martin had about that was 'sad', something in the head, dark and heavy, like your neck muscles couldn't hold up your skull and brain and face. It was sad that so few people liked Latin.

With his feet and legs and hips mostly, although his back and many smaller parts too — walking uses over two hundred muscles (two hundred and one? two hundred and ten? eleven? numbers just didn't stick) — Martin opened the door, walked across the patio and down to the beach. He stopped beside the girl. She looked up at him and smiled.

"Hello," she said, "my name is Allegra. I'm from Italy. Do you like *stellarina* — starfish?" The way the words arrived at his ears made him think of the word 'neat' again.

Beside her lay a big book. *Ovidius: Metamorphoseon libri*, it read. In Latin.

THE INTERVIEW

Olivia-Rose

What was your first impression when you read "Latin?" [original story title]
I thought "autism" in the first paragraph, when it talks about the loud noises.

Does this remind you of your life in any way?
I get the not knowing the senses and the noises and everything. It brings back memories when I was at camp at one time. It was really loud. I had to go outside, it was too loud for me. Yet other noises don't bother me.
   I also like the Latin aspect of the story.

What do you like about it?
I love Latin. I have a thing for Latin. A wonderful language. If you learn it, you get to the root of things, you learn how to spell a lot of things.

What else?
I don't think I like the aunt. She was mean to the boy.

Have you had people like that in your life?
Yes, my older cousin, who judges people all the time. She says mean things about everybody and says that what she says is the truth about them. It reminds me of that. That's been an issue for me. She says that when someone says something nice about me that person didn't really mean what they said. Or things like "He would never touch you because of your weight" or "She can't be your friend, she is my age" or "Everybody in my family has blocked you [on social media] and don't want to be with you." It may have a grain of truth though, sometimes, and that makes me doubt things.

What's that like for you?
As someone on the spectrum, it's more difficult for me to slough it off. When you're on the spectrum, words are stuck forever in your head, 24/7. As a child, other people would get over things but not I. E.g., my grade 4 teacher, Madame Freman, sent me to the principal for drawing green bunnies. There is no such thing as green bunnies, she said. It was awful. I will never forget that.
   Years later, a friend gave me green plush bunny for Easter and I named it Freman. That's a good revenge.

Anything else in the story that reminded you of your life?
I can't do two things at the same time. I cannot multitask.

The double meanings of things like sarcasm are really hard for me to tell. Sometimes I use it myself but it's difficult when others use it. But I know when I'm being sarcastic. "It was so nice of you to abandon me." Or "I enjoyed being beaten up."

Do you see anything positive or hopeful in this story?
The fact that Allegra is going to be his friend. I liked the last paragraph. "I'm from Italy. Do you like starfish?" — that is hopeful. I like that he smiles at her.

How about friends in your life?
It's hard for me to make friends. It's hard for me to know that someone is my friend unless they tell me. Even if I've spent quite a bit of time with them, unless they say they're my friend, it's hard for me to tell. Friends can be fickle too, they can come and go. Sometimes, you think you know somebody but you don't. One person I've known asked me for $500 for his business and he had a "the world screwed me over" mentality. When we hung out, I got angrier and angrier. It was not good. I'm glad I'm not friends with him anymore. He was falsely positive. He sounded like he was upbeat on the surface, but underneath it was negative, negative, negative. The more you got to know him, he talked about how everyone screwed him over, my grandmother screwed me over, the autism community screwed me over, my mother screwed me over, my father screwed me over. He didn't place any responsibility on himself. Perhaps some of his actions could have contributed to his problems, but he thought he was the faultless person.

I take full responsibility for my actions. Like letters I've written to my family that were not very nice. It's damaged relationships and I'm taking responsibility for it and repair the damage. My cousin says the damage is done. But I can work on it.

Has there been anyone like Dr. Polt in your life?
My current counsellor. If I have an email communication at work that has gone wrong, she tells me exactly how it is, what's going on. She gives me good rules for things.

What's an example of a good rule?
E.g., how I need to think straight, or when I'm stressed at work, to work quietly and not talk to anybody that morning. That happened at the anniversary of my father's death. I can always email her and vent. That makes it easier for me to stay positive.

How were things before you met that counsellor?

I had issues at work. I was so angry and also, in other group situations, I did not know how to calm down. I also had a boss who made things worse. I got into a lot of trouble with her. She had this fake smile and there was something off about her. When she left, I was supposed to go to her office and hug her goodbye. I refused. That got me into a lot of trouble. I didn't know how to express myself and then overreacted. I got into trouble because I didn't feel comfortable. I made a scene and I got into trouble for that. I was really loud, said "Don't touch me." It was awful. I felt disrespected. But now I have a new supervisor and it's so much better.

Anything else you'd like to say?

Lying and truth is difficult for me. People don't tell me things not to hurt my feelings or they otherwise withhold information. I don't think that's nice. If people don't tell me what they don't like about me, how can I know? For example, if someone clicks their pen and it gets really annoying, doesn't that produce more anger if you don't tell them?

I like the rules a friend has given me. Three emails a week, no more. Rules really work for me. If you give me a hard and fast rule, that really helps. If you say something like "sometimes" — what does that mean? But if you say, you can send me three emails a week, then I can do that.

If you were to meet young Martin, what would you say? Would you give him any advice?

He is nice. I don't know what advice to give him.

Always ask for clarification. Ask people to be upfront and to tell him if he's being annoying. Give him rules he can follow.

Isabella Mori

The Research

Introduction

Olivia-Rose's first reaction is "I thought 'autism' in the first paragraph, when it talks about the loud noises." She, too, is very sensitive to auditory stimulation. She shares Martin's interest in Latin and doesn't like the aunt, who just does not seem to understand the young man. Like Olivia-Rose's cousin, the aunt is neurotypical, someone who experiences the world and herself in expected ways and cannot put herself in the shoes of someone who thinks differently. She often becomes judgmental when people don't conform. Olivia-Rose demonstrates in some detail how painful that is. With that, she expresses something that is not only hard for people on the autism spectrum but is probably experienced by everyone interviewed here: stigma, or the judgment for being perceived as 'other'. Some interviewees, such as Johnson and Gabrielle, talk about it directly. In the chapter on aphasia, the research discusses it at some length. But Olivia-Rose is the most outspoken about it.

Olivia-Rose dispels the myth that people on the autism spectrum are not interested in friendship. It's just that the rules of friendship are hard for her to grasp — and no wonder, because friendship is one of those things with an expectation that everyone just knows how it works. (Whether that is actually the case is questionable, but somehow most neurotypicals seem to squeak by.)

It's also interesting that Olivia-Rose understood the story just as it was intended. Of course, I had no expectations of interviewees interpreting a text I gave them in the same way I did, but there is something intriguing about the fact that it was a person on the autism spectrum who intuited the night language of the story pretty much the same way I did when I wrote it.

A last example of where Olivia-Rose aligns with the story is in the parallel between Dr. Polt and her own counsellor, who guides her through the maze of human relationships the way Dr. Polt does Martin.

The Autism Spectrum

Olivia-Rose felt that the most interesting topic to delve into after our interview was friendship as experienced by people with high-functioning autism (HFA). HFA is a subset of Autism Spectrum Disorder (ASD). The DSM-5 describes ASD as "persistent deficits in social communication and social interaction across multiple contexts ... restricted, repetitive patterns of behaviour, interests, or activities [which] cause clinically significant impairment in social, occupational, or other important areas of current functioning."

People on the high-functioning end of the autism spectrum tend to have challenges around back-and-forth conversation, sharing or reciprocating emotional content, making eye contact, or understanding body language, all of which can lead to difficulty with relationships. People on the spectrum often have a need for repetition and routines and can have very specific and narrow interests (such as Martin's interest in Latin and anatomy). Many, like Olivia-Rose, are highly sensitive and distressed by sensory input such as noise or touch. Imagination also seems to work differently for people with HFA. Psychologist Simon Baron-Cohen and colleagues have developed a questionnaire in which people with HFA agreed with statements such as:

- I find it difficult to imagine what it would be like to be someone else.
- New situations make me anxious.
- I find it hard to make new friends.

and disagreed with statements such as:

- I am good at social chit-chat.
- I find it very easy to play games with children that involve pretending.

Deficits vs. Neurodiversity

Baron-Cohen and colleagues investigated the similarities between people with HFA and those who had not received that diagnosis, specifically people who may exhibit similar traits, such as computer scientists, physicists, and teenagers who had won the UK Mathematics Olympiad. It turned out that a small percentage (3.3) of science students had traits quite similar to people with HFA. A pronounced ability to notice patterns and the urge to pursue interests — both items on the questionnaire — are useful to all scientists but come naturally to many people with HFA.

This shows that the historical way of looking at people with autism, specifically HFA, does not paint an accurate picture. Expressions such as "inappropriate use of eye contact," "failure to develop friendships," "impairments in communication," "problems with the pragmatic and social aspects of language," "impairments in imagination," and "rigid and repetitive behaviours" point to a problem-based view and are found frequently in the literature, writes psychologist Charlotte Brownlow. Hence, some researchers started questioning these ideas, stating, among other things, that "what counts as impairment is culturally relative."

This is connected to the notion of neurodiversity (now often referred to as neurodivergence), a term coined by scientist Judy Singer, who is also autistic. Neurodiversity challenges the assumption of autism as a disorder to be eradicated, prevented, treated, or cured. Related to this is the term 'neurotypicals' — people whose thinking and interacting is more mainstream and who often "assume that their experience of the world is either the only one, or the only correct one." (For a delightful and thought-provoking reading on this, visit the Institute for the Study of the Neurologically Typical.)

What Is Friendship?

Here are some characteristics of friendship as found in the literature:

- Acceptance
- Affection — the parties like each other and show it
- Conflicts resolved to everyone's satisfaction
- Cooperation, equality and reciprocity (e.g. benefiting equally from the relationship)
- Desire on the part of each party to spend time together
- Emotional support
- Having fun together
- Honesty and trust
- Intimacy (e.g., self-disclosure, discussion of personal topics)
- Listening to and understanding each other
- Loyalty (e.g., standing up for a friend in his/her absence)
- Practical support (e.g., volunteering to help in a time of need)
- Sharing (e.g., news of success, ideas)
- Similarity.

Of course, it must be noted that some of these may be more Western notions. For example, in a study by psychologist Marina Doucerain and colleagues that compared Russian with Canadian friendships, friendships in Russian contexts are described "as deep, very close, and a strong bond, with frequent communication and (almost unconditional) help in adversity as essential features." Canadian concepts of friendship showed up as "a lighter relationship, with greater emphasis on congeniality and the sharing of pleasant activities, or 'having fun.'"

Olivia-Rose and Friendships

While the section on deficits vs. neurodiversity questions many assumptions regarding autism, Olivia-Rose's interview shows no such challenges. When it comes to her friendships and relationships, most of them seem to be with neurotypicals. She wants to know and follow relationship 'rules', talks about the hurt she has experienced in relationships, shares her difficulties around communication, and lets us know how difficult it is for her to make and maintain friends. In this, she is not alone. Occasionally, the question arises whether it is even necessary or desirable for people with HFA to have friends, but all in all, most people with HFA do want friendships. Olivia-Rose certainly wants to have friends, as does Martin in the story. Says speech pathologist Erinn Finke:

> Autistic people want to experience more than just integration or inclusion within communities, they want to belong … Belonging is the feeling of security and support when a person is accepted and valued for being their authentic self. … Belonging is experienced best through relationships, and is core to the neurodiversity movement.

Friendship Rules

In his master's thesis in psychology, Elliott Newton states "there is no formal agreement between friends, it is generally an unspoken bond. There are no rules, or lists of instructions." That makes things difficult for Olivia-Rose and other people with autism. Lists like the ones above (presumably generated by a neurotypical sample) are extremely rarely discussed among friends and would only be partially helpful. A person with autism might have to spend some time deciphering precisely what it means, for example, to show affection, acceptance, or emotional support, especially in a neurotypical environment. An interviewee in Sophie Chappell's psychology PhD thesis on friendships and intimate relationships among people on the autism spectrum explains:

> With people with Asperger's it's harder […] because they don't sort of know the social […] unwritten rules, and they find it difficult to be naturally intuitive, or naturally […] considerate to other people, the needs of other people.

This is partly because they can find it difficult to imagine or understand other people's thoughts, feelings, and desires (referred to by researchers as having a 'theory of mind'). Another reason is that many people with autism simply have not had enough opportunity to learn and practice neurotypical friendship skills and are often used to relationships characterized by power imbalance, e.g., with parents, teachers, or counsellors.

Erinn Finke found differences between friendships by neurotypical people and friendships by persons with an ASD diagnosis. While both groups valued similarity of personality between friends, the ASD group was more interested in concrete arrangements when connecting with friends (e.g. meet for specific activities), as opposed to 'just chatting', and thought their friends see them mostly as someone to have fun with as opposed to neurotypicals ('NTs') who see themselves most importantly as a support to their friends. Persons with ASD also enjoyed more online-only friends.

Verbal Communication

This is also the case for Olivia-Rose and Martin, who have good relationships with their counsellor/therapist. Both communicate well with those professionals and appreciate what they learn from and with them. Martin, for example, is in the process of learning about sarcasm, something that Olivia-Rose also finds a bit baffling. A person says one thing but means another; why is this strange thing called irony and not a lie? Irony is ever-present in neurotypical language; psychologist Raymond Gibbs Jr. found 4.7 instances of irony once every two minutes in spoken communication. People on the spectrum typically "have no clue what [others'] intent may be" (one of Newton's participants) and have to painstakingly learn about forms of communication like that.

They are also often very honest — sometimes brutally so — and like to be specific and explicit. When NTs know that, it can be quite helpful. Participants in Newton's exploration of how adults on the spectrum experience friendships with NTs states that the participants in his study "welcomed being told when they were talking too much or overstepping a mark." They valued "clear, non-abstract language, and setting boundaries such as agreeing to change the topic after five minutes." This is similar to the email rules appreciated by Olivia-Rose or to the rule Martin learned about saying 'thank you' when someone does something nice for him. And Olivia-Rose's observation that she needs to be told whether or not someone is a friend is echoed almost exactly by one of Newton's participants who did not know that friendships had been formed until somebody told him.

Hurt

Olivia-Rose was ordered to hug someone goodbye. While this is hardly acceptable under any circumstance, it is particularly difficult for people on the spectrum, who are often highly sensitive, and therefore adverse, to touch. Sociologist Hanna Bertilsdotter-Rosqvist's observation about public spaces come to mind, which she admits are shared social spaces but "in essence neuro-separate space, dominated by NTs and [...] often experienced as hostile by autistic people."

Being ordered to hug someone could be interpreted as bullying, which is something many people on the spectrum have experienced. It was difficult to find research on bullying of adults with autism, but research on children with high-functioning autism shows they are four times more likely to be bullied than those without any obvious disability. People with autism often find the conscious and unconscious social codes in the NT world hard to understand and follow, so are therefore exposed to bullying, ridicule, rejection, and isolation.

Olivia-Rose refers to Martin's aunt and her older cousin as 'mean' and mentions how she speaks disparagingly of her relationships, including romantic ones. One hopes she had met someone like Louise in Rebecca Ellis's master's thesis who, after being in quite a few unhealthy relationships as a teenager, wants to tell other young women about her experience and all the reading she has done since. An example is the writing of Maxine Aston, a psychologist specializing in assisting people with high-functioning autism in the area of intimate relationships, who says in her book *The Other Half of Asperger Syndrome*: "the success or failure of a relationship does not depend upon the neurological condition of either partner, but instead on the compatibility of their personalities, values, goals and interests, commitment to the relationship and whether they really care."

Also difficult for Olivia-Rose was 'sloughing off' hurtful words: "When you're on the spectrum, words are stuck forever in your head, 24/7." Interestingly, this goes against at least one research article, by psychologist Lorna Goddard and colleagues, which found that people with HFA performed lower on autobiographical memories (that is, memories about themselves) than others. As a possible reason, the authors of the paper cited that people with HFA tend to have lower visual memory. Visual memory is an important aspect of autobiographical memory. However, the difference in scores of memory retrieval and use were such that there could have been an overlap in the areas of negative and neutral memories, and it is precisely a negative memory that Olivia-Rose recalled.

How good that at least one person understood her and gave her the green bunny.

Bibliography: Chapter Five

Argyle, M. & Henderson, M. (1984). The rules of friendship. *Journal of Social and Personal Relationships*, *1*, 211–237.

Aston, M. (2014). *The Other Half of Asperger Syndrome: A Guide to Living in an Intimate Relationship with a Partner Who Has Asperger Syndrome*. The National Autistic Society.

Bauminger, N., Solomon, M., Aviezer, A., Heung, K., Brown, J. & Rogers, S. (2008). Friendship in high-functioning children with autism spectrum disorder: Mixed and nonmixed dyads. *Journal of Autism and Developmental Disorders*, *38*(7).

Baron-Cohen, S. (2019, April 30). The concept of neurodiversity is dividing the autism community. *Scientific American*. https://www.scientificamerican.com/blog/observations/the-concept-of-neurodiversity-is-dividing-the-autism-community/

Baron-Cohen, S., Wheelwright, S., Skinner, R., Martin, J. & Clubley, E. (2001). The Autism Spectrum Quotient (AQ): Evidence from Asperger syndrome/high-functioning autism, males and females, scientists and mathematicians. *Journal of Autism and Developmental Disorders*, *31*, 5–17.

Bertilsdottir-Rosqvist, H.B., Brownlow, C. & O'Dell, L. (2015). "What's the point of having friends?": Reformulating notions of the meaning of friends and friendship among autistic people. *Disability Studies Quarterly*, *35*(4).

Brownlow, C. (2010). Re-presenting autism: The construction of 'NT syndrome'. *Journal of Medical Humanities*, *31*(3), 243–255.

Bukowski, W.M., Newcomb, A.F. & Hartup, W.W. (1996). Friendship and its significance in childhood and adolescence: Introduction and comment. In W.M. Bukowski, A.F. Newcomb & W.W. Hartup (eds.), *The Company They Keep. Friendship in Childhood and Adolescence*, 1–19. Cambridge University Press.

Chappell, S. (2011). *Friendship and Intimate Relationships in People on the Autism Spectrum* (Doctoral dissertation, University of Warwick).

Doucerain, M., Benkirane, S., Ryder, A. & Amiot, C. (2018). Being a droog vs. being a friend: A qualitative investigation of friendship models in Russia vs. Canada. *Russian Psychological Journal, 1*(15), 19–37.

Ellis, R. (2016). *Exploring Individual Perceptions of Adults Diagnosed With Asperger Syndrome Using a Cultural Framework* (Doctoral dissertation, University of Sunderland).

Finke, E.H. (2022). The kind of friend I think I am: Perceptions of autistic and non-autistic young adults. *Journal of Autism and Developmental Disorders*, 1–18.

Gibbs, R. (2000). Irony in talk among friends. *Metaphor and Symbol, 15*, 5–27.

Goddard, L., Howlin, P., Dritschel, B. & Patel, T. (2007). Autobiographical memory and social problem solving in Asperger syndrome. *Journal of Autism and Developmental Disorders, 37*(2), 291–300.

Hall, J.A. (2012). Friendship standards: The dimensions of ideal expectations. *Journal of Social and Personal Relationships, 29*(7), 884–907.

Institute for the Study of the Neurologically Typical (2002). Archived at http://erikengdahl.se/autism/isnt/

Little, L. (2002). Middle-class mothers' perceptions of peer and sibling victimization among children with Asperger's syndrome and nonverbal learning disorders. *Comprehensive Pediatric Nursing, 25*(1), 43–57.

Newton, E. (2018). *"Neurotypicals are snowflakes, they get offended over the slightest thing": Exploring How Adults on the Autistic Spectrum Experience Friendship with Neurotypicals* (Doctoral dissertation, Leeds Beckett University). Retrieved from https://inclusive-solutions.com/wp-content/uploads/2019/01/Neurotypicals-are-snowflakes-they-get-offended-over-the-slightest-thing.pdf

Sedgewick, F. & Douglas, S. (2023). *Understanding Autistic Relationships Across the Lifespan: Family, Friends, Lovers and Others*. Taylor & Francis.

CHAPTER SIX

"The Monastery"

Yoga and Substance Use

The short story "The Monastery" imagines how random circumstances can lead to changing a person's trajectory of drug use — in this case, through arduous exercise.

The interview was done with Piper, a musician and writer in his late thirties who is in recovery from bipolar disorder and substance use. Piper stresses how different his approach to recovery is from that in the story. What has helped and shaped him are yoga and voluntary participation in the twelve steps as laid out by Alcoholics Anonymous. He sees recovery "as a long journey rather than something quick … a spiritual journey, surrendering, understanding to see how our Higher Power works in our life. Not a pill or even a treatment." Piper also does not classify yoga as exercise; the exercises (or 'asanas') are only a small part of it, hardly mentioned in the Patanjali, yoga's original text.

Research tentatively agrees that yoga (mostly portrayed as exercises and/or short moments of meditation) can be helpful with addiction. Whether involuntary participation in substance-use treatment is effective is a hotly debated topic.

THE STORY

The Monastery

Reporter: Dr. McAngus —

Sean: Call me Sean, please. Brother Sean if you need a title.

Reporter: Brother Sean, then. So — you have become an expert on addiction. You're a psychologist. That started your treatment method, I presume?

Sean: I wish it was that sophisticated. And it wasn't really a treatment method. It was much simpler and more selfish on my part. Honestly, I was just bored, all by myself up there at the old monastery at Broadmore Castle.

Reporter: So, how did it start?

Sean: Well — I was the last surviving brother at Broadmore Castle. I had been the youngest, all the other monks were — oh, I'd say at least two generations older than I. When I decided I did not want to be a psychologist anymore and became a monk, I imagined always to be surrounded by others who had left the worldly life behind. But that wasn't how it turned out. The last one to die was Brother Allan, nine months before Blair came along. So it was just me and the dog, Rufus. I didn't know what to do with myself. There is only so much cleaning and praying and gardening you can do.

Reporter: And then?

Sean: And then Blair showed up.

#

Blair opened his eyes. He had no idea how he had landed in the room — tiny, almost like a jail. Cheap wood panels, an open closet space that didn't fit more than what the five bent coat hangers in it could carry, a nightstand without a lamp, and a rickety plastic chair. A nondescript crucifix hung on the wall opposite the narrow bed with a hard pillow and a fake camel hair blanket.

To his right, a window. Blair got up and looked out: a breathtaking view down a steep cliff and across the empty Scottish landscape.

But never mind. Where was it? In the jacket, of course. He looked around, then under the blanket, under the bed. Where the fuck was his jacket? And the envelope with his stash? And why was it so cold? He shivered and knew it wasn't only because of the chill. Just a bit, just a little hit would help, he knew. In two paces, he was at the door, opened it, and ran out into the long, cold corridor.

"Hello? Hello??"

Far at the other end, past who knows how many windows, he saw the corridor bend; there must be something just around it. He ran towards it. Around the corner, more corridor. He approached a window with the sun shining through. An inner courtyard: a square, a few bushes, a simple fountain, well-kept — and empty. The chill he felt just a minute ago turned into sweat. His heart beat faster than it should, surely? And was this a headache coming on?

What was this sound? He whirled around. Again, that sound! Oh. A creak — his feet on the old hardwood floor. Where was his room? Better run back, find it — ah, there, the open door. And the jacket hanging from a hook at the door! How could he have missed it earlier? Sweet, warm relief washed over him.

Now! Now he could — where was it? Not in the breast pocket where he usually put it. The envelope with a tiny plastic bag inside, full of three hundred pounds worth of pure. He had just bought it. No, not in the other pocket. Everything felt dry now and parched, his hands hurt at every furious brush with the jacket's leather, even the lining. Two, three, four times, he went through each pocket — empty, empty, fucking empty! He ran to the window in the cell — no one there. No cars near or far. Just cliff and landscape.

Breathing had become hard, but it didn't matter. What mattered was that his life needed saving because he would die without a hit. Die. His throat closed up. Running out of the cell, he started sobbing. Down the hallway, to the left, around the next corner. Where was everyone? Anyone? Another corner, back again, maybe he had missed something?

And indeed he had. The second time around, he noticed a narrow set of stairs. Down, down, down he clattered and met no soul. The courtyard? He spied a toolbox in a corner, ripped it open, realized with the bit of intelligence still left that there was no rust — there must be someone, where are they?

"Hel-*loo*!" He hollered again, his chest reverberating, "Where *are* you?"

No answer, except a faint barking.

A dog. Where there are dogs, there are people. He spied an archway leading out of the courtyard. Indeed, a big dog — German shepherd? — stood at the bottom of the cliff, slowly waving his tail, barked some more, and casually walked away.

"I'm coming, I'm coming!" Blair yelled.

But how to get to the dog? Search as he might, he could not find a way down the cliff, no stairs, no secret pulley, nothing. And no one, absolutely no one in this place, not even after opening every door he could find.

He raced up the stairs again. *Sweating like a pig*, he thought to himself, pausing for a moment at the landing to fumble with his shirt buttons. Hot! He was so hot! And so fucking thirsty! Amid a jumbled recollection that pigs didn't sweat, his disorientation was complete — how come there were hallway windows to the *outside* now? Blair half-lunged, half-stumbled to the nearest one — same fucking nothing but that fucking dot of a dog!

How he finally found his way to the rickety wooden stairs leading five thousand miles down to that sorry excuse of a garden he never knew. Somehow, he ended up collapsing in front of a man in a dirty brown robe. Somehow, a moment later, he found himself sitting on a wooden bench, drinking one glass of water after the other. When he was finally done, he didn't waste any time.

"I had a jacket. There was an envelope in it and I need to get back to Edinburgh."

"You need to get that envelope to Edinburgh?"

"No, you idiot!" For a fraction of a second, he took note of a far-away admonishment, something about not calling brown-robed men idiots. Never mind. "I need the envelope! The envelope! Get it?"

The other man nodded. "Yes, yes. I understand. I did find an envelope. With a little plastic bag with — sugar in it, maybe?"

Nodding vigorously, Blair grabbed him by the arm. "Where is it?"

The man searched his face. "Come, Rufus," he called to the dog. Paused. Seemed to think. "In the kitchen," he finally said. He gently shook off Blair's hand and stood.

"But where is the kitchen?"

The man, walking off, raised his hand, pointed back up to the castle and left without a word.

It didn't occur to Blair to ask where in the castle exactly, so relieved was he. Up, up to the kitchen! He took the first flight of stairs without pausing, a little slower the second, walked up the third, decided this must be where the kitchen was. Panting, his shirt long since ripped off, he found the kitchen, five hours later or maybe five minutes. There on the counter was his envelope! Thank God, thank God! He tore it open and — what the *fuck*? There was some blow in the little Ziploc bag all right — enough for one tiny line! He snorted it greedily. Relief, anger, tiredness, and exhilaration coursed through his veins in competing swirls. Dizzy, he sank to the floor. Its waxy, clean smell rose to him like a ghost, filling his nostrils to bursting. A fly crawling across the floor stood in sharp black relief against the slanting sun; he could count the hairs on its legs, see the round sucking cups on its feet.

But of course, that didn't last. He now had a mission: make that scrawny bastard in the shit-brown dress cough up the rest of his stash. Blair drew a splinter from the floorboards as he raised himself up. His head buzzed from the coke and from falling down.

Down. He needed to get down! The stairs? Where were they in this maze of wood and windows? He ran up and down the corridors, getting lost, screaming, hollering, but finally found the stupid rickety stairs again. Maybe they weren't five thousand miles long, only three — who cares, all he wanted was to find that stinking asshole who had stolen his stuff.

When he got down to the garden, he heard a voice from above.

"Hey, you! I found some more!" Around Blair whirled, back up the stairs, when halfway up he heard "In your room!" Completely drenched in sweat, bare-chested, barefoot, he found his room eons later. Before he pounced on the baggie, he drank the whole of the two carafes of water that had appeared on his windowsill, sparkling in the setting sun.

There was nothing in the baggie.

Blair spent the next three days in a zigzag of up and down, racing, chasing, dragging himself from the kitchen to the garden to the hallways to the stairs to his room and other, empty ones. He completely forgot about Edinburgh.

More and more water he consumed, then the occasional soup and sandwich. There appeared coffee and eventually, a hard pillow with dreamless sleep. Sometimes there was something in the baggie, sometimes not, but always less than before.

Five days later, Blair sat at the kitchen table, an empty plate before him, a half-full cup of coffee in this hand. He contemplated a baggie sitting innocently beside a can of evaporated milk. He felt his heart beat from the run up the stairs, oxygen plumping every cell, and no draw towards the few white grains in the baggie.

The man in the brown robe appeared before him.

"I don't even know your name," Blair said.

"Sean." The man stretched out his hand.

A smile, the first in a week, spread on the younger man's face. He shook the proffered hand, warm and firm. "Blair."

Reporter: So — this gentleman, Blair, appeared.

Sean: He'd totalled his car on the road just below. Miraculously, he was pretty much unharmed, had just blacked out. So I carted him up to a room on that hidden elevator we have. For some reason, I thought to check his pockets and, wouldn't you know it, there was a baggie of cocaine. Something made me take it out.

Reporter: God?

Sean: Oh, I don't know. I wouldn't go as far as that. Maybe mischievousness, that's more like it. Yeah, mischievousness. Boredom. When he showed up, I started playing a game on him. The hidden elevator helped. But then —

Reporter: Then …?

Sean: Then somehow the game started a life of its own and a week later or so, he was sober. I think for him it was all the running around, up and down, what did the trick. He became a parkour runner after that, you know?

Reporter: Yes, we talked to him. And because you're a psychologist, you realized the mechanism of his recovery, I assume, and started applying this method to others?

Sean: Oh no. Really, psychology — that life's behind me. No — it all just happened. It wasn't until a year later that Blair brought another person, a girl, up to the castle. Nothing had worked for her, so he thought, why not try Brother Sean? But a totally different game showed up for her.

Reporter: What did you have planned for her?

Sean: I don't think you understand. I said the game showed up. There wasn't any planning, not for a long time. I get it — you'd like a noble intention, an altruistic motive. But let me repeat — the truth is that I was bored, I needed something to do, so I just played around. For that girl, it was grooming the dog, good old Rufus. It wasn't until some months and a few people later that I realized we had something there. I still don't plan anything. All I know is that there are games, activities, whatever you call them, that work for people. I wait for them to reveal themselves. Decreasing the dose of whatever they're hooked on seems to work, and it looks like you have to make sure there aren't any rules they understand — the element of surprise is important — only there's something else to do beside using. Then we play the game. That's all. I'm nothing but your buddy who plays this game with you that gets you better, at least for a while.

THE INTERVIEW

Piper

What are your first thoughts in terms of how this story may or may not relate to your own experience?
Interesting thought that addiction can be cured by the whimsical intervention of another. That is not grounded in any recovery or spiritual background. That was not my recovery experience.

Was there anything at all that you could relate to or was it all completely foreign?
I guess if there was some relationship, it was in a metaphorical sense. You don't know what's going to be helpful and what not.

Can you say more about that?
The monk seemed to pluck a couple of ideas out of the air for each of his clients and, bingo, that seemed to help. There are many things in life where you go, oooh, that might help — kind of serendipitous.

Has there been any serendipity in your recovery?
Everybody's life is entirely serendipitous. That idea is part of my program — that we appreciate God's gifts for us.

Can you give an example of that?
I guess waking up in the morning. You might have died in your sleep. You don't know. You open the curtains, there is still a world out there, there wasn't a nuclear holocaust while you were asleep. And so it goes on.

How would you connect this to your personal recovery?
It is gratitude for those things.

How does gratitude help you in your recovery?
It is an attitude for those things around you that perhaps you cannot control and shifting to that attitude of gratitude. For a lot of people, this is part of their recovery, as opposed to resentment, being a victim, things not under your control, frustration at not being able to control things that are outside of your control. This is a spiritual program of recovery. As opposed to somebody saying do this or this or this.

Who would that somebody be?
In the story, that would be Brother Sean. This is somebody else initiating the recovery, not the person.

In your life, has it happened that somebody tried to initiate your recovery?
It started when I was at school and people around me had better ideas about what I should be doing than what I did. So I left school. I think it was confrontation on all fronts, not just drugs. Identity, future, past, clothing, all kinds of things. Teachers who didn't like it when we went to school with safety pins in our ears. It was enough so I felt angry enough to soon leave home and school to live in a forest in a tent.

What did your parents do or not do that made you want to leave home?
I guess by the time I left, it wasn't my home anymore. I didn't feel at home anymore. I was living in a different world from them and the worlds did not overlap. I didn't keep in touch with them, perhaps neither party was interested in the other.

Other people haven't instigated recovery for you...
Philosophically, I am part of an approach that scorns that interventions can be effective.

Can you tell me more?
From a twelve-step perspective, the first step, the engine of change, is surrender. Not to somebody else, but just saying I can't do this anymore. We don't believe in intervention. We snicker. At a meeting, people would laugh at this story. It would be a humorous part of the meeting.

Is that because people have had experience with that and it didn't work?
Possibly. But with the twelve steps, it's a fairly sophisticated framework for spiritual recovery that we have and interventions don't fit in that schema. The bedrock of this is surrender, not intervention by somebody else.

So when you read the story, was it a little bit like sitting in a meeting and snickering?
Yes, for two reasons. One, because we tend to see recovery as a long journey rather than something quick. Two, because we see it as a spiritual journey, surrendering, understanding to see how our Higher Power works in our life. Not a pill or even a treatment, if truth were told.

If the castle were a metaphor of a treatment centre, there would be skepticism. Like a doctor treats a patient. That's not how it works.

What would you say then is the theme of your reflections on this story?
Addiction is a long, complex malady and to resolve that is often a long journey. Recovery is not an instance, it is a process. We do have tools to help us do that. And I think the most valuable tools I have are yoga, Buddhism, and the twelve steps. They are not really three different things. We do have the tools to achieve spiritual recovery. It's not a mystery.

Did you see any similarities between your doing yoga and the physical aspects of the story — all the running?
I would not necessarily put yoga in a physical practices category. The asanas, the poses, are just one of eight parts of yoga according to Patanjali, the authoritative text on yoga. In Patanjali's yoga sutras, it is the one that is least mentioned. The Bhagavad Gita, the most revered book in India, is also a yoga book but there is no mention at all in it of the asanas. The Bhagavad Gita is two thousand, three thousand years old. The invention of asanas is quite new, in the last 150 years.

My impression is that this interview did not stir many 'hot' emotions in you. Would you be all right with finishing this interview?
Yes.

THE RESEARCH

In the interview, Piper says:

> Addiction is a long, complex malady and to resolve
> that is often a long journey. Recovery is not an
> instance, it is a process. We do have tools to help us
> do that. And I think the most valuable tools I have
> are yoga, Buddhism, and the twelve steps.

As can be seen from the interview, Piper was not overly impressed with the story; still, he suggested focusing on yoga and recovery from substance use. Since Piper stressed the spiritual/esoteric aspects of yoga, let us begin with that.

Yoga and Yoga in the West

While not reporting on research or pointing specifically to how yoga might be helpful in substance-use recovery, Thomas Matus, a Benedictine monk with a PhD in Comparative Mysticism, provides some thoughts in the medical journal *Substance Use and Misuse* that share some similarities with Piper's approach to yoga. Matus cites yoga researcher Stefanie Syman, who talks about Western approaches to yoga as "sanitized, sanctioned, and family friendly" activities. For example, during the White House's 2009 annual Easter Egg Roll, Michelle Obama reportedly pronounced, "Our goal today is just to have fun. We want to focus on activity, healthy eating. We've got yoga, we've got dancing, we've got storytelling, we've got Easter egg decorating."

This is far removed from the original Indian texts that Piper and Matus refer to. There, the ultimate goal of yoga is liberation (*moksha* in Sanskrit; the end of the cycle of birth and rebirth). Yoga itself refers to a type of harmony — the words 'yoking' as in 'yoking together' and 'yoga' have the same roots. Says the Bhagavad Gita:

> Yoga is a harmony. Not for him who eats too much,
> or for him who eats too little, not for him who sleeps
> too little, or for him who sleeps too much. This is
> the yoga that gives peace from all pain.

There are many yogas; the yoga of the Bhagavad Gita is one of them and is the one that Indian gurus such as Yogananda and Vivekananda[5] brought to North America. Theologian Elizabeth De Michelis traced the history of yoga in the West, stating that with colonialism in India came a tremendous change and, around 1885, its original form turned into what she calls 'modern yoga'. With the current focus on posture, what most people understand to be yoga nowadays is what she calls 'modern postural yoga'.

Piper would probably be happy with what Matus says: "what unites the various schools of yoga is the basic principle of psychophysical practice that leads to inner silence and focus on the Ultimate." Matus also mentions that the goal of yoga is "perfect autonomy." Taken together, the idea of working towards liberation, autonomy, and harmony (especially in connection with moderation) are naturally attractive to people seeking a way out of substance use.

Yoga and Substance-Use Recovery — Early Research

Moving on from this very brief sketch of yoga as a life practice that encompasses much more than physical yoga poses or asanas — what does the research say about yoga and substance-use recovery?

One of the earliest research articles in English, by Lois Goldberg and Gloria Meltzer in 1975, studied twenty-two participants at a methadone clinic, ten of which underwent a 'yoga therapy program' consisting of "relaxation techniques, yoga exercises, and mantra chanting." They assessed thinking skills and impulsivity and detected no difference between those who did and did not choose the yoga program; however, five, or half, of the yoga participants requested detoxification versus two of the group who did not choose the yoga therapy program. Today, when it is much easier to carry out studies with larger groups, some would see the results as so small that they are almost anecdotal. However, a small number of study participants as well as a fuzzy (or even no) definition of yoga can still be seen in newer studies.

Random Controlled Trials: Encouraging

In 2014, physiotherapy researcher Paul Posadzki and colleagues defined yoga as "a part of Ayurvedic medicine that can consist of one or more of the following: specific postures, breathing exercises, body cleansing,

5   The Indian Hindu monk Swami Vivekananda (1863–1902) was central to the introduction of the Indian philosophies of yoga and Vedanta to the West and is often thought to have brought enough awareness to Hinduism to grant it the status of a major world religion.
    Paramahansa Yogananda (1893–1952) was a yogi and guru who, largely through his book *Autobiography of a Yogi* introduced millions of people in the West to yoga and the spirituality associated with yoga.

mindfulness meditation, and lifestyle modifications." The researchers were interested in evaluating the evidence of effectiveness of yoga as a treatment for alcohol, drug, or nicotine addiction. They searched fourteen electronic databases for randomized controlled trials where any type of yoga for any type of addiction was compared with any type of control and found eight randomized controlled trial studies worth including. In seven of them, yoga brought about significantly better results for participants compared to control interventions. Posadzki and colleagues concluded that although results were encouraging, it was difficult to determine any benefits due to methodological flaws in all the studies and the relatively small number of participants (the smallest group studied was twenty-four, the largest ninety-six).

The yoga in the studies varied from breathing only to a combination of meditation, stretches, and poses (asanas). One study had participants do yoga for forty minutes, six days a week for eight weeks; another had them do hatha yoga once for thirty minutes. That is, the studies did not use yoga in directly comparable ways and a wide variety of types of yoga were used:

- hatha yoga, a practice of asanas (postures), practised along with controlled breathing and meditation
- Iyengar yoga, a form of hatha yoga focusing on standardized, precisely aligned asanas that can be tailored for individuals
- vinyasa yoga, a form of hatha yoga that emphasizes the continuous flow of movement between postures and pays close attention to linking breath with the movements
- Yoga nidra, a deep relaxation technique
- pranayama, the practice of voluntary regulated breathing while the mind is directed to the flow of breath
- sudarshan kriya yoga, a type of breathing yoga.

How Yoga Is Helpful and Therapeutic Suggestions

A few years later, psychiatrists Siddarth Sarkar and Mohit Varshney did a literature review of seventeen studies (including the eight studies Posadki had discussed) and proposed possible reasons why yoga might be helpful in dealing with addiction: stress reduction (e.g., via breathing exercises that help reduce heart rate, blood pressure, and cortisol); improved mood; social connections that are often built in yoga groups; coping and controlling cravings; and overall health improvement.

Sarkar and Varshney also made therapeutic recommendations. They felt that yoga for substance use might be most accepted by people already familiar with yoga and suggested that it's best to wait to introduce yoga once the person is out of the acute withdrawal stage, that it should be coupled with other treatment such as medication and/or counselling, that promotion of yoga should last at least a few weeks, and that reminders to practice yoga for a longer duration of time would be helpful.

Substance Use and Exercise in General: Good Results

Sport psychologist Dongshi Wang and colleagues performed a meta-analysis about how exercise in general might be an effective treatment for substance-use disorders. They looked at twenty-two studies, four of which used yoga. Two studies had participants struggling with nicotine use, one with alcohol, and one with heroin. For all of the twenty-two groups, the researchers were quite enthusiastic about the findings, especially in terms of high abstinence rates in participants with drug use.

Wang and colleagues classified exercise types into low, moderate, and high, as well as aerobic and mind-body exercise. Yoga falls into the low/moderate and mind-body groups. Both outperformed the other types of exercise on every test: abstinence rates, withdrawal symptoms, and the anxiety and depression that often come with substance-use disorder. People struggling with drug use tended to score better on all measures. However, another study, by public health researcher Victoria Gunillasdotter and colleagues, also showed the superiority of yoga over aerobic exercise in facilitating the recovery of individuals with alcohol use disorder.

Largest Single Study — Yoga Makes No Difference

The largest single study on yoga and addiction I found was a doctoral dissertation in psychology by Joseph McDaniel that compared one hundred persons in treatment facilities that incorporated yoga to a second group of one hundred persons in treatment facilities that did not use yoga. These two groups of people filled out a survey which asked questions about improvement in substance use, health, personal responsibility, and community integration. McDaniel found no difference in the responses of the two groups (those who used yoga and those who did not), suggesting that generally, yoga may not have any effect on drug treatment outcomes. McDaniel did not explain what type of yoga people were engaged in or how often.

In the Words of Yoga Program Participants

Finally, let's hear what participants in yoga programs have to say.

Women Who Have Experienced Trauma

Social work researcher Amy Smoyer conducted a study of a trauma-informed yoga program for low-income women with substance-use disorders. Women with problematic substance use often have survived significant trauma, something that can interfere with accessing and successfully completing treatment. Smoyer interviewed ten of the thirty women who participated in her study and found that the topics discussed almost exclusively were about relaxation, mindfulness, and movement. She noted specifically that participants were happy with the relatively low level of exertion in the classes, something that coincides with Wang's observations above.

Here are a few samples of Smoyer's interviews. Only one refers directly to substance use:

> I can go to yoga and it just makes me feel like I don't need to go use. I'm better than that. I'm healthier than that. It keeps me on the right frame of being healthy and not using … it's helping me focus on being healthy.

Many of the other interviews refer to the types of experiences that are often associated with problematic substance use, such as racing thoughts, high stress, and mood swings:

> I've been sleeping better since I started yoga. My mind doesn't race, I don't wake up racing.
>
> I felt very less stressed, and very less anxious. And I have very, very high anxiety problems where it's, it's bad. So, it helps, it definitely helps.
>
> If I ever get worked up on the outside or get too excited or get too upset or whatever the case may be, I can just sit back and breathe on it and take a few seconds, take my time, and that's a lot yoga has to offer as well. It teaches you to take your time, at your own pace, so that's definitely something that I'm going to take with me.

Interviews with Prisoners

Criminology researcher Azra Karup captured the insights and experiences of prisoners doing yoga, asking, "How do prisoners experience yoga and what meanings do they attach to their practice?" She was also interested in the consequences of prisoners practising yoga. Karup personally interviewed eleven prisoners and also read through one hundred and fifty letters on the topic. Most of the prisoners were male. In regard to that, Karup writes:

> The nurturing, slow paced nature of yoga stands in stark contrast to the broader context of prisoner culture and other forms of exercise available, described by Carl [an interviewee] as a 'sort of full pelt training [where] you are not in control because you are always trying to go harder, faster, stronger'. In these activities' competitiveness, speed, and physical strength are the markers of success. This may be caused by, and perpetuate, dominant ideals of masculinity that can contribute to more aggressive and hostile prison cultures.

While the study was not specifically about prisoners with problematic substance use, it should be noted that generally, around 70% of prisoners deal with substance use. Below are some quotes from prisoners that directly talk about it.

> You get the best buzz ever through meditating, and there is not a drug in the world that could ever come anywhere close.
> I never ever thought anything could replace the void filled by drugs until I discovered meditation.
> This practice has made me realise that suffering, craving, unsatisfactioness [sic], expectations and all possible states of mind or feelings arise, exist and pass away right here, inside my mind.
> I started to do the yoga every morning … and instead of blocking out my feeling with exercise, drink and drugs … I learned to sit with my feelings, accept my feelings and I have gone from strength to strength.

Can Involuntary Treatment Be Successful?

Even though I could not find more than one large study on yoga and addiction, and not many others that have used methodologies that allow for strong conclusions, it still seems that yoga is a promising approach to help people deal with their substance-use problems, which is similar to what Piper said in the interview. What diverges from Piper's experience is that the study participants were all 'in treatment' and they did not always have a choice as to whether to partake in yoga or not. Piper made it clear that he disagreed with any treatment that is not self-initiated.

Whether involuntary treatment of substance use is effective, regardless of whether it includes complementary approaches such as yoga or exercise, has been a hotly debated topic for decades. Psychotherapist and addictions specialist Stefanie Klag and colleagues surveyed thirty years of research on the effectiveness of compulsory treatment, concluding that it has "yielded a mixed, inconsistent, and inconclusive pattern of results." Klag and colleagues suggest that research is needed to:

- "clarify what sort of clients, in what settings, respond best to what type or combinations of pressures and coercive strategies, if any"
- "investigate the nature of coercive measures themselves, how they exert their impact on individuals, and the results they produce in terms of retention and treatment outcomes"
- "provide an indication of how much pressure is enough, or too much, and how long coercion should be used to achieve the maximum benefit."

Spirituality

This points out the stark difference between Piper's approach, which emphasizes spirituality, surrender, and no outside 'treatment', on the one hand and most scientific approaches on the other, which shy away from spirituality. Only one of the studies discussed so far — Smoyer's — mentioned the connection between spirituality and yoga. What Piper's approach may come close to is referred to as 'devotional fitness' by religious studies researcher Martin Radermacher. Radermacher discusses it exclusively in a Christian context. (It may be interesting to note here that the twelve-step approach Piper feels so strongly about was originally built on a Christian framework.)

Radermacher mentions one program that particularly made me think of Piper, "Shaped by Faith" by Theresa Rowe. This program is built on the idea that in the pursuit of whole-person wellness, all areas of life should be centred on (the Christian) God. In the book by the same name, every chapter has the organizing principles of "Shaped by Life," "Shaped by Fitness," "Shaped by God," and "Shaped by Prayer." Except for "Shaped by Fitness," these are topics discussed in the twelve steps, as is the topic of surrender, which is also frequently mentioned in Rowe's program.

Piper does not primarily see yoga as a physical activity. The researchers whose work I investigated were not very articulate regarding how they classified yoga. That underlines a point that surfaces particularly in this chapter: Most scientific research finds it hard to delve into the more organic side of human experience, avoiding concepts such as surrender or spirituality and its holistic nature. They are mostly all about treatment and intervention.

Piper and "The Monastery"

A final question: Was Piper a good fit for the story about the monastery? At first glance, it looked like he was because of his experience with cocaine and movement; however, he soon pointed out that he did not agree with Brother Sean's intervention and also did not agree with yoga being classified as physical exercise.

In research (and in life) there is a bias towards confirmation — we like to shout out loud what confirms our ideas and downplay what doesn't. But why ignore all the times when there is not a fit? The reality is quite possibly that true, planned successes constitute the minority of our experiences and the rest is a middling muddle of situations we stumble into and, if we have the energy, make the best of. And sometimes serendipity helps along a bit.

BIBLIOGRAPHY: CHAPTER SIX

Canadian Centre on Substance Abuse, Graves, G. & Thomas, G. (2004). *Substance Abuse in Corrections FAQs*. CCSA-CLAT.

De Michaelis, E. (2007). A Preliminary Survey of Modern Yoga Studies. *Asian Medicine: Tradition and Modernity*, *3*(1), 1–19.

Goldberg, L.S. & Meltzer, G. (1975). Arrow-dot scores of drug addicts selecting general or yoga therapy. *Perceptual Motor Skills*, *40*(3), 726.

Gunillasdotter, V., Andréasson, S., Hallgren, M. & Jirwe, M. (2022). Exercise as treatment for alcohol use disorder: A qualitative study. *Drug and Alcohol Review*, *41*(7), 1642–1652.

Karup, A. (2016). *The Meaning and Effects of Yoga in Prison* (Master's thesis, University of Cambridge).

Klag, S., O'Callaghan, F. & Creed, P. (2005). The use of legal coercion in the treatment of substance abusers: An overview and critical analysis of thirty years of research. *Substance Use & Misuse*, *40*(12), 1777–1795.

Mascaro, J. (1962). *The Bhagavad Gita* (translated from the Sanskrit with an introduction by Juan Mascaro). Penguin Books.

Matus, T. (2013). Dharma, Yoga, Tantra. *Substance Use & Misuse*, *48*, 1180–1186.

Posadzki, P., Choi, P., Lee, M. & Ernst, E. (2014). Yoga for addictions: A systematic review of randomised clinical trials. *Focus on Alternative and Complementary Therapies*, *19*(1).

Prabhavananda, S. & Isherwood, C. (1953, 1969). *How to Know God: The Yoga Aphorisms of Patanjali*. New American Library.

Radermacher, M. (2012). Devotional fitness: Aspects of a contemporary religious system. *Scripta Instituti Donneriani Aboensis*, *24*, 313–343.

Rowe, T. (2008). *Shaped by Faith: 10 Secrets to Strengthening Your Body & Soul*. Guideposts.

Sarkar, S. & Varshney, M. (2017). Yoga and substance use disorders: A narrative review. *Asian Journal of Psychiatry*, *25*, 191–196.

Smoyer, A. (2016). Being on the mat: A process evaluation of trauma informed yoga for women with substance use disorders. *The Journal of Sociology & Social Welfare*, *43*(4).

Syman, S. (2010). *The Subtle Body: The Story of Yoga in America*. Farrar, Straus, and Giroux.

Wang, D., Wang, Y., Wang, Y., Li, R. & Zhou, C. (2014). Impact of physical exercise on substance use disorders: A meta-analysis. *PLoS ONE*, *9*(10), e110728.

Yogananda, P. (1946). *Autobiography of a Yogi*. Harper Collins.

CHAPTER SEVEN

"Purgatory"

PSYCHOSIS AND PSYCHIATRIC HOSPITALS

In "Purgatory," a story written in lyric prose, the protagonist has a psychotic break and he is hospitalized. When he is discharged, his journey through the hospital's maze of hallways parallels the journey of his mind.

The person who was interviewed for this portion was Shannon, a woman in her thirties. Psychosis brought her to the hospital over two dozen times. This was often complicated by problematic drug use. Her psychiatrist was doubtful that she would ever recover, seeing that "she seemed to be in her own little world, staring into space, crawling on the floor, giggling, mumbling and chanting to herself, and sprinkling herself with water and dirt, for 'purification'."

Shannon now works in the mental health field and has just finished her master's degree.

After reading the story, Shannon felt a kinship with the man's experience as he went through seclusion, met nurses and fellow patients, and continued on his path to recovery. Those are the topics explored in the research section.

THE STORY

Purgatory

The gates of hell are open night and day;
Smooth the descent, and easy is the way:
But to return, and view the cheerful skies,
In this the task and mighty labour lies.

Virgil, *Aneid*, Book 6

Like many older institutions in this city, the buildings of St. Mary's Hospital were a mishmash of an annex here, a tunnel there, a bridge, a wing, a stair, a ramp. None matched, not quite. Over the decades, the hospital had turned into a warren, a purgatory of confusion. Third floors had become second; numbers were odd on one side, even on the other, but not everywhere. In building 3H, room numbers jumped from three to eight for no apparent reason.

On one of those between-floors — between the basement and the ground level — was EPT: Emergency Psychiatry Treatment. In 1968, a young, ambitious doctor of psychiatry had had enough verve and, more importantly, moneyed connection, to wrench the fate of psychiatric patients away from doctors obsessed with fixing broken bones and reattaching retinas. He built for people with unhappy minds their own sanctuary. The only hitch: though the donors freely gave money for education and such things, they showed no interest as to aesthetics nor, indeed, as to location. So EPT got stuck "somewhere" — that somewhere was an in-between with hardly any light. Only three windows turned to the outside, and even there, a thick hedge blocked most sunlight.

In 1981, our young, ambitious doctor long gone off to Harvard or the Mayo Clinic or wherever young ambitious doctors go, a kind administrator found a little money, bought chairs cushioned in cheery orange, painted all counters green, and found some art from a small gallery gone broke.

Nothing has changed since then. It's 2015 now. EPT is a dark place, a place of suffering and yet of healing. One quarter sanctuary, two quarters purgatory, and one a mystery.

Here's Hans, a man of undetermined age (well — no: determined by some scribbles on a chart, immediately forgotten). He came in, hand broken, bloody with glass — the window he had jumped through. The window and the void beyond? Who knows. Clearly to him, at that moment, and with those voices in his mind, the only sensible thing to do. Just then, police were driving by, heard splintering noises, stopped, and found the shivering man curled on the ground, bloodied, but mostly whole except two fractured bones in his left hand. They brought him in and closed the door. No one can leave here on a whim; only a doctor-god can let a patient out.

His third day at the EPT, Hans has resumed the medication that had seemed the source of all the evil in life not long ago. Behind a screen, days one and two: a fog of needles, doctors in suits, security guards, nightmares, a padded, dark room way too hot to breathe in. Wrestling. He can't remember who or what he fought with. Demons? Another patient? Hospital staff?

But now, day three, he likes his nurse. He sleeps quite well. This comes about, he feels, from knowing someone's there, someone who cares, someone who knows, someone who keeps him safe. He takes, and willingly, what's given to him, too tired of questioning, too tired of suspecting, now that the pills help him suspect much less. The voices still there by his side, they murmur more and scream less often. They speak more now in what Hans read somewhere is called, strangely, 'word salad'. *Arugula, cucumber, matos, matos, matchmakers making egg salad.* Less of the "Die!" variety, the voice hungers not so much to speak, but craves the sound of splintering, of crashing, smashing, of crunching bones and wet, dead splattering. Instead, a little bit of mumbled word salad — *romaine, abstain, contain* — is fine with him.

Hans watches others, wonders, vaguely, what is on their minds as they pick fights, play cards, scream, hug each other, swear at nurses, write them adoring notes, do not accept their doctors' orders.

Hans watches as Jill cries, Jill who can't stop her memories of three little ones unborn and whose mother comes, day in, day out, in vain hopes of consoling. Jill's husband is long gone, to find another woman, one who will give attention just to him, to cheer him up, one who will not forget to put on make-up every day and pretty shoes.

Hans watches Norm, who won't say anything, and Peter P., who doesn't seem upset at anyone or anything, a guy friendly enough to nurses and to doctors as long as they engage in endless small talk with him.

"Nice weather, nurse."

"Hm."

"Nice weather, I said, nurse."

"Nice weather, Peter."

Peter has staked out meaningless nothings around him — beyond that, he shares not a bit. He sleeps and sits, waiting in limbo until they find a place for him to stay where he won't smash everything he finds — chair, sofa, table —

to pieces. Not that he's angry. It's just — he needs someone to talk to, right? And it's not fair when people don't make time for him. Not fair.

There's Clara, admitted for her first time and could be for her last. Perhaps she just needs time away, a few nights' sleep, some medication, and a friendly word. There's quite a few like her. A rock suddenly comes smashing through their hearts and minds, the shock is horrible, they pick the rock up, throw it back or bury it, and that is it. Maybe they find a way to glaze their windows with much thicker glass, maybe luck has it that a rock never again comes crashing through.

Many a rock has come through Hans's windows. Many a window has been smashed, both ways. It started when his mother jumped and hasn't really ended since.

They took his boy away. "Too dangerous," they said, after his wife had found him, twenty-one years ago, standing out on the balcony, holding their child, Hans not willing to come in, to move away from the abyss up on the nineteenth floor.

Today, Hans wants to heal.

And then there's Gretchen, Gretchen the nurse. Gretchen is suffering. Ash blond her hair and blue her eyes, her skin a porcelain beige — and dry, dried out from smoke and sorrow. Gretchen comes in each shift, her limbs heavy, her voice tired, heart filled to the brim with boredom and with dread. She's seen it all. Seen people bent on suicide admitted one morning and leave again a day later, dead the next. Seen furious husbands, sleep-deprived brothers, and innocent girls come to the hospital equipped with vials full of coke hidden in places who-knows-where. Seen social workers who don't give a shit; seen doctors who don't think they're God, they *know* it; seen other nurses gossip, laze about, and snarl at patients. There was a time — but when was that? — when she saw so much more, when she saw kindness and compassion, when she saw hope — oh, hope, hope, hope ... but that was years ago. Or aeons.

Gretchen is suffering. Gretchen can't hear when Jack, her young teammate, tells her of someone, a woman with depression, whose face lit up when Jack sat down and listened to her tell of her three cats. Can never feel Hans's friendly eyes on her. Won't read the book Sibyl, the old psychiatrist, gave her about the mountains that Sib knows Gretchen once loved so much.

Gretchen is suffering. Her heart is blind.

One night, Hans dreams. It wakes him up. He cannot sleep. Nurse Gretchen, tired, wants nothing more than be alone with her crocheting — pink, black, beige — behind the desk. But Hans insists. Gretchen gets up, about to charge him with obstreperousness, even 'aggression' (a word highlighted in purple in the chart, a word that's not erased that easily), when something stops her and she listens.

"I dreamt," Hans says, "of a strange place in Italy. There was a cave. There was a woman. She looked like Sibyl, the psychiatrist." Here, Gretchen flinches. She never feels comfortable with Sibyl and her books that she schleps with her everywhere she goes. She finds her quietness irritating. She doesn't like when Sibyl, finally dispensing words — not many — says things that make her shiver because they touch her in a way too deep. She doesn't like her voice, it makes her think of — no. Memories are useless.

But Hans goes on.

"This old woman looked like your mother. That's — in the dream. 'Cause I don't know your mother. But there in Italy, I knew her. It was important that I knew her, nurse, you see, and that is why, Gretchen, I'm telling you. In my dream there, I knew your mother. She looked a bit like you, just older. Softer maybe?"

Gretchen takes Hans's chart, writes, "Dreams. Ideas of reference." Her hand shakes just a bit. She changes pens.

"That's interesting," she mumbles. Neither of them know what that's supposed to mean. Hans, nevertheless, takes it as an invitation.

"Her hair was longer than yours, wavier, and she wore skirts. Another thing I knew about her, don't ask why — this woman didn't like the feel of pants." Their eyes, Hans's and Gretchen's, are drawn to Gretchen's grey-blue slacks that she wears every day. They're super practical.

"Well, thank you, Hans," she chirps, "And now it's off to bed with you. Need pills?"

He looks at her, wants to continue. Gretchen turns round, away from him — there's things to do, she now remembers. Tasks that are far away from folks who don't wear pants.

Hans raises a hand and clears his throat.

"Si—"

"Now, now," says Gretchen, remembering vaguely what it's like to smile, to smile a real smile.

Hans stops. He may not have the words for it, but — Hans understands. Something in him knows about the drums we carry deep inside us, how much it hurts when outside voices make their old hides thrum. He has received so many good things in this hospital; no need to push it. He goes to bed. His face relaxed, a friendly light dancing in his green eyes, he wishes a good wish for Adam B., his roommate. And off he goes, to dream again.

The next day, he is discharged, just before lunch. Collects his things, walks down the hall. A nurse looks at her chart, nods, buzzes the heavy steel-frame door open for him. And he is free. Hans has a dim sense that it's spring, the twenty-fifth of May. Disorientation sets in now. Where to? A grey, bare corridor stretches before him, grey to the left, grey to the right. A light bulb flickers, another has gone out completely. Far down the right, an empty stretcher. He walks down that side of the corridor. His sneakers squeak on the waxed floor. He smells nothing, tastes nothing, but here in this hallway that very nothing smacks of — he cannot tell. It's not just any nothing. An image rises — no, two rise! — of fire, one, and brimstone; the other of cool, dark cave walls, ancient and dank.

Hans has arrived at the stretcher. Three books lie there. He looks around and hears his father's strict, cold voice: "Got nothing to do with you, boy, go, move on!" His father was a harsh man, strict, malicious even. Rebellious, Hans does not heed what the man says, his dad's advice always expensive to his soul. He takes the books. Further ahead, a fork. As soon as he gets there, he is faced with three more choices: keep going on, go left, or halfway to the right. Hans' head reels. He wants to go back, back to the safety of old EPT. But there's no way, or already too many, to find the path back to that place. There's nothing left but to go forward.

And then: another human being! A woman in high heels. Will she be friendly, helpful? Hans slows down, there's hesitation in his steps. His mouth feels dry and yet he forms the words, "Excuse me?"

She is, turns out, Italian, knows little English. But as a Jehovah's Witness (which Hans finds out immediately), she knows what to do. She does not know the way as he had hoped; instead, she smiles at him and hands him three *Watchtowers*.

"Don't take a thing from these cult idiots! Imbeciles all!" Hans hears.

Polite nevertheless, Hans takes the pamphlets, bows, smiles back.

"Ciao!"

Remembering that word from a trip long ago ignites a small and happy feeling in his chest. Slowly, he walks on, but then he stops.

"Don't take a thing from these cult idiots!" He did not obey that voice. What's more, he knows whose voice it is — not one of *those* voices: it is his father's. More yet: a voice not from outside but from inside. A voice that's knit from memories, from *his* memories. He knows he can react in any way *he* chooses. He knows, there in his heart, that this voice must obey *him*, and not the other way around.

An "Aaaaah" falls from his chest. He looks down on the pamphlets. It's unlikely he'll read them, but they gave him something. He's grateful.

Amidst these musings, Hans has walked deeper into the labyrinth. He looks up, sees pipes above him and doors that say, "Keep out! Hazardous Waste!" and "Boiler Room." Where is he now? Will he find his way out? He hasn't had lunch yet and breakfast was ridiculous. His blood sugar is low. He sits, right beside "HVAC 2," down on the floor.

Small. Hans, yes, feels small. He says the words out loud.

"Small. I feel so very small." He says it with his voice, no other voice commands him. Something inside him likes these words. They speak the truth. The truth is good.

"I feel so small." He repeats it, he tastes the words deep in his mouth, deep in his heart, deep in his feet. What to do now? He does not know.

"No, I don't know." Another truth.

"I feel small. I do not know." Hans laughs, a small laugh, a content laugh — this truth, it feels so comfortable. It sits well, fits his limbs, his soul, and fits his mind.

"Yes, I feel small."

Down in the cave, down in the labyrinths, the gods can see a man sitting beside the door to those who control all the weather in this vast old place. Heat, ventilation, air conditioning. Hot, cold, it's up to them. Hans controls nothing.

Without much thought, he leafs now through the books he found out on the stretcher. Grins to himself, remembering going against his father's harsh commands. Leafs through one, then another, *Anatomy of Peace*. The third one, a small, dog-eared paperback, a textbook copy of Virgil's *Aeneid*, Latin on one side and on the other, English. He's trying to feel guilty for taking books that weren't his, but he can't go there. The first book has its cover missing. He shakes it. Something falls out. Three bits of paper. A recipe for brownies and a recipe for soup. The third one is a doodle. "This way out!" a sign reads on it, with stars and smiley faces, pointing to a big open and pouty mouth with flowers sprouting off one side.

Hans looks up. Gets up. Picks willy-nilly one of the three branches of the labyrinth, comes to an end soon. A door greets him and he walks out.

It's spring. May twenty-fifth. The sun shines on a bench in a small garden with peonies in bloom. Not far off, gleaming beneath blue skies, a street sign: "9th Avenue."

Hans nods, smiles, and walks on.

THE INTERVIEW

Shannon

As you read this story and think of your own experience, what comes up for you?
Two things: I can really identify with being locked in the isolation room. And the other thing is how Hans feels comfortable in the psych ward. There is a real dichotomy between being in the hospital hating it, hating being detained under the Mental Health Act, and at the same time liking the single bed in a room where you know your meals are brought to you, where someone looks after you. And then the other people in the hospital — going out for a smoke together, laughing, having fun.

What is it about that dichotomy that holds interest for you?
It's the dialectical thing. Two things can be true at once. When I ran away from the hospital barefoot and got chased by the security guards through the neighbourhood and then put into an isolation room again, experiences like that were traumatic.

But when I was manic or hypomanic, it was like a party in there. You get like five or six people together, it gets exciting. People feed off of it. There's a group of us sitting around, being loud, out on the steps, being 'crazy' until the nurses go "You need to go to bed now."

I loved movie night with potato chips and chocolate. Getting people to bring me smokes. Going out for smokes with people, depending on what ward you're in. I've been in one where you can only go out four times a day with the security guard. That was hell.

But in other wards, I remember nurses saying you do need to spend some time in the ward. There were people playing guitar and singing. At times, I was thinking I was in a band. And then there was always the psych ward boyfriend.

Being locked in the isolation room — can you talk more about that?
When they picked me up from a treatment centre, I was in full psychosis. I remember a cop handcuffing me. Somehow I managed to get out of them and the cop had to put them on tighter! Next thing, all I remember is waking up on a bed, thinking I was going to get wheeled onto a stage and break out of it like Criss Angel and perform. In reality, I got wheeled into a small room with nothing but a mattress on the floor and a steel toilet. But I was so unwell, I

was not even banging on the door. I remember there was this white powder on the floor, probably some cleaning product, thinking it was coke, snorting it.

There were other times I would be banging on the door. "Please let me out, let me out." I was so unwell I was in the open psych ward and I wanted to go to a nightclub and I couldn't get my boyfriend at the time to take me. I hated so much that I couldn't get out. So I took seventy Tylenols. At least I would get to the ER — I just wanted to be in a different part of the hospital.

I've overdosed on pills, but never with the intention to kill myself. I took the pills and then I told someone that I did it. People talk about a cry for help. When someone cries for help, they need help! It's not simply a call for attention.

Have you met anyone like Gretchen in the hospital?
I met one who was a man. I was in an acute ward like EPT. I had no clothes or change of clothes, so my mom brought me fresh underwear. He said you can't store that here. I asked him, do you like your job? They had quite the range of nurses there for sure. He was a complete asshole.

There was another nurse in a locked ward and I got a short pass. I left the psych ward, went home, went and got cocaine, went back to the hospital, and I got put from that closed ward to a completely locked nothing. The first one had a couch, your own room, a piano. This side had nothing. Isolation rooms, maybe four or five of them in a row. And I just hated that guy so much for moving me. It's hard to explain what it feels like to be locked up.

What else comes up as you read the story?
I could relate to the different characters. Some people hating it, some people admitted for the first time, whereas I have been admitted thirty times. There was this guy, he was a dad and his daughter came to visit him and, a day later, he jumped out of a window and killed himself.

There was this guy named Ken that I had a crush on and we'd go out for smokes together. He kept telling the docs he was suicidal. They'd discharge him and a few days later he'd come back. One day, I went over to his place. There was a pack of cigarettes on his front porch. I had this intrinsic feeling that he was going to do something and told the people in the hospital. They called the cops. He had OD'd on alcohol and pills. That to me brings up a failure of the hospital system that they don't listen to people. They don't take suicide seriously until they almost die. That's seriously fucked up.

Then with Peter in the story, I could relate to the small talk. Some people don't get very deep. A huge range of people there.

I was always — remember the two different sides — I often thought it was a party. Okay, let's be in a band together, let's do drugs, let me sit on your lap, even have sex with different guys. I also got extremely taken advantage of a number of times. This guy was hospitalized — he conned me, gave me a check to cash and it bounced. You meet all sorts of people in the hospital. One woman was glorifying sex work. Lots of bad ways people can influence each other.

Another part of the story is about voices. Do you have experience with that?
Never really experienced hearing a voice audibly, but I would often think I thought I heard something. Not like a loud male voice coming into my head. A lot of times in the psych ward, I was extremely paranoid. It still happens to me today. I think I hear people talking and it's about me. Not that I heard voices specifically, but I'd get confused and I'd hear people talking quietly and think it's about me.

Anything else that comes up for you about the story?
Reading about Gretchen also reminds me of the nurses that were nice. One helped me a lot with diet and weight gain. "I'm the voice inside your head," one nurse kept saying to me, the voice to help me make good choices.

One time when I was in hospital, I had foot problems. Every night, a nurse would come and bring me a basin with warm water to bathe my feet.

The title of the story is "Purgatory" — did that resonate?
I do relate to that. I was in a place like that. I met this guy in hospital and we went to the Downtown Eastside to get drugs. I had a business card from the psych ward with me; they give them to everyone on a pass so that they know where to come back to. It was two in the morning; we had done crack and marijuana. I came back to the hospital to a security guard, showed them the card, here, this is me. They walked me through the tunnel and back to the hospital. The hospital had an isolation room ready for me. The tunnel was surreal. I thought I was in a movie.

When I used to smoke weed, it always made me think I was in a movie, the star, and everyone around me were actors in the movie. That time, smoked weed after the crack and we came up on that circular thing on the Cambie Street Bridge — I remember laughing and being so tripped out and shouting, "This is a movie," and Chad said, "Life is a movie!"

What would you say to people who are maybe not as far in their recovery as you are?
I sometimes give a talk called "High Maintenance." It's about how to be successful in recovery. Not that I am high maintenance for others. I have to be high maintenance to myself. Eat, sleep, move well, think well. Exercise is

super important, especially when I'm depressed. I need to be healthy in all areas of my life. It's quite a bit of work. If you are new in your recovery and you feel like life is shitty, hang on, you just need time to get better. If your brain has been in psychosis or you've used drugs, your brain needs time to get better. But just trust it, you will feel better, you just need some time to ride it out.

This year, I got nominated for the Courage To Come Back Award. My doctor, who has treated me since 2011, wrote me a letter of reference for it. Here's an excerpt from it:

> ...she seemed to be in her own little world, staring into space, crawling on the floor, giggling, mumbling and chanting to herself, and sprinkling herself with water and dirt, for 'purification'. Hospital staff were very worried about her safety. It was hard to imagine at that point that she would ever get well. Over the next few weeks, however, we finally found a combination of medications that seemed to be helpful, and she slowly improved...
>
> ...Looking back over the last 7 years, I think that Shannon has improved remarkably. I don't want to give the impression that this has been an easy task. It has been, and continues to be, hard work, every step of the way. I am proud of Shannon, for her courage and determination in fighting her illness and in using her experiences to help others.

THE RESEARCH

Shannon suggested we take a closer look at some research on psychosis and recovery.

In a psychotic state, a person's perceptions, thoughts, and experience are quite different from those of others around them. For example, Shannon thought that the seclusion room was a stage and sprinkled herself with water and dirt for purification. In the story, Hans heard voices and felt that the most sensible thing for him to do would be to jump through a closed window.

People almost always recover from extreme psychotic episodes like that. But what about long-term recovery such as Shannon is enjoying? And what is recovery? We'll begin by exploring the use of this term and its history.

A Brief History of Recovery

The term 'recovery' in the context of mental illness is one that has traditionally been used more by persons with mental health or addiction challenges than by clinicians. What is recovery? We'll look into that in more depth below. For now, let's use psychologist Larry Davidson's definition: "Recovery is learning to live better in the face of mental illness."

The first person to use the term in the context of mental illness was John Perceval in the 1830s. The son of an English prime minister, he wrote *A narrative of the treatment experienced by a gentleman* which details his three years with schizophrenia. A hundred years later, in 1939, the first edition of the book *Alcoholics Anonymous* starts with the words: "We, of Alcoholics Anonymous, are more than one hundred men and women who have recovered from a seemingly hopeless state of mind and body," recovery being a central concept in AA. The term was also prominent in the mental patients' liberation movement in the '60s and '70s, then slowly came to be used by clinicians in the 1990s. While it is now widely adopted by them, it still cannot be found in the DSM-5 (the *Diagnostic and Statistical Manual*, 5th edition), the principal psychiatric authority for clinicians in North America and other parts of the world.

Recovery — Definitions

'Recovery' in mental illness is a much-debated concept, and people new to it in this specific context sometimes wonder, is it the same as a cure? Or is it similar to what groups like Alcoholics Anonymous talk about? And what or who is recovering or recovered?

One definition frequently found in North America is by SAMHSA, the U.S. Substance Abuse and Mental Health Services Administration:

> Recovery is a process of change through which people improve their health and wellness, live self-directed lives, and strive to reach their full potential. There are four major dimensions that support recovery:
>
> o   health — overcoming or managing one's disease(s) or symptoms and making informed, healthy choices that support physical and emotional well-being.
> o   home — having a stable and safe place to live.
> o   purpose — conducting meaningful daily activities and having the independence, income, and resources to participate in society.
> o   community — having relationships and social networks that provide support, friendship, love, and hope.

This definition contrasts somewhat with what a client-focused research group of Maori in New Zealand determined to be fundamental processes of change, which they gave the acronym HEART:

> Hope
> Esteem
> Agency
> Relationship and connection
> Transitions in identity

This group created another acronym, RECOVER, encompassing recovery strategies:

> Reading, researching, and learning from others about mental health
> Emotional growth
> Change of circumstances, or recovery-enhancing life changes
> Others — experiencing social support
> Virtues — practising them (we will discuss those later on)
> Etceteras — additional recovery strategies
> Repeating strategies that work and realizing that recovery takes time

Here are two more definitions of recovery:

> Psychologist Emily Treichler: Recovery is the lived experience of the person, encapsulating hope for a better future, empowerment, social connectedness, personal meaning, and quality of life.

> Psychologist Patricia Deegan: Recovery is an attitude, a stance, and a way of approaching the day's challenges. It is not a perfectly linear journey. There are times of rapid gains and disappointing relapses. There are times of just living, just staying quiet, resting and regrouping. Each person's journey of recovery is unique.

Themes we find here, then, are health, self-directedness/empowerment, home, purpose, social connections, hope, quality of life, and uniqueness. Both Shannon's and Hans's stories clearly echo with the themes of health and social connectedness. From the point of view of psychiatrists, their mental health improved. Their social connections with hospital staff, fellow patients, and for Hans, the mysterious Italian woman, were short but meaningful. Although not as clearly, the theme of purpose also resonated: Shannon is now helping others and there is a vague purposefulness with which Hans finds his way out of the warren of hospital hallways, which parallels how he finds his way out of the torment of his inner voices.[6] It is also here, as he realizes that he has some say over his father's voice, that he literally becomes self-directed.

Recovery as Process

Related to the question of how to define recovery is: who decides a person is recovering or has recovered? Several studies have found that there can be a contrast between what patients think about this as opposed to what clinicians and occasionally others such as family think. The major difference lies in a tendency where persons with lived experience of mental illness experience recovery as a process, whereas others see it as an outcome.

In 2019, psychiatric rehabilitation researcher Jaap van Weeghel published a major study that surveyed twenty-five meta-analyses and systematic reviews on the topic of recovery, each review itself covering anywhere between three

---

6 I do not wish to insinuate that the voices that people with psychosis often hear can be reduced to self-talk or remembering someone else's voice. However, this 'inner speech' can be entangled with auditory hallucinations. *See* Rosen et al., 2018, in the Bibliography.

and one hundred and fifteen studies. Van Weeghel talks about the difference between personal (process-oriented) and clinical (outcome-oriented) recovery. Surveying the work of researchers such as Mary Leamy, Bethany Leonhardt, and Emily Treichler, the process of personal recovery includes:

- something that emerges as a person actively makes their way through life, often using the word 'journey' to describe that, and alluding to nonlinear processes
- 'subjective' and unique experiences
- dealing with psychological and social difficulties such as loneliness, stigma, loss of personal identity, and feeling that others do not hold them in esteem
- a focus on strengths
- more like a disability to be managed than a disease to be cured
- a higher rating of quality of life than rated by clinicians.

While this is not a comprehensive list, it gives a taste of how many people in recovery from mental illness describe their processes.

Recovery as an Outcome

Clinicians in the studies surveyed by Leonhardt and van Weeghel often describe recovery as:

- an outcome after a successful treatment
- determined by someone other than the individual (e.g., a clinician rating of symptom severity; often, the clinician's judgment is called 'objective', as opposed to the person's own experience being 'subjective')
- focused on what clinicians perceive as odd, unusual, or diminished behaviours or thoughts (e.g., little insight into one's mental illness) and psychosocial impairments
- concepts such as functions, abilities, and symptoms (interestingly, Treichler and colleagues found no reason to believe that functional measurements — e.g., physical involvement in daily activities — tracked significantly with how well individuals felt they were recovering)
- "about making people independent and normal."

The advantage of outcome-based approaches to recovery is that it is easier to measure success, however that is defined. Leonhardt and colleagues found that across twenty-four studies, on average, 51% of people with prolonged psychotic illness such as Shannon's eventually had no more symptoms (e.g., auditory hallucinations), 25% significantly improved psychosocial functioning, and 19% both.

An Integrated View

Of course, there are many attempts towards integrating these views (and in practice, this is more common than as portrayed in the research). Psychologist Paul Lysaker and colleagues suggest combining observable outcomes with the person's subjective rating of their internal and external lives.

Rehabilitation psychologist Ilanit Hasson-Ohayon and colleagues further propose a framework large enough to accommodate a range of approaches as well as room for disagreement between consumer and clinician. A way of doing this is to take a dialogic approach. Such an approach typically includes a good amount of talk therapy. According to psychology researcher Aitana Fernández-Villardón, dialogic approaches are "based on egalitarian interactions, in which a basic feature is that each participant feels heard and listened accordingly … It fosters the co-existence of multiple, separate, and equally valid 'voices' within the treatment." Fernández-Villardón surveyed thirteen research articles on the topic of dialogic approaches in the treatment of individuals diagnosed with psychosis and found benefits such as improved symptoms, decreased hospitalization rates, higher participation in the labour force, and positive results in terms of interpersonal communication.

Both Hans's story and Shannon's interview — both, of course, only small snapshots of experience — seem to point vaguely towards either an integrative view or one that favours clinicians' assessments, 'vaguely' because an in-depth analysis of their recovery experience is probably not nearly as important to them as simply "living better in the face of mental illness."

Living Better

Shannon talks about how she has to be "high maintenance to myself" to be successful in recovery: "Eat, sleep, move well, think well. Exercise is super important … It's quite a bit of work." This reminds one of the "virtues" mentioned in the Maori study above. They include:

- good general health practices
- keeping away from situations and stressors known from experience to worsen mental ill health

- recognizing warning signs of impending mental health problems and taking preventative action
- using medication thoughtfully and in a considered way to maintain recovery
- emotional release
- psychological/cognitive techniques to overcome thoughts and behaviour symptomatic of ill health
- spiritual practices
- pushing at the limitations that have arisen as a legacy of the mental health problem.

Hans is still early in this round of his recovery. We can almost hear Shannon reassuring him, "hang on, you just need time to get better." However, in reflecting on the voices he hears, he seems instinctively to use techniques to overcome thoughts and behaviours symptomatic of ill health and to push at limitations. One could also read a spiritual component into his surrender to "I am small" and "I don't know," followed by emerging into the light.

Seclusion

Seclusion was another experience that Hans and Shannon had in common (Shannon refers to it as 'isolation'). The Canadian Patient Safety Institute explains that "restraint and seclusion are behavioural management interventions that should be used as a last resort to control a behavioural emergency. Behavioural emergencies are often the result of unmet health, functional, or psychosocial needs." Seclusion "involves confining a person in a room from which the person cannot exit freely." Also known as 'safe rooms' or 'quiet rooms', the physical design can range from windowless 'padded cells' to rooms with calming colours, windows, safe patient-operated vents for fresh air, access to calming tools, etc. According to an evidence review conducted by the British Columbia Ministry of Health, the therapeutic value of seclusion rooms is at best questionable.

Sophie Staniszewska, a nurse-researcher, found five studies where patients reported that seclusion was helpful, necessary, and/or made them feel safe. (According to psychiatrist Juliane Mielau and colleagues, this opinion tends to occur more often with patients who have better insight into their illness.) Staniszewska's findings are illustrated in a patient quote from a study by nursing researcher Raija Kontio and colleagues: "I thought I was in heaven, feeling much better when I was restrained. I did not have nightmares, I was safe."

On the other hand, in nine studies surveyed by Staniszewska, patients felt they were not given sufficient reasons for seclusion, that seclusion was used as punishment, and that they were degraded, humiliated, treated in an undignified manner, or that their rights were violated. In Kontio's study, one patient noted: "I felt fear and anger, especially toward those who put me into the seclusion room. Nurses and physicians used power and authority over patients. I didn't know where I was and how long it lasted, it was terrible."

Still, when psychologist Eva Krieger asked patients who had experienced a range of restraints, the majority preferred seclusion over forced medication, mechanical restraint (e.g., 'straightjackets'), or manual restraint (holding).

What about Hans and Shannon? Neither of them was fully aware during their seclusion. Hans does not comment on it at all, and when Shannon does, she is not entirely negative about it. Neither is the research that was surveyed, which is somewhat surprising given the BC Ministry of Health's negative evaluation. At an intuitive level, seclusion — literally being locked up and alone — does not seem to be a favourable option, but not all patients are opposed to it. Is it perhaps that less coercive methods are just not available enough and seclusion is the lesser evil? It should be noted that there are efforts underway in some hospitals to change this. One example is Safewards, a program focused on reducing tension and conflict in psychiatric hospitals by using ten interventions (e.g. "know each other", "talking it through") to engage hospital staff and patients in a positive and proactive way. Another is the High and Intensive Care model. Focusing on recovery-oriented care, it gives particular attention to connectedness, self-determination and self-management.

Relationships

In the research on recovery as well as in Hans's and Shannon's experience, connections with each other play an important role. In their extensive study, Leonhardt and colleagues observe that "social connection was the overall most important aspect of recovery identified by persons diagnosed with serious mental illness." Roberto Mezzina and colleagues talk about "social recovery as a way to regain identity, personal power, and citizenship with communities."

For his part, Hans observes other patients around him, tries to build rapport with Gretchen the nurse, and has an epiphany triggered at least in part by the encounter with the mysterious Italian woman. Shannon speaks enthusiastically about the relationships, romantic and otherwise, that she had with fellow patients and compares helpful encounters with staff with less helpful ones.

Relationships with Staff — Positive Experiences

Patients commonly report that when they are in a psychiatric hospital that their relationship with staff "is the most important therapeutic factor … empathy, interest and understanding, in addition to a safe therapeutic environment, have meant the most," according to psychiatric researchers Lisbet Borge and May Solveig Fagermoen. Patients appreciated staff being kind-hearted, even "like family." They liked it when staff asked the right questions, gave them a sense of security, and knew when to push and how to give feedback. They often encountered staff who made them feel seen and understood, gave them a sense of equal worth, and helped them "find their way to their inner selves." Staniszewska and colleagues, who surveyed seventy-two studies on the experience of patients in psychiatric hospitals, add the important element of respect.

These positive relationships with staff are echoed in some of Shannon's story: "'I'm the voice inside your head,' one nurse kept saying to me, the voice to help me make good choices." and "One time when I was at [the hospital], I had foot problems. Every night, a nurse would come and bring me a basin with warm water to bathe my feet."

Relationships with Staff — Negative

In Hans's story, on the other hand, it seems that nurse Gretchen is struggling between dedication and burnout. She reminds one a little of Shannon asking one nurse, "do you like your job?" (although the connection between burnout and job satisfaction among people working in psychiatry is unclear).

When psychiatric nursing researcher Willem Nugteren looked at the experience of patients in psychiatric wards, he found four overarching themes, three of them dealing with negative experiences with staff: inappropriate use of ward rules, lack of time for patients, and feeling humiliation:

> When staff or associated authority figures are involved in insensitive, inappropriate, neglectful, or abusive actions, this is referred to as 'sanctuary harm.' These stressful events invoke in consumers a response of fear, helplessness, distress, humiliation, or loss of trust in psychiatric staff.

Relationships with Other Patients

A quote from a patient in a study that analyzed the role of social factors in recovery from psychosis, by Mezzina and colleagues:

> Yes, it's easier talking with people who've been sick.
> They understand you … A healthy person who's
> never been sick can never understand a psychotic
> person … I feel I'm not alone with my sickness …
> Here I feel like I belong. Like with my pal … she and
> I talk a lot about feeling ill, having things go against
> you … We don't cope so well with our existence
> when it blows up a storm like an ordinary healthy
> person can do … we have to struggle twice as hard
> to attain what an ordinary healthy person can.

In another study, Lisbet Borge found that socializing with other patients was a core experience for most patients in a psychiatric hospital. (As nurse-researcher Inger Johansson put it, fellow patients made the place "feel alive and home-like.") This was definitely the case for Shannon; in about half of the interview, she mentions fellow patients, most of it in the context of what psychologists Anna Galloway and Nancy Pistrang refer to as companionship and friendship. Shannon talks about "going out for a smoke together, laughing, having fun … it was like a party in there … There were people playing guitar and singing. At times, I was thinking I was in a band." Galloway and Pistrang add that "naturally occurring peer support (i.e., spontaneous interactions without structure or roles) in inpatient settings has received little research attention." Indeed, it was quite difficult to find research on the topic.

As can be imagined, such interactions can also lead to conflict, for example when Shannon is conned, or when, in Hans' story, Peter turns to rage when people don't engage in small talk with him. Several researchers point to this, particularly when closeness to others is unwanted but unavoidable, when it is hard to see a fellow patient suffer, or when conflicts that arise in therapeutic groups remain unresolved.

However, it appears that generally, patient-patient interactions are helpful. Apart from the reasons already mentioned, that is also because it allows people to feel they are more than a patient. For some, it is almost like being part of a family. Patients have more time to interact with each other than staff does and they help each other. Says one patient in Galloway and Pistrang's study:

> You get taken under someone's wing … if you're
> sitting on your own at dinnertime, somebody will
> come by and will talk to you … we do that to new
> people … anyone who's new on the ward, you say

'Can I sit with you?' and if they say 'no', that's fine, and if they say 'yes' … you start conversations.

BIBLIOGRAPHY: CHAPTER SEVEN

Alcoholics Anonymous (1939/2001). *Alcoholics Anonymous*. AA World Services.

Bateson, G. (ed.) (1962). *Perceval's Narrative: A Patient's Account of His Psychosis 1830–1832*. The Hogarth Press.

Borge, L. & Solveig Fagermoen, M. (2008). Patients' core experiences of hospital treatment: Wholeness and self-worth in time and space. *Journal of Mental Health*, *17*(2), 193–205.

Bowers. L., James, K., Quirk, A., Simpson, A., Stewart, D. & Hodsolla, J. (2015). Reducing conflict and containment rates on acute psychiatric wards: The Safewards cluster randomised controlled trial. *International Journal of Nursing Studies*, *52*(9), 1412–1422.

British Columbia Ministry of Health (2012, September). *Secure Rooms and Seclusion Standards and Guidelines: A Literature and Evidence Review*. https://www.health.gov.bc.ca/library/publications/year/2012/secure-rooms-seclusion-guidelines-lit-review.pdf

Canadian Patient Safety Institute (2017, September). *Mental Health Care: Seclusion and Restraint*. https://elderadvocates.ca/seclusion-restraint-in-mental-hospitals/

Davidson, L. (2012). Considering recovery as a process: Or, life is not an outcome. In A. Rudnick (ed.), *Recovery of People with Mental Illness: Philosophical and Related Perspectives*, 252–263. Oxford University Press.

Deegan, P. (1988). Recovery: The lived experience of rehabilitation. *Psychosocial Rehabilitation Journal*, *11*, 11–19.

Fernández-Villardón, A., García Carrión, R. & Racionero Plaza, S. (2022). *Exploring a Dialogic Approach in Tackling Psychotic Diseases: A Systematic Review* (Doctoral dissertation, University of Deusto).

Galloway, A. & Pistrang, N. (2018). "We're stronger if we work together": Experiences of naturally occurring peer support in an inpatient setting. *Journal of Mental Health*, *28*, 1–8.

Hasson-Ohayon, I., Kravetz, S. & Lysaker, P.H. (2017). The special challenges of psychotherapy with persons with psychosis: Intersubjective metacognitive model of agreement and shared meaning. *Clinical Psychology & Psychotherapy, 24,* 428–440.

Johansson, I., Skärsäter, I. & Danielson, E. (2009). The meaning of care on a locked acute psychiatric ward: Patients' experiences. *Nordic Journal of Psychiatry, 63*(6), 501–507.

Kontio, R., Joffe, G., Putkonen, H., Kuosmanen, L., Hane, K., Holi, M. & Välimäki, M. (2012). Seclusion and restraint in psychiatry: Patients' experiences and practical suggestions on how to improve practices and use alternatives. *Perspectives in Psychiatric Care, 48,* 16–24.

Krieger, E., Moritz, S., Weil, R. & Nagel, M. (2018). Patients' attitudes towards and acceptance of coercion in psychiatry. *Psychiatry Research, 260,* 478–485.

Lapsley, H., Nikora, L.W. & Black, R.M. (2002). *Kia Mauri Tau! Narratives of recovery from disabling mental health problems.* Wellington: Mental Health Commission.

Leamy, M., Bird, V., Le Boutillier, C., Williams, J. & Slade, M. (2011). Conceptual framework for personal recovery in mental health: Systematic review and narrative synthesis. *The British Journal of Psychiatry, 199,* 445–452.

Leonhardt, B.L., Huling, K., Hamm, J.A., Roe, D., Hasson-Ohayon, I., McLeod, H.J. & Lysaker, P.H. (2017). Recovery and serious mental illness: A review of current clinical and research paradigms and future directions. *Expert Review of Neurotherapeutics, 17,* 1117–1130.

Lysaker, P.H., Yanos, P.T. & Roe, D. (2009). The role of insight in the process of recovery from schizophrenia: A review of three views. *Psychological, Social and Integrative Approaches, 1*(2), 113–121.

Maslach, C. & Leiter, M. (2016). Understanding the burnout experience: Recent research and its implications for psychiatry. *World Psychiatry 15*(2), 1–9.

Mezzina, R., Borg, M., Marin, I., Sells, D., Topor, A. & Davidson, L. (2006). From participation to citizenship: How to regain a role, a status, and a life in the process of recovery. *American Journal of Psychiatric Rehabilitation, 9*(1), 39–61.

Mielau, J., Altunbay, J., Gallinat, J., Heinz, A., Bermpohl, F., Lehmann, A., et al. (2015). Subjective experience of coercion in psychiatric care: A study comparing the attitudes of patients and healthy volunteers towards coercive methods and their justification. *European Archives of Psychiatry and Clinical Neuroscience* (2015, April 22).

Nugteren, W., van der Zalm, Y., Hafsteinsdóttir, T.B., van der Venne, C., Kool, N. & van Meijel, B. (2016). Experiences of patients in acute and closed psychiatric wards: A systematic review. *Perspectives in Psychiatric Care, 52*(4), 292–300.

Ostrow, L., Adams, N. (2012). Recovery in the USA: From politics to peer support. *International Review of Psychiatry, 24*(1), 70–78, 10.3109/09540261.2012.659659

Rosen, C., McCarthy-Jones, S., Chase, K., Humpston, C., Melbourne, J., Kling, L. & Sharma, R. (2018). The tangled roots of inner speech, voices and delusions. *Psychiatry Research, 264*, 281–289

Substance Abuse and Mental Health Services Administration (2020). *Recovery and Recovery Support*. https://www.samhsa.gov/find-help/recovery

Treichler, E., Li, F., O'Hare, M., Evans, E., Johnson, J. & Spaulding, W. (2019). Psychosocial and functional contributors to personal recovery in serious mental illness. *Journal of Mental Health, 19; 28*(4).

Van Melle, A., Noorthoorn, E., Widdershoven, G., Mulder, C. & Voskes, Y. (2020). Does high and intensive care reduce coercion? Association of HIC model fidelity to seclusion use in the Netherlands. *BMC Psychiatry, 20*(1), 1–7.

Van Weeghel, J., Van Zelst, C., Boertien, D. & Hasson-Ohayon, I. (2019). Conceptualizations, assessments, and implications of personal recovery in mental illness: A scoping review of systematic reviews and meta-analyses. *Psychiatric Rehabilitation Journal, 42*(2), 169.

CHAPTER EIGHT

"Pink Dragon"
THE LONELY PINK DRAGON

In the poem that begins this chapter, a pink dragon sits in a restaurant — an out-of-place creature all alone, surrounded by people in their element.

Johnson is a musician and writer who has recently retired to what he calls 'Paradise', a quiet place on the coast. He lives there with his wife of almost thirty years, a dog, and a library full of books and videos.

Johnson's upbringing was very difficult; he scored high on the Adverse Childhood Experiences questionnaire. When given a number of stories and poems to choose from, he focused on "Pink Dragon," because loneliness was such a core experience of his childhood and youth, even though he was often among scores of people. He found ways to triumph over loneliness and the destructive blueprint of his family of origin: "June 27, 1975. Worst day of my life. The crossroads that day was a vow not to be like the rest of my family. A conscious vow."

The research section delves into the phenomenon of loneliness, discusses relationships with peers and parents, and describes how some people overcome loneliness.

THE POEM

Pink Dragon

"never on good friday,"
mumbled the pink dragon,
and sighed over a dish of
marbled curry chicken,
"never on good friday
have i, pink dragon, had a friend
hold my spiky tail."

his spiky tail with
orange pink polka dots,
his spiky tail all alone
in a chinese restaurant.

all around him
were grandmothers with white hair
pampering their gapped-tooth grandsons,
middle-aged lovers
twinkling eyes
over cups of hot green tea,
waiters and waitresses
chattering in cantonese —

but the pink dragon
sat alone.

his beautiful tail twitched sadly.
and out of a dragon eye with long purple lashes
rolled a long, salty dragon tear.

The Interview

Johnson

I'll read you a few pertinent sentences from your email [from an email exchange we had in preparation for this interview].

> I have grown to have a dim intolerance for poetry,
> cuz I've grown to have a dim intolerance for poets,
> the poets in my family either causing or suffering
> the most tragedy ... "Pink Dragon" — the concept
> of 'home' has always affected me, 'coming to
> home' meaning 'finding peace'. Growing up, I had
> a war zone, not a home, and didn't begin to find
> peace until I met my wife, grew up, married, and
> found my own home. I hope the dragon finds his.
> Everyone should.

Are these sentiments you still have, a week or so after you sent that email?
Poetry doesn't do much for me. I wrote a fair bit when I was younger before I started writing songs. Most poetry I know is navel-gazing, introspective stuff. It doesn't move me, partly because of the ambivalence I have towards poets and poetry. Just not my curriculum.

But I liked "Pink Dragon" because it told a story. Coming back home. Trying to find happiness and contentment, obviously feeling loneliness, feeling sad, hoping, wishing — all emotions that press buttons in me. Find that home, find that peace. I hope that pink dragon can find that, too.

Tell me about home, loneliness, hoping, wishing — it pushes your buttons?
That comes from growing up. My home life was a battlefield. I had a picture in my mind from friends with loving families. Mine was not like that. Very tense all the time and so wishing it was something different, better, realizing that I was growing up without it.

You have to make your way in the world so, if you have that kind of lack of home, you have a choice. You can deal with it or not. You can survive with it or not and I managed to deal with it, managed to survive, managed not to inflict it on anyone else. That's something I don't respect. I grew up with lots of others who had crappy lives too. They couldn't handle it, they were users and losers, would blame their home life: "I had a shitty home life so I can be a shit for the rest of my life." I don't buy that. It took a hell of a lot of self-restraint, though. But the fact that, after all those years, I found love and peace, and home is the happy ending that I hope the pink dragon gets.

What does the pink dragon mean to you?
Not sure that he is a dragon or a man. If it isn't a man, what the heck is a pink dragon doing in a Chinese restaurant? The pink dragon strikes me… why a dragon, why a pink one, why a Chinese restaurant … what do they mean to me? Somebody who stands out, very much alone, maybe the way he looks in an otherwise communal place. Somebody who is solo, so different, so isolated.

Somebody solo, different, isolated …
I never felt that I fit in. I was the loner, I was the isolated one, the youngest, the one that vowed to be different. I wound up being the butterfly, a part of all groups but not a member of any when I grew up. Ironically for a loner, I had hundreds of friends, too many to know what to do with. "Oh you know, this guy is a musician, etc." That was really just a persona. I just wanted to be alone and go within myself and do my own thing, be with my own things. All these groups of friends I had, and I had an unbelievable amount of friends … one talent I have is that I know excellent people. But by and large, I never feel I am one of them except for very select groups.

The pink dragon is not sitting in a park bench at midnight with no one around. He is sitting in a Chinese restaurant, he is at least among people, he is being seen, still trying to be part of what's going on and hoping that by the end of it … 'will happiness be there when I come?' like you say in one of your poems. When I come out, when someone finds me? The dragon is visible, is trying.

In terms of the dragon, are you thinking of others or yourself?
I was thinking of myself. That's how I approach everything I read: how does it relate to me? Then I can learn more about myself. However, when I mulled the poem over, I was also thinking of others, you know, there's gotta be a lot of other pink dragons around.

It's funny that I think this right now … the things that make an impression on me … I think about a time, forty years ago, I was on a bus, maybe to get concert tickets, on the Stanley bus, this guy came on. I can still picture him: tall, thin, gawky, big nose, weird-looking face, dressed nerdily, little brown bag in his hand, and I remember thinking, I'm glad I'm not that poor schmuck. But I hope he did okay. That guy could be the pink dragon.

You see so many people with lives of pain and you wish things could be better for them, that they could have happy endings. I wish everyone could.

Here's the pink dragon, he's so hopeful, why would you not wish him the best? One person could say he's just a loser — but what's inside of me is that I look at the pink dragon and I wish him the best.

In my late teens and twenties, I was a mess. Over half of my life, I've been a mess. When you're an intelligent mess, you hope that one day you won't be a mess.

When I hit thirty, after half of my life trying to kill myself, I realized I'm still here. Part of me felt like a failure. But then I thought, if I'm gonna be around for a while, I should probably do something with myself. It was then that I started to grow up, mature, get responsible. Interestingly, that was also the year when my wife and I started to go out and became a couple.

But I was self-destructive for a very, very long time.

You said, "When you're an intelligent mess, you hope that one day you won't be a mess." Can you say more about that?
I guess someday you hope not to be a mess at all. I say that because I've seen so many people who have not had as much in the toolbox and have had horrific childhoods like I did and never got over it and inflicted their childhood on everyone else for the rest of their life. If you're an intelligent mess, you got more in the toolbox, you recognize things can be different, and that's the road I ended up going on.

I had a lot of crossroads that I walked up to and managed to, in the end, take the right turn, with a bit of help from some great people. There's a story I read. There is this milquetoast woman, she was married to this brute of a husband. She was the silent "yes sir, no sir" type of wife, makes the dinner, etc. Then the brute husband dies. Everyone wonders how she is going to manage. And then, she starts to blossom. By the end of it, she is absolutely a changed person and a line near the end was that … it has to be in you for it to come out at all.

You need that inner toolbox.

And you had that inner toolbox, and you call it intelligence.
Yes. I guess that's one word for it.

Can you talk about one of the crossroads?
June 27, 1975. Worst day of my life. The crossroads that day was a vow not to be like the rest of my family. A conscious vow and, at some point, I probably said it out loud that I was going to be something other than this. Something goddamn different. And I started down that fork in the road. Led to an awful lot of grief and more crossroads, but it did in the end turn out the right way to go.

How did you want to be different?

I think it was the first time that I consciously realized that I did not want to hurt people who hadn't hurt me first. This is the way I wanted to be. I chose to be defensive rather than offensive. I would take the first punch, I wouldn't throw it. People over the years have found that I'm perfectly capable of throwing that punch. If you don't see that in people, you can be awfully surprised. My brother once remarked that I was so easy-going. And he was surprised when I laughed. I said, "I'm your brother, do you really know fuck-all? I'm not easy-going, I'm self-controlled."

It was the self-controlled aspect that was the mechanism that made it possible for me to live every day, to be able to function. The loneliness was the environment that I was in, but the self-restraint was what made it able for me to live within it. If I reacted to everything the way I grew up, I would have seriously hurt someone. The self-restraint allowed me to function.

There's a song by Alice Cooper — *I may be lonely but I'm never alone.* That's how I felt. A complex answer to what sounds like a simple question, but it's a simple question that doesn't have a simple answer.

Interesting. Often people talk about how it's the other way round: "I'm alone but not lonely."

I was the guy moving from room to room at a party. Often I would slip out, go around in various stages of intoxication, sometimes vandalize stuff, then return to the party. Sometimes it was noticed that I was gone, sometimes it wasn't. I was in a group of people but really not of that group of people.

That reminds me of what you said of the pink dragon: "Somebody who stands out, very much alone, maybe the way he looks in an otherwise communal place. Somebody who is solo, so different, so isolated."

The pink dragon is lonely in community. You can be lonely and you can still try to communicate and reach and touch, stay in some kind of contact, maybe it works out, maybe it doesn't. For years when I was a kid, I had no close friends but couldn't stand being at home evenings. I would leave the house, lying to my mother I was going to this person or that person, and I would walk for miles, would walk around the neighbourhood, to the PNE, Hastings, Kootenay Loop[7], anywhere where something might happen. There might be some kind of event that would take me out of where I was in my head. I would walk, oh my God, I would walk for hours and hours and get home at three a.m. I was armed a lot of the times and it was lonely, almost as if I tried to find somebody, anybody, just trying to be out there, trying, searching for something, and I did that for so long.

7 Areas in East Vancouver

Do you still consider yourself lonely?
No. I still consider myself a loner, but not lonely.

People have many turning points in their lives. What's one of yours that changed you into someone who is not lonely?
Finding a group of people finally that I felt to be a part of. I had other groups of people previously. For example, I was a counsellor at a camp when I was fourteen and they were a great bunch of people. But of course when the camp goes, everyone goes back home and then I lost them all. The person I was becoming in that group, I lost that person too. That led to a lot of the loneliness and walking around.

Quite by accident towards the end of grade eleven, I managed to get a very good friend. We would go to his place and rock and party and get drugged up and then, quite by accident, I became involved with the people in the senior year who did the yearbook. Wound up with these people, going out partying afterwards, and they were pretty close to each other and they all knew me. They were all pretty suspicious of me because I had a bit of a reputation. But we all wound up having a great time and clicked. Saw that we had a hell of a lot in common. One of them was instrumental in smoothing over the worries the others had. We had a marvelous time in the summer with all sorts of escapades and then running the yearbook. They are still among my closest friends today, forty years later. In fact, just last week we threw ourselves a sixtieth birthday party with a great big dinosaur cake. And it was in that group I finally found myself to be part of something. I was accepted and I didn't have to throw on a mask because I was different. Every group needs a person like me and I became that type of person in that group. That was a huge turning point.

That sounds a bit accidental, but is it really?
It was. When you're in a rock band like had I been in music for years and years, you chance upon each other. It's karma that brings people together. I had known those people, but the circles of life all turned, but they all turned in a different direction and we all converged, especially that first night. All the circles converged and we suddenly realized what a great group we were and still are. Yes, accidental.

And that's the meaning of life. That's the magic of life.

The magic of life. Pure accident.

Starting from a low point in life, feeling such a failure. I wasn't just going to give up or drink myself to death. I'll reinvent myself and go into a different direction. It's what's in your toolbox. If you give up, then you wind up on the street.

Let it be magic!

THE RESEARCH

When I approached Johnson, knowing that he would be an interesting person to interview, I suggested various topics to him and a number of stories and poems. He chose "Pink Dragon" and the topic of loneliness.

Loneliness is often referred to as an epidemic (further exacerbated by the pandemic that started in 2020) in terms of global health. It is seen as a critical determinant of health. The stress of loneliness, in addition to decreasing mental health, can also have physiological effects, such as heart disease, diabetes, and earlier death.

What Is Loneliness?

On the face of it, the term 'loneliness' seems self-explanatory; however, bringing the concept into sharper focus shows more of its complexity. Such a focus can also help distinguish it from similar terms, which we'll see is important in this case.

To begin with, loneliness can come from being alone, but being alone is not the same as loneliness. For example, when Johnson talks about wandering the streets at night, he does not talk about loneliness, he talks about being alone.

Sometimes a desire to be alone can lead to isolation, which can lead to loneliness — but again, those are not exactly the same thing. Here is what some researchers say about the nature of loneliness:

Loneliness is "a perception of diminished social relations or that they are inadequate," say psychologists Liesl Heinrich and Eleonora Gullone in a widely cited article on the mental health consequences of loneliness. Also highly influential, to this day, is sociologist Robert Weiss's 1973 theory of loneliness, which talks about the difference between two types of loneliness: 'emotional loneliness', which stems from a lack of intimacy with close individuals, including parents, and 'social loneliness' because of insufficient relationships with peers. Johnson also tells us in his interview about something that psychologist Janet Younger writes about: one can feel lonely despite being with others. As well, she mentions a related term, 'alienation': a disconnection from oneself, others, God/transcendence, or nature.

Loneliness in Youth

Johnson shared quite a bit about being lonely when he was young. Pamela Qualte is a psychologist who studies loneliness across the lifetime. She and her colleagues point out that a certain amount of loneliness is typical among younger people. In the general population, loneliness peaks in those years, then again after a person turns eighty. Positive attitudes towards aloneness, such as Johnson experienced, also tend to emerge in adolescence. "Time alone might be deliberately used, for example, for emotional self-regulation and identity development" adds psychologist Marlies Maes, one of Qualter's collaborators. Interestingly, other researchers cited by Maes found that such positive attitudes towards being alone were associated with lower emotional stability and higher openness to experience; both these attributes fit Johnson as a young man.

The Quality of Relationships

One of the things that stood out in Johnson's interview was how he evaluated the quantity ("hundreds of friends") and quality ("I never felt that I fit in") of his friendships as a young man:

> I never felt that I fit in. I was the loner, I was the isolated one, the youngest, the one that vowed to be different. I wound up being the butterfly, a part of all groups but not a member of any when I grew up. Ironically for a loner, I had hundreds of friends, too many to know what to do with. "Oh you know, this guy is a musician, etc." That was really just a persona. I just wanted to be alone and go within myself and do my own thing, be with my own things.

When psychologist Gerine Lodder and colleagues investigated friendship quantity and quality in adolescents, they found that that research participants who felt lonely tended to evaluate some friendships as 'low quality'; however, their friends did not necessarily share that view. Such a disconnect probably only emphasized the feeling of loneliness. Maybe that was also the case for Johnson, especially since younger people generally tend to increasingly long for quality, more emotionally close friendships.

Relationships with parents also play a significant role in how young people experience loneliness. As can be expected, high-quality relationships not only with peers but also with parents contribute to psychological well-being. Research participants in a study by psychologists Gay Armsden and Mark Greenberg who had good relationships with parents tended to agree with statements such as "my mother respects my feelings" or "I feel my father does a good job as my father" and disagree with statements such as "my mother has her own problems, so I don't bother her with mine" or "I don't get much attention from my father." In addition, psychologist Miri Scharf and colleagues found that the more accepting and child-centred that parents were towards their children — something that did not happen in Johnson's life — the less children felt lonely around their parents. Also, Maes and colleagues found that youth who enjoyed being alone tended to feel lonely around their parents. All of this makes Johnson's experience around loneliness seem almost inevitable.

What Motivates Us To Overcome Loneliness?

It turns out that we have a biological signalling system that tells us when we have not sufficiently connected with others. Qualter and colleagues state: "When a person is rejected by others, the 'social hurt' activates the same regions of the brain that would be activated if the person stubbed their toe, what we would normally call 'real' hurt." Because we try to avoid that pain, we are often quite motivated to overcome it. Some factors make that difficult though, such as low self-worth and low trust of others, something that can come quite easily in persons who grow up in conflicted families, such as Johnson.

Who Finds It Easier To Overcome Loneliness? Locus of Control

Another factor is external and internal locus of control, an influential concept pioneered by psychologist Julian Rotter in the 1950s, which relates to what we believe is the cause of our experiences. A person with an external locus of control may feel that, for example, their successes are due to luck and that negative experiences are about something that has happened to them, without much influence or responsibility on their part. Conversely, a person with internal locus of control might believe that skill or hard work led to their successes or that they don't need to be victims of circumstances.

Some researchers, such as psychiatrist Mohammedreza Hojat, suggest that those who are chronically lonely have an external locus of control. Low self-worth, low trust of others, and an external locus of control can lead to negative thinking. As an example, this could take the form of interpreting social interactions in a negative light ("he said he was busy, but I bet he just doesn't want to talk to me"), which in turn could lead to prolonged loneliness. Psychologist Jeffrey Arnett even talks about loneliness as "caused by the weakness of personal communication and socialization skills."

Was Johnson motivated by the pain of loneliness and helped by an internal locus of control to change things around? He tells us:

> You have to make your way in the world so, if you have that kind of lack of home, you have a choice. You can deal with it or not.

and:

> When I hit thirty, after half of my life trying to kill myself, I realized I'm still here. Part of me felt like a failure. But then I thought, if I'm gonna be around for a while, I should probably do something with myself.

"Let it be magic!" Johnson says of how positively life can evolve. Hopefully, all the pink dragons in the world can find that magic, too.

BIBLIOGRAPHY: CHAPTER EIGHT

Armsden, G.C. & Greenberg, M.T. (1987). The inventory of parent and peer attachment: Individual differences and their relationship to psychological well-being in adolescence. *Journal of Youth and Adolescence, 16,* 427–454.

Arnett, J. (2007). Emerging adulthood: What is it, and what is it good for? *Child Development Perspectives, 1*(2), 68–73.

Barjaková, M., Garnero, A. & d'Hombres, B. (2023). Risk factors for loneliness: A literature review. *Social Science & Medicine, 334,* 116163.

Centres for Disease Control and Prevention (2023). *Health Effects of Social Isolation and Loneliness.* Retrieved from https://www.cdc.gov/social-connectedness/risk-factors/

Heinrich, L.M. & Gullone, E. (2006). The clinical significance of loneliness: A literature review. *Clinical Psychology Review, 26*(6) (2006, October), 695–718.

Hojat, M. (1982). Loneliness as a function of selected personality variables. *Journal of Clinical Psychology, 38*(1), 137–141.

La Placa, V. & Morgan, J. (2022). The social construction of loneliness and global public health. *Social Science Perspectives on Global Public Health,* 189.

Lodder, G., Scholte, R., Goossens, L. & Verhagen, M. (2017). Loneliness in early adolescence: Friendship quantity, friendship quality, and dyadic processes. *Journal of Clinical Child & Adolescent Psychology, 46*(5), 709–720.

Maes, M., Vanhalst, J., Spithoven, A.W.M., Van den Noortgate, W. & Goossens, L. (2016). Loneliness and attitudes toward aloneness in adolescence: A person-centered approach. *Journal of Youth and Adolescence, 45,* 547–567.

Nayyar, S. & Singh, B. (2011). Personality correlates of loneliness. *Journal of the Indian Academy of Applied Psychology, 37,* 163–168.

Qualter, P., Vanhalst, J., Harris, R., Van Roekel, E., Lodder, G., Bangee, M. & Verhagen, M. (2015). Loneliness across the lifespan. *Perspectives on Psychological Science, 10*, 250–264.

Rotter, J. (1966). Generalized expectancies for internal versus external control of reinforcement. *Psychological Monographs: General and Applied, 80*, 1–28.

Scharf, M., Wiseman, H. & Farah, F. (2011). Parent-adolescent relationships and social adjustment: The case of a collectivistic culture. *International Journal of Psychology, 46*, 177–190.

Steinberg, L. & Morris, A.S. (2001). Adolescent development. *Annual Review of Psychology, 52*, 83–110.

Weiss, R.S. (2008). *Loneliness: The Experience of Emotional and Social Isolation*. MIT Press.

Younger, J.B. (1995). The alienation of the sufferer. *Advances in Nursing Science, 17*(4), 53–72.

CHAPTER NINE

"When the Doorbell Rings"

Hope, the Hidden Message: Responding to Intimate Partner Violence

"When the Doorbell Rings" features a mysterious visitor who delivers a letter to an old couple, promising hope to Mrs. Hapley, the abused wife.

When Violet encountered the story, it reminded her of her and her mother's life as an abused wife and child. As a child, she grew up in an extremely violent family, and she has also encountered domestic violence as a young woman. She sees in Mrs. Hapley "every wife, sister, daughter, mother … She is every black, LGBTQ, disabled, Indigenous person who had to put herself aside for someone else."

Violet and her family live on Canada's East Coast, where they enjoy living in a heritage home. She has a life-threatening illness. She looks back on many years as a social service worker and activist.

The research portion looks at the intersection between intimate partner violence and hope, with attention to the wide variety of forms that resistance fuelled by hope can take.

THE STORY

When the Doorbell Rings

At the sound of a motorcycle roaring, Laura Hapley moves the curtain aside and looks out the window. Instead of passing by, the machine stops. A tall person dressed all in black swings their legs off and gently places their helmet on the seat. The light of the setting late September sun surrounds the apparition with a halo of gold. Laura lets the curtain fall.

A moment later, the doorbell rings. Laura hesitates, then opens the door.

"Mrs. Hapley?"

"Yes…?"

"And Wally Hapley?"

"My husband, yes. And you are…?"

The woman is tall, very tall. Broad-shouldered, dressed in black leather from boots to gloves. She hands Laura a business card.

"I am sorry to trouble you, Mrs. Hapley. My name is Arch. Michaela Arch." The business card features name, email address, telephone number, and a logo in gold showing a sword stuck through a dragon. "Could I speak to Mr. Hapley, too, please?"

Laura looks at the business card. A faint smell of something like incense emanates from it. "He's busy. What is this about?" She glances towards a door in back.

The tall woman produces two envelopes from her jacket, cream coloured, also with a golden logo, this one showing wings. The backs are closed with a red seal.

"I need to speak to you and him together. There is a request for you to read these documents in my presence."

"Laura!" A voice from the back. "What is it?!"

Laura looks over her shoulder, moves towards the voice, hesitates, returns to the door.

"Please." Her voice is low and urgent. "I will tell my husband. He cannot be interrupted right now."

"I do apologize for inconveniencing you, Mrs. Hapley, but unfortunately he will have to come out." The tone is firm, friendly, polite. "It is important. It cannot wait, I'm afraid." Ms. Arch smiles at Laura, a friendly, warm beam.

Still smiling, she shouts, "Mr. Hapley?" She does not have to raise her voice much. Deep and resonant, it carries easily.

"Laura! I'm busy!" Laura's eyes open wide, flicker, then close.

A little dog appears behind her. It curls around her legs like a cat, looks up at the stranger, does not bark. Beside the entrance stands a small table, on it a vase with flowers. Lilies and sunflowers — an odd combination, but beautifully arranged.

Ms. Arch briefly bends down to pet the dog, whose tail slowly begins to wag. She straightens and looks down the hallway.

"Mr. Hapley, we need you here! Could you spare a moment, please?"

A thump and out from a door down the hallway rushes a man in his early seventies, his hair almost white, well-groomed. He carries himself with a professorial demeanour — sure, apparently, of his importance. He shoots a look of great annoyance at Laura, then the tall woman.

"Who let you in?" He turns to his wife. "Laura!"

Laura's eyes dart to Mr. Hapley, then the vase. The little dog's tail disappears between its legs.

"Whoever you are, I'm busy and you're trespassing. Leave or I'll call —"

"— the police," finishes the woman. Her black leather crackles faintly as she takes a small step forward.

"That would be quite all right. Suit yourself. In the meantime, Mr. Hapley, Mrs. Hapley, I have two documents that I have been asked to witness you read in my presence."

"Who asked you?" Mr. Hapley steps forward, too.

"Move!" he hisses at the dog.

Laura flinches, starts to bend down to the dog but, with a glance at her husband, just gently shoos it away with her foot.

"Please open and read these documents. This is yours, Mrs. Hapley." The woman extends one to Laura.

Wally snatches it. "I can read both. We are a married couple. We have no secrets from each other."

The tall woman takes the envelope from Wally Hapley and returns it to Laura. Laura looks at Wally, a question on her face.

"I'll read it later," he snarls, "I'll probably have to explain it to you, anyway."

A low, quiet, growl emanates from the woman dressed in black.

"That will be enough, Mr. Hapley."

Laura Hapley slowly opens the letter, hands shaking.

Wally Hapley tears open his envelope, throws it towards the little table. It slips to the ground.

> Wally, years ago when the doorbell rang, you opened and the man said, 'If you ever lay hands on Laura again, I will kill you.' It is time to remember this now. You were spared. But now you need

to remember. Each time you are about to raise your hand against Laura, remember it and act accordingly. Each time you are about to raise your voice against her or threaten her. Each time you are about to raise your hands or voice against someone or something who Laura loves, or threaten them, remember. Remember, act accordingly, and you will live in peace. If you need help to carry out this request, contact Ms. Arch.

Laura reads her letter:

Laura, years ago when the doorbell rang, it filled you with both hope and dread. You kept both alive. Sometimes hopes bears fruit; here we are, your protectors. You are a beautiful, creative, wise, and compassionate woman. You may not be fully aware of it yet, but it is never too late to realize. You are not alone and you are more powerful than you think. Please remember that. If someone, anyone, raises their voice or their hand against you, or threatens you or someone you love, remember you are not alone, remember you have protection, remember your power, and act accordingly. Do that, and you will live in peace. If you need help, contact Ms. Arch.

Four hands tremble. Two rest folded, relaxed, strong.
Ms. Arch looks at Wally until he returns the gaze. "You understand?"
Wally nods, hypnotized.
"If you understand, say, 'yes, I understand.'"
Wally clears his throat, mumbles, "Yes, I understand."
The tall woman looks at Laura. Her eyes are already trained on her. "You understand?"
Laura nods. "Yes," she says, her voice quiet but steady. "Yes, I understand."
"Please shake hands."
Their hands reach out towards each other. One thin, elegant, olive brown, moving one inch, then another, perceiving, as hands do and as the conscious brain rarely notices, the small change in the atmosphere as the other hand approaches — a tiny rush of air movement, ever so much more warmth — and a bigger hand with a few stray hairs on its back, a bit bony now in older

age, shaking a little, with a bead of sweat appearing in the lifeline crease. They touch. And grasp. And hold.

"Apologize."

"I apologize," both say, simultaneously.

"You know who needs to apologize."

Laura looks at the stranger, then her husband. Wally's head is bent. Slowly, he lifts it.

"I apologize," he says, almost whispering.

Michaela Arch nods and returns to her motorcycle. The little dog runs along for a moment. Nobody scolds it as it lets out a happy little yip, wagging its tail in the wake of the quickly receding tall woman in black leather.

THE INTERVIEW

Violet

Because of her illness, Violet tires easily when reading, so I read the story to her.

What is your first reaction to this story?
Who sent her? It's like a demand from a will. Someone sent the woman with the two letters, which also sounds like a will or a death request. And the letters are personal. All those years ago… Who sent her to them?

Would you have wished for something like that to happen at any time in your life?
I would have loved to have seen my mother and father being told to apologize.

Who would have done that?
My old teacher, Mr. Woolsely, would have done it. He knew a lot about my family's secrets. I think he threatened my father once. There was an incident where I had been injured on the school grounds. Mr. Woolsely brought me home. My father was there. He said, "She better show up in school tomorrow. She's not so sick that we don't expect her to be in school tomorrow." Mr. Woolsely was my high school homeroom teacher but also my guidance teacher for that year. He knew stuff. I always saw him as a bit of a hero. In the books I read as a young kid, he was a lot like one of those hero characters.

I imagine this woman, Michaela Arch, would have silenced Mr. Hapley with a look. He immediately became submissive. Mr. Woolsely had a look like that, a don't-fuck-with-me look.

Did you dream about this kind of rescue?
Yeah! Always dreamed someone would come and set my father straight and tell my mother to get out of that damn armchair. "You have kids to look after, woman!" "And you" — my father — "keep your hands off those children."

Were those dreams helpful or harmful?
When I was very young, it was helpful. I believed in rescue. Up until I was twenty, twenty-two, I still believed rescue was possible. Not until I'd been in therapy, I realized that I had to be my own rescuer, that it wasn't going to come from another place. It took me a long time to take responsibility for the

stuff that I was creating and inviting into my life. Because if I were to rescue myself, I had to stop the things I needed rescuing from.

I have a hard time imagining that Mrs. Hapley is that old, that she still lives with someone who she is so afraid of. For me, it would have been, there's no way I would put up with this for as many years as my mother did. If I'm in charge because I'm an adult responsible for children, I have to *be* in charge.

And your mother?
I don't think she believed in rescue. I believe she believed that was her lot in life. She just kept her head down, kept her eyes averted. "He's on a rampage, send one of the children into the room to see if he's all right."

That sounds strange: "see if he's all right."
That's what she would say, "Your dad sounds unhappy, see what he needs." And that was my job. Thrown to the wolves.

Wolves… so what do you think about the dog?
My father would have stared the dog down until he whimpered. Kicked him across the room if he thought that was necessary. And my mother would have done exactly the same thing Laura did — reach down to protect him but then change her mind mid-motion.

So your mother could protect neither the dog nor the children.
Or herself.

Like that man in that story, anything my father did was more important than anything that goes on in the house. He was a foreman in a factory. He would come home and, if it was cutting the grass day or whatever, the entire mood of the day was "what is he doing?", "don't disturb him." My dad thought he was pretty friggin' important. And my mom treated him like he was important. Yup.

The woman that came and showed them the business card — in my imagination she is either a cop or a private detective or someone executing a bequest.

This is the second time you're mentioning the idea of a will.
Maybe that's the space my head is in right now.

There is an air of authority of that person. And it would have been on that business card. Name, email, telephone number, but not company or anything. Why is that business card important enough to get you in the door when someone already said three times, no, he's unavailable. And the narrator makes a point of describing the business card but doesn't say the name. What gives her the authority to have to speak to you both at the same time? Who sent you? With what authority?

There are three circumstances in my life that they have that kind of authority... police, lawyer, government.

Did you ever dream that one of those would show up?
Police, police, police! I thought they'd be a hero. In my prayers at night, I would pray that God would send someone to come to our house. So ultimately, it would also be God.
[At this point, I read the story to Violet for a second time.]
Now I'm replaying the story... Archangel Michael! If I follow this through as a message from God, who are the mister and missus? Mr. and Mrs. Hapley get a message from Archangel Michael, "Stop what you're doing."

Who is Wally that he needs to apologize? He is an abusive husband. He's a dick who thinks he's more important than God. Who is Mrs. Hapley? Is she every wife, sister, daughter, mother? She is more than that. She is every black, LGBTQ, disabled, Indigenous person who had to put herself aside for someone else. Because the someone else thinks they are more important. Mr. Hapley thinks he's more important than anything she could ever possibly say. Every time she asserts herself, he beats her back. Mr. Hapley thinks he's more important than even God. Who could come to his door and say "Wait a minute?"

What do you think of Michaela, Archangel Michael?
She has a big ego, just like Mr. Hapley. She has been sent to deliver this message and maybe she feels like she shouldn't have to hand over a business card, just take her word for it. When I think of the Archangel Michael, all I can think of is John Travolta in *Michael* who is sent to earth to deliver a message.

When you prayed, was it like that?
I didn't think the angels would be so much like us, so human. My rescue, what I imagined my God intervention, was very much like the stained glass windows in church. What the crucifix in the church looks like — it looks just like that. You could see the halo just like in Sunday school. Very churchy.

Do you think a story like this is hopeful or too far off?
You have to have some hope to understand this story. You wouldn't make the connection that Michaela Arch is Archangel Michael. The hidden message is, you have to have hope. If you don't have that hope, then it's too far out there, there is no way it could be like that.

Isabella Mori

How would you describe the overall feeling of the story and the interview?
I think the story is on the side of hope. If you have at least a bit of hope, that story is evidence that your hope is correct. For me — I know I'm hopeful. It's evidence for me. Yeah, I get it. I make all my connections through a hope filter. So you don't even get into my life if you're not a part of hope. Beliefs, art, stories, music — if you don't have hope, you don't get in. I don't have room. I want to be so full of hope that there is no room for doubt.

THE RESEARCH

Violet wished for the research part to focus on the intersection of hope and intimate partner violence (a term frequently used today instead of 'domestic violence').

Violet speaks of the hopes she had as a child: "Police, police, police! I thought they'd be a hero."

This is exactly what happened in the case of Rona, a South African mother of three who had been imprisoned by intimate partner violence. Months after a fateful visit from a police officer, who she called "man of hope," she wrote this letter to him:

> Dear man of hope,
>
> I think the work you do deserves more than what I can put on paper. In December 2000, an angel in the form of a police officer came to my rescue. He had been called to my house to attend to the violence about a thousand times before that day. This time, he said to me: "If this is how you want to die, then die here. This is it."
>
> These harsh words were like a bucket of ice water. However, it was then that I realized that I was going to die and I was allowing this to happen.
>
> That day, I decided I was going to make a difference to my life and the lives of my three children.
>
> And I still make a difference. I wish I can make a difference in other women and children's lives, but even if I cannot give it to them directly, I want to give it to you, the man of hope, to give to the women and children.

Rona further recounts that the officer "was sympathetic … he talked to me as if he really understood … I think the policeman's heart broke when he saw me." This made it possible to see herself with more compassion and, she states, "his words carried me towards hope."

The parallels between Rona's experience, Violet's interview, and Mrs. Hapley's story are striking.

Reasonable Hope: Doing vs. Feeling Hope

Rona's account appears in a case study by family therapists Elmarie Kotzé and Kaethe Weingarten, along with their colleagues, who illustrate how a community of police officers and therapists came together and learned how to have, hold, and 'do' hope.

It leans heavily on Weingarten's ideas about what she calls 'reasonable hope'. She contrasts hope as a feeling with hope as an activity. In her view, hope as a feeling comes with unrealistic expectations of the culmination of an ever-upward movement. Her view of this type of hope is similar to the wishful thinking that Violet had as a child.

But Violet eventually decided to move from wishful thinking to action. Her words "I had to stop the things I needed rescuing from" (again, so similar to what Rona expressed) imply hope, hope for something attainable: you can only stop something that you think you have at least some control over.

This attainability is one of the features of Weingarten's reasonable hope. Other features are:

- Reasonable hope occurs in relationship with others. Hope is sustained by those with whom we hope together. Being South African, Weingarten leans on the concept of ubuntu, which is often translated from the Zulu as 'humanity' or "I am because we are," a belief in a universal bond that connects all humanity and which transcends individualism.
- Reasonable hope is not about accomplishing goals, but about aiming towards them, sometimes in very raggedy fashion, but always seeking pathways that may lead to those goals.
- Reasonable hope is not black and white. It functions in a vast grey zone.
- Reasonable hope is not destroyed by doubt, contradictions, or despair — it makes room for these experiences.

"Hopelessness thrives when the future is perceived as known, certain, and bleak." In reasonable hope, the future is open and uncertain, but/and we have some influence over it.

We can imagine that, in the story, Mrs. Hapley feels she knows exactly what her future will bring: more threats against her little dog, more demanding voices, more belittling, more broken vases, and perhaps also bones — until an angel comes, in the form of Michaela for her, and in the form of the "man of hope" for Rona. In both cases, hope suddenly springs up in an accidental, new, and fleeting relationship. It's hard to do hope alone. For Violet, a therapist helped.

Intimate Partner Violence Statistics

Let's look at some grim statistics from Canada:

- In 2011, close to 40,000 intimate partner violence (IPV) crimes against women were reported to police. Less than 25% report such crimes; the actual number is closer to 200,000.
- The rate was double for Indigenous women.
- In 2011, 89 people died of IPV, most of them women.
- In 2015, 48% of all solved homicides of women were related to IPV. In contrast, men were most often killed by casual acquaintances.
- 63% of IPV victims had been victimized more than once prior to calling the police; 28% had been victimized more than ten times before contacting police.
- Women report more serious forms of violence than men. In 2009, three times as many women who reported IPV indicated that they had been sexually assaulted, beaten, choked, or threatened with a weapon by their partner in the previous five years.
- The conviction rate for IPV crimes is lower than for other crimes. In the province of British Columbia between 2002 and 2012, the rate was 49% as opposed to 70% for non-IPV cases.
- In the U.S., on a single day in April of 2014, 12,058 beds were counted for women fleeing IPV and their children.

Looking at the numbers above, there is much need for hope but also much reason for its absence. Among the many adverse effects of IPV are hopelessness, a lack of confidence in finding and keeping housing, financial and healthcare resources, and low self-esteem. IPV brings thoughts of suicide with it, as well as Post-Traumatic Stress Disorder. But it also brings strategies to deal with the violence and it brings resistance.

Just as in Chapter 2, it should also be mentioned that women are not the exclusive victims of IPV. Cherami Wichmann, a researcher with the Department of Justice Canada, points out that men comprise about 20% of all IPV cases reported to police in Canada. About 20% of those are homicide victims. Men report IPV less frequently to police. When they do, it results less often in an arrest or a police record. Indigenous males represent a much larger proportion (44%) of intimate partner homicide victims (women represent 21%). Furthermore, each year between 2009 and 2017, more than 2,300 incidents of IPV involving same-sex partners occurred in Canada; 55% involved a male victim and a male accused.

Helplessness

When discussing intimate partner violence, the question of "why didn't she do anything about it?" almost always comes up. The answers to this could fill a small library.

In the late 1970s, psychologist Lenore Walker interviewed 403 battered women, which led her to the theory that when women saw none of their actions leading to positive changes, they began to feel futile, often resulting in learned helplessness. This was a groundbreaking idea at the time because it challenged a widely held perception that women's behaviour was the cause for the abuse; instead, Walker looked at how the abuse was a cause of their behaviour. From this, other theories evolved. In the late 1980s, sociologist Edward Gondolf interviewed 6,612 victims of IPV in shelters and also surveyed 1,000 women in the community. From this, he developed a theory that holds that battered women tend to be anything but inactive in their attempts to stop violence as it grows more frequent or severe. This also held true for Violet's mother, who did eventually break free from the abuser by fleeing to a shelter.

Women's Strategies To Deal With Intimate Partner Violence

Both Mrs. Hapley and Violet's mother used methods such as keeping things quiet for the abuser and doing whatever the abuser wanted. When investigating how to assess such methods, psychologist Lisa Goodman and colleagues categorized these behaviours as placating. However, rather than seeing this as a sign of helplessness, they saw it as part of a whole range of strategic methods, which they listed in categories such as placating, resistance, safety planning, informal (e.g., talking to a friend), formal (e.g., trying to get help from clergy), and legal ones. The placating category includes courses of action aimed at changing the abuser's behaviour without changing his sense of control, maybe even supporting it.

Placating and resistance strategies were the most frequently used, even though they were actually often not the most helpful. The five most effective strategies were:

- talking to family members, used by 69%

- safety planning by having important telephone numbers close at hand, used by 50.1%
- talking to an IPV program, used by 49.3% of the women
- hiding important papers, used by 44.2%
- sending kids to friends/family, used by 41.5%.

The least effective strategy, also used by the least amount of women — 23.5% — was getting legal assistance.

Resistance

For Goodman and colleagues, resistance in IPV includes strategies "intended to change batterer behaviour and possibly the balance of power in the relationship by challenging his sense of control." They also point out it may not be that effective. Conversely, "external help seeking, as opposed to private attempts to manage the violence, is critical to women's ability to end the violence in their lives. Strategies that involve engaging family and friends seem to be particularly helpful." It is interesting to note that external help played a crucial role, too, in Violet's and Rona's lives, as well as for Mrs. Hapley in the story.

However, in the sometimes decades-long time before the violence ends, there can be subtler forms of resistance that Goodman did not include in her study, perhaps because it is a different way of thinking about resistance. In an article on everyday resistance to violence and oppression, psychologist Allan Wade points to "small acts of living":

> ...any mental or behavioural act through which a person attempts to expose, withstand, repel, stop, prevent, abstain from, strive against, impede, refuse to comply with, or oppose any form of violence or oppression (including any type of disrespect), or the conditions that make such acts possible, may be understood as a form of resistance.
>
> ...
>
> Any attempt to imagine or establish a life based on respect and equality, on behalf of one's self or others, including any effort to redress the harm caused by violence or other forms of oppression, represents a de facto form of resistance.

Examples of these are:

parody, lying, withdrawn muteness, feigned ignorance, thinly veiled contempt, muttering, or a credibly performed deferential bow.

Stephanie Dornschneider, who researches international relations, applies this to the oppression of Palestinians in occupied lands, an angle that Violet, the former activist, would have appreciated. Dornschneider adds to Wade's examples the avoidance of confrontation and visibility (similar to Mrs. Hapley not wanting to call her husband or not openly protecting the dog), as well as persevering, "a sustained effort to overcome challenges in spite of failures and setback." In our context, it would be something like struggling to maintain a 'normal' life in the face of daily violence. Violet feels that her mother did not engage in this type of perseverance when she did not "get off that armchair."

In hoping for the police or God to intervene, Violet very much imagined a different life. In contemplating how to protect her dog and not making any great efforts to shield her husband from Michaela, Mrs. Hapley engaged in resistance. These are indeed small acts of resistance, but sometimes that is all the oppressed person can, or feels she can, do — always born out of experience: the oppressed person has very good reason to believe that harm will come to her or those she holds dear if she shows too much opposition.

Sometimes the only place of resistance lies in the privacy of the abused person's mind (perhaps when even perseverance is too hard). Dwelling in this privacy is sometimes labelled as dissociation; Wade laments that, stating that it often involves creating not *dis*- but *imaginative* associations that can be life-saving. Seen that way, none of the acts just described are really small: "Any act of resistance in such circumstances is inherently and profoundly significant."

Wade cites radical feminist therapist Bonnie Burstow who writes about resistance as a continuum. On one end of it are isolated actions ('private actions', as Goodman refers to them) which may not have much effect on the violence but which remind the abused person that they have not been treated with respect. On the other end is collective action against the patriarchal forces that perpetuate violence against women and children. Regarding isolated actions, Burstow's own words could not be more powerful:

> Some women's acts are limited, individual, and border on resignation, but even here is a core of resistance that is poignant and meaningful. In this category we find the housewife who stops cleaning up and just sits there unhappy and "unable" to do anything … her being is rebelling … Although

the refusal may not be happening on a reflective plane and refusal is only one dimension of what is occurring, this woman in her own way is going on strike.

It is fitting that Violet suggested as a theme for this chapter, "Hope, the Hidden Message." Hidden even in resignation, then, can be a kernel of resistance and hope.

BIBLIOGRAPHY: CHAPTER NINE

Beattie, S. & Hutchins, H. (2015). Shelters for abused women in Canada, 2014. *Statistics Canada: Juristat*.

Burstow, B. (1992). *Radical Feminist Therapy*. Sage.

Department of Justice (Canada) (2018). *Making the Links in Family Violence Cases: Collaboration Among the Family, Child Protection and Criminal Justice Systems. Annex 1: Family Violence Statistics*.

Dornschneider, S. (2023). Exit, voice, loyalty… or deliberate obstruction? Non-collective everyday resistance under oppression. *Perspectives on Politics*, *21*(1), 126–141.

Gondolf, E. & Fisher, E. (1988). *Battered Women as Survivors: An Alternative to Treating Learned Helplessness*. Lexington Books.

Goodman, L., Dutton, M., Weinfurt, K. & Cook, S. (2003). The Intimate Partner Violence Strategies Index: Development and application. *Violence Against Women*, *9*(2), 163–186.

Johnson, D., Johnson, N., Perez, S., Palmieri, P. & Zlotnick, C. (2016). Comparison of adding treatment of PTSD during and after shelter stay to standard care in residents of battered women's shelters: Results of a randomized clinical trial. *Journal of Traumatic Stress*, *29*(4), 365–373.

Kotzé, E., Hulme, T., Geldenhuys, T. & Weingarten, K. (2013). In the wake of violence: Enacting and witnessing hope among people. *Family Process*, *52*(3), 355–367.

Taha, F., Zhang, H., Snead, K., Jones, A.D., Blackmon, B., Bryant, R.J. & Kaslow, N.J. (2015). Effects of a culturally informed intervention on abused, suicidal African American women. *Cultural Diversity and Ethnic Minority Psychology*, *21*(4), 560.

Wade, A. (1997). Small acts of living: Everyday resistance to violence and other forms of oppression. *Journal of Contemporary Family Therapy*, *19*, 23–39.

Walker, L.E.A. (1979). *The Battered Woman*. Harper & Row.

Weingarten, K. (2010). Reasonable hope: Construct, clinical applications, and supports. *Family Process*, *49*(1), 5–25.

Wichmann, C. (2021). Male survivors of intimate partner violence: A summary. *Victims of Crime Research Digest No. 14*.

CHAPTER TEN

"Bicycle Creatures"

No Expectations: The Families of People with Substance Use

"Bicycle Creatures" is a story in which a bicycle courier is asked by a mother to find her son, "half-angel, half-demon," who has become homeless because of substance use.

Meredith, the person interviewed for this chapter, is a retired mother of three. One of her children has spent many years struggling with serious addiction. For almost twenty years, Meredith has facilitated a support group for families and friends of people with challenges around substance use.

Meredith's experience is that when a person is deeply entrenched in substance use, nothing much can be gained by trying to talk them into treatment when they are not interested. Instead, "you make connection, connection without expectation … 'I care about you, I love you, I think about you, here is something that connects us' but not 'you need to come home, you need help, you can't live like that.'"

Despite the fact that a large portion of people who problematically use substances never enter formal treatment and that there are many families who use Meredith's approach, there is next to no research on it. The third part of this chapter looks at what little could be found, as well as approaches that come close to it.

THE STORY

Bicycle Creatures

What a bright morning! All the windows are open. A fresh breeze blows through the rooms, carrying with it a faint scent of the roses down in the garden. I snatch my keys from the wooden bowl on the counter and bound down the stairs. A short, faint echo clatters through the house.

The bike by the door, ready. Its all-black frame calls out an invitation just for me; no one else would ever feel attracted to its darkened spokes, the springs under the saddle black, the brake lines, the pedals, everything black.

Open the door and down the street. The bicycle is my horse, my lover. I don't need a boy or girl between my legs. The saddle pressed against my seat where all the nerves converge, the wind in my hair, what more could I possibly want? I fly, I fly, and the speed is more than measured metres rushing by; speed surges through my loins, my mind, my soul.

I am a courier. I bring people things. Parcels, pizza, documents. Weaving through traffic is my meditation. Only extreme awareness lets you thread between a semi and a Harley in the middle of the road just as the light turns green. The road is my cathedral, the high-rises to the left and right its sacred walls.

My bike and I, we ride beyond the cathedral. Up the hills we go and, where others strain, we revel in our strength, my bicycle with its carbon fibre triangulated frame, I with my muscles and tendons. We're one, a carbon-based — no, not a monster: a cyborg, a mythical creature, a sphinx on wheels.

But we are not silent like a sphinx or shy like a unicorn. We are right here, right before your very eyes. When you open the door and see us with our offering from Foodora — a portobello burger with arugula salad — your eyes light up with my clear-voiced hello. You can't hear the whisperings of my bicycle's springs as they breathe out, but I can and I know they greet you, too.

And then there are times when the mythical connects and you, the bicycle and I weave fairytales together. Today, your eyes and mine meet. Yours fall on the black, black bicycle. You speak:

"Do you have a moment? Can you… can you do a delivery for me?"

Twelve times out of thirteen, I say no to a new customer. But this is the moment to say yes.

"I don't know the exact address, though."

Yes. This is a job for my bike and me. I saw it in your eyes right away.

"Come in," you say.

I follow you into the kitchen. Without a word, you bring an apple pie out of the fridge, take a fifty from your wallet, disappear into the hallway, and return with a Naloxone kit, the magic bundle that reverses overdoses. You put it all in a bag, hesitate, close the book sitting on the counter, and add it to the package. You go to your phone, scroll, and show me a picture.

"This is what he looks like."

His blue eyes are bloodshot, hair cut at weird angles, probably with bad scissors, scabs on his cheeks. A huge smile lights up his face.

I recognize a fellow mythical creature. A two-headed monster, half-angel, half-drugs.

"Lyle," you say. "His name is Lyle. This is where he was last week." You show me the address on the phone. "But I don't know. Maybe you won't even find him. Just keep this, then" — you wave at the package — "or give it to someone else. There'll be someone else's son."

I nod. You ask for my number so that you can text the picture.

"Don't worry about the address. I know the area," I say. "Just the picture."

You pay me. I don't take your tip.

I text Josh to take over my deliveries for the next two hours.

This must be done well.

My bicycle turns left instead of right; we need a moment of composure. After a few minutes down the hill at breakneck speed, so fast we almost kill a pigeon, we find ourselves at the dyke. We slow down. We wait.

And the melody comes. I start whistling it. A lilting uprise of air through lung and lip, accompanied by the crackling of tire on gravel, little pebble-drums beating against the black rubber, soft now in its sudden slow motion. The notes rise, tweet high in a trill, then soar down, muddy about in a low G, then settle around the steady A, where the melody weaves in and out, then softly quietens.

Yes. The melody will show the way.

And off we are again, down the rest of the dyke, then right, eight kilometres down Gromer Road, beside a pig transport all up and down the bridge, and finally, there we are, in the heart of the city, its dirty, angry beating heart, where all the tears and hope and garbage collect.

He's not at the Raven Hotel, the last address. Doesn't surprise me. The melody isn't right.

Not at Trinity Mission, where they recognize him but "No, Lyle, haven't seen him — what, for a week?" Not at the library across the street, where the hungry go for a bit of quiet and soul feeding.

Slowly, we ride through West Alley. I nod to Hersh, rummaging through his pile of bags. No use asking him, his mind is too far gone. I can't see anyone else I know. Over to Eastmore Street. I scan the faces, so many of them,

Chinese, Fijian, Haida, men, trans, women. Lyle is not among them. The melody urges me on, tells me not to stop and talk to them; I'd be distracted.

In my backpack, I can feel the package. Did she bake the apple pie hoping it would make it to her son? I didn't ask for her name. But I know her. Lyle's mother. Did she always have a fifty at the ready for him? How many times has she shown up at the pharmacy, asking for a Naloxone kit? Do they have the same taste in books?

My bicycle turns into the lane between Eastmore and Washington. Wanda waves to me, "Hey Jules, over here!"

"Can't!" I yell, "Later!"

I could have asked her but my bicycle moves on, driven by the melody.

Bradley Road, Dasher Alley, the back of the library. My bicycle keeps on going.

We turn left into the lane behind McSheridan, with all the restaurants and their dumpsters.

The melody starts to rise. I whistle. One, two, three times.

A baby rat races across the asphalt broken by the roots of a lone old fir tree, its little feet light like a water bug on a pond. Against the tree leans a bicycle. Recognition hits me; it's Edwina's, the one that disappeared last week, a thirty-speed folding Morana, painted ugly brown in hopes it wouldn't get stolen. I step down to take a closer look and take out my phone to call Edwina. Lyle's photo is still up. I look at the Morana again. Now I notice — behind it, on the ground, swathed in a black hoodie and loose brown pants, squats a guy, getting a needle ready.

"Hey!" I say.

He doesn't look up, keeps fumbling with his stash.

"Hey! You!" Louder now. "Whose bike is this?"

He looks up.

"Hey! It's — you're Lyle!"

He squints at me.

Incongruously, I show him his picture.

"That's me!" The two words slowly ooze from his mouth.

"Lyle! That bike… your mother…"

Where do I start?

He drops the needle. "My mother?"

I dig the bag out of my backpack, unpack the pie, the book, the fifty, the kit.

The first thing he goes for is the book. *Breathing Under Water*, by Richard Rohr.

"I love Richard Rohr," he mumbles, then starts thumbing through the pages. "*The result has been spiritual disaster*," he reads. Thumbs some more. Then sighs. "That was the first of his books I read."

I see that his right index finger is all bloodied up.

"Here!" he says as he finds another passage. *"How you do life is your real and final truth."* Looks up at me. "So? How do you do life?"

I squat down, give him a hug, stand up.

"Watch that bicycle here for me, will you?" I point to Edwina's steed. "It's my friend's. I'll tell her you have it and it's safe with you."

My bike has me get back up. "And call your mom!" I call to him as I ride off. I turn my head at the end of the lane; he still has the book in his hand.

I need to text Edwina. But for now, the wind whistles in my ears as my bike and I fly to the tune of our truth.

THE INTERVIEW

Meredith

Meredith, in your email you said you resonated with some things, for example, the book. Can you tell me more about that?
I think that I related to that because, for all of us parents who have loved ones that are struggling, there are some deep-rooted needs to remain connected to the child that we knew before substance use came into the picture. And that is an absolutely perfect example of what we talk about as parents — focusing on that book title, or a cartoon, or a favourite superhero that your loved one liked — and when you try to make connection when you can, it's about talking about those things as opposed to all the issues. That book absolutely represents what we experience trying to hang on to the person, the child.

What other connections did you find?
The care package idea — that she had a care package ready at all times; whenever she had opportunity to make it to her son, she would use the opportunity. The courier idea was brilliant, I don't think anyone had ever thought of using a courier. I think we all have this care package ready and we're ready to deliver it however we can at any time. The example I always use, our loved ones are on an island and we are on the shore. They can row across to us; when they get to us, we have everything they need to get better. But often they won't get on the boat. But we show up every day, wave to them, wait for them to get in the boat. Using the courier is reaching him on the island. He's on his island, he won't come home, he won't get help.

Those parts stood out for me. The connection part. And that she didn't have expectations. No note, how are you doing, do you have a place to stay. That's exactly what we're talking about all the time in my group. How do you make connection, connection without expectation? "I care about you, I love you, I think about you, here is something that connects us" but not "you need to come home, you need help, you can't live like that." In fact, it was the courier that said "call your mom." The courier had an expectation.

This reminds me now of talking to my son who has this YouTube channel on exotic animals. When I call him, I'm dying to ask: have you called your disability worker, have you talked to your doctor, etc. But instead I listen to him about those animals, just listen, keep that connection going even though I have a list of questions I want to ask.

It's hard to keep that connection going without the expectations. Certainly in my group, we talk about it a lot. For some parents, not getting a call and not hearing is sometimes better. When they hear from them, then maybe there is an expectation on their loved one's part, often for money, and they have to respond to that and they are fearful of the communication. On the one hand, "Why I am not hearing from them?", and on the other, "They're gonna want something."

And then there is the other one, when you don't hear anything, you reach out and there is nothing. "What am I doing that that person is not responding?"

How do you make a connection and try not to have an expectation? It's really working, though. Like a text message, "Do you remember Boxie, auntie's old cat, hope you're doing well, love you!" — those kinds of messages tend to get responses.

Putting that book in the package is a subtle message. "The only expectation is I want to know you're alive and, if you get this, I know you're alive."

Letting go of expectations is very hard. Can you talk a little about the journey to get there?
Exactly that. It's a journey. I'm thinking of a grandparent right now who is suffering greatly. They get intellectually that the more expectation they show in their communications, the more their granddaughter retreats. "But I don't have anything positive to say!" they say. Well, so you don't say anything. But they're having a horrible time with it. They're getting counselling to help with the emotional part of it. And of course, that journey is different for everybody. For some, the emotional part is so deep and rooted, in perhaps their own lives, and a support group is not going to be enough. Reading about how to best communicate can help.

You have to accept where people are.

Others are more like me, extremely practical: give me a tool, give me something new, give me a new idea, I will try it. When I can actually take an action and don't have to be mired in the emotional place and can't take any step, that frightens me more than anything. By God, if there's something I can do! Even just for myself.

There's an in-between. There are people really emotionally not able to do anything practical and those who have been through a long journey and have let go of expectations, or at least communicating them to their loved one. There is all kinds of shades in-between.

Those tools that I just mentioned, with the people in my support group, I can't have any expectations around those tools either: "Here I'm handing you a tool, just use it." Maybe they'll use it, maybe they won't. But for me, even when I was in the thick of it, in the trenches, I was all get-to-the-support-group, all about coping, surviving, this is not going to get me, I refuse!

I relate to the mother who is doing something practical and loving. She could be active, she could make that pie, she could have that ready, she had a plan, when that courier comes, maybe this is the way to get the care package there. Even if there is no expectation about results or change — what it is, it's therapeutic for *her* to keep on believing and doing something. You're doing it for yourself actually! I can visualize her in the kitchen, it's all on the counter, all ready, she's ready.

But their first concern is probably their loved one. When you tell people they're doing it for themselves, how do you make that palatable for them?
The idea that you're doing it for yourself, you can only acknowledge that in a place where it's safe and you would only say it if you say it about yourself, not about someone else. But here, the mother decided it's the best way to show love at the time, and it's good for *her* to do that. Whatever you do, you'll probably think "I'll be judged," but that's what you can do at the time. There's so little you can do, the son or daughter or whoever is not in your life right now. At the time, it's the best way to show love, you have no other way to show it.

There isn't anybody on earth who can understand that except for people who have gone through it. I don't even talk about this with the rest of my family. They have expectations!

So you retreat into yourself and seek support from people who understand, and read, and you inform yourself, maybe go to a counsellor, you find your own path to deal with it. When you trip up, for example, loan your laptop to your son, not knowing you'll ever get it back — other family members would say, are you crazy, but in the group we say, okay, you took the risk, and that's okay. No judgment. You had decided at the moment you would take that risk. No one understands except for people who've been there.

What can guide us in that journey is really what I call 'the toolbox'. Where your coping tips are, where your strategies are, where you find ways to learn to be patient, where you learn about things like the Stages of Change, find out how siblings cope — when all these issues arrive, having the toolbox and having that guidance helps tremendously. You don't have to look to anybody else except this toolbox that has been compiled by people who have experience with these challenges.

… and to have a toolbox big enough for you to create your own tools?
Yes! I'm reminded of when my son had this big accident and I travelled all the way across Canada to see him and I had all these things I wanted to do

for him and say to him. And he just put his hand up, said *stop,* I just want to visit with you.

A big thing in my toolbox is 'The List' — a tool that helps you figure out what's for you to do and what's for the loved one to do. So my question when I visited my son ended up, how do I go about handling what *I* need to handle? What's on my list and what's on his? The toolbox is your compass put together by people who have walked that path. No one in your family, in your workplace, not some counsellors can help you. They do not walk that path, they do not get the calls at two in the morning, they're not there when your child comes for nothing but a shower and then steals your husband's computer, these other people don't experience what you experience. That's why I'm putting a handbook together with all the tips I've ever found.

Do you come across families who say families' experiences are all well and good, but advice for me needs to come from a professional?
Yes! We often have professional presenters — counsellors, doctors, etc. — and when we announce that, people come in droves. People are thirsty for knowledge, always searching for that answer, always wanting to hear from the expert. I categorize that as education. Learning is great. It's soothing to find out, okay, this is an illness. Then you can understand. It's very important to hear from the experts, but to think that it's going to be *the* solution, that it's going to fix things… There is no fix, there is no solution. That is the difference.

I don't know how many presenters I've brought to the group — Guy Felicella [an inspirational speaker who has recovered from substance use], workshops, lawyers, etc. It's about empowering the family member and making them more resilient. The more knowledge you acquire, the more confident you can be in how to react to your loved one. That's why Addiction 101 [a multi-week workshop on substance use] is so great, because you find this understanding. When addiction first enters your life, it hits you like a bomb and there is this sudden and immediate learning curve. I recognize the importance of the expert. But often when families leave these workshops, they feel they've learned something but also wonder, how is this going to help in my situation? How can I apply this?

What do you think of Lyle being "half-angel, half-drugs"?
I get a zing in my chest. You don't even recognize your child but you gotta hang on to the image of your child. The person, not the drug. Separating the disease out from the person. The person is there. They're just not healthy in this state.

Also, the contrast between the kindness of the hug — but also he had stolen her friend's bike. They contrasted each other very well in that situation. His world included stealing that bike. But he had to be held accountable. She didn't let it go. That really struck me. That's a contrast — that is so hard for us to deal with as family members. This disease criminalizes the person. Families get stolen from. Then they're in court, then you visit them in jail. This whole world you're thrown into, oh my God, when he was a boy and we found five dollars, we went to the police! Contrast that with you can't have them in your house because they'll steal, their whole day would be spent with "What can I steal?" You get thrown into this world of dishonesty. The stolen bike really triggered something for me. This whole world. It's very rare that a family doesn't have to go to the police, to court. And often we're relieved when they're in jail, at least they're in a kind of gated community.

Where is the hope in all of this?
The hope is that there is always hope. I have this huge sign that says 'Hope' in my room. I pretty much have a gallery in my room of hope artifacts.

Hope is always hanging, never on firm ground. There is nothing you can do about the situation. But hope just resides in you, in the world, not only in our particular situation. We hope there will be a vaccine for Covid-19, a cure for breast cancer. They're working towards it and there's this hope bit. It exists pretty much in every aspect of life. If you have a family member who gets Covid, there is a hope for treatment.

In twenty years, I have seen absolute miracles. I get pictures from families that were coming to group, they were hopeless, is there ever going to be change? And then the pictures arrive, showing their loved ones, married, children.

Recovery — the success stories are largely on the person's terms when they start to really get it that nothing about using drugs is working. You have no control over that realization that they want to make a change, you have no choice. Maybe you can influence something a bit and you can keep on loving them, supporting them the best you can while protecting yourself, and in the end it rests on hope. I have a son who is nineteen years sober who went from using heroin to successfully getting suboxone treatment now [a prescription medicine that treats opioid type substance use]. That is hope, and I hold on to it, and I hold it for all the two hundred people in my group.

There are some really difficult situations that some of our families find themselves in but so many of them are still pretty optimistic about where their own life is going and I'm thrilled how well they're taking care of themselves — meditating, walking, having a positive perspective on life. You'd think they'd be wanting to jump off the cliff, but I'm just amazed how well they are managing.

Isabella Mori

THE RESEARCH

In the U.S. in 2019, close to 8% of the population, or 19 million people, officially had a substance-use disorder. About 73% of them struggled with alcohol use, 39% with drug use, and 12% with both. Many more actually use these substances; there is a large grey zone of those who clearly struggle but have no diagnosis, those who use somewhat problematically, and those who use with few apparent consequences. Also:

- 51% of prescription drugs were obtained through friends or relatives, most of it given to them for free.
- 50–60% of people recover from substance use.
- Approximately 10% of people struggling with substance use end up in treatment.
- An estimated 20% or more have a family member with a substance-use disorder.

This chapter is about these families.

A Scarcity of Research

Meredith was most interested in research on families who focus on keeping the connection with a loved one who is using substances, without any expectations. She and the families she works with have decades of experience with that approach. However, after two months of trying, I found only one paper that talked directly about it. Why?

One potential factor is that the majority of research is on treatment, yet according to the U.S. National Survey on Drug Use and Health in 2019, 90% of problematic users of drugs or alcohol are not in treatment. Lyle, the lost young man in the story, has no intention of doing anything about his drug use. He is part of the under-researched majority.

The families of people who use drugs are also under-researched. When families are mentioned at all, they are usually listed as an add-on, e.g., "the voices of those in recovery as well as their families."

When research does focus on families and it is not in the context of treatment, the problems they experience are understandably front and centre. There is also some research on coping, but there are only a few indirect indications that coping includes simply staying in touch with their loved ones.

We will begin with the one paper that is very similar to Meredith's approach, then will go into some detail on three approaches that come close.

Overcoming Stigma With Dialogue — A Mother's Story

Melissa Dee LeMar's master's thesis in communication is an autoethnography project in which she describes her experiences as a mother of a woman using opioids. Autoethnography is a form of qualitative research. Similar to a memoir, the author describes personal experiences but deepens it through detailed self-reflection and places it in the context of relevant research, often from a wide variety of fields, e.g., from psychology to social work to political science.

LeMar traces the journey from stigmatizing her daughter's addiction to building and maintaining a relationship with her through dialogue. Just like Meredith, who talks about the importance of education and information, LeMar wishes she had known more about addiction when she began her journey — but all she understood about it was what she had learned from the media. This was mixed in with advice, comments, and judgments from people around her who knew just as little. This is reminiscent of Meredith when she says "other family members would say, are you crazy?" and one hopes that LeMar, too, had a group where people were learning with her and accepting of her choices, without judgment.

Had LeMar known more, she could have been more supportive of her daughter, including educating her own friends and family so that they could be less stigmatizing in turn. When LeMar did not heed her friends' and family's advice to "kick her out," she was stigmatized as well and, for example, labelled as an enabler. She felt like a failure as a mother — hadn't she told her daughter to "just say no" to drugs? LeMar experienced stigma by association or 'courtesy stigma', where not only the person struggling with addiction is seen as deviant and flawed but also the family.

LeMar asserts that dialogue can combat stigma. Dialogue is more than simple conversation; in dialogue, individuals consider others' opinions, hear about experiences new to them, and gain insight into perspectives they had never thought of. This aids in respectful, open-minded, mutual understanding and in deepening relationships.

'Stigma Days' vs. 'Dialogue Days'

LeMar divides her experiences into 'stigma days' and 'dialogue days'. On 'stigma days', when her daughter said she was going out for the evening, LeMar would ask where she was going, who she'd be with, and what time she'd come home, treating her like a high school girl instead of an adult. LeMar's intentions were good and her fears rational and understandable, but the path she took was full of accusation and interrogation, reinforcing the power dynamic of a parent-child relationship. She implied that her daughter's addiction was a conscious choice, that she did not want to get better, and that she couldn't be trusted. This resulted in closed-off conversations.

Just like in the case of Meredith and her group members, who want so much to ask all sorts of questions — Have you gone to the doctor? Do you have a place to stay? — these parent-child interactions don't seem to be productive.

On 'dialogue days', LeMar's scenario was different.

> I would respond with encouragement that she is getting out of the house and doing something positive. Instead of allowing the 'what if' questions to come flooding forward in my mind, I would reflect on the triggers and simply tell her, "I love you." Knowing that she is a person that has value and has free agency to make choices in life, I would suspend my judgment or my fear and allow her to be a 'Thou' that is deserving of my full respect. I would also try to not judge her friends as they are individuals who have value as well. This type of trust would allow her to tell me about what she was doing and encourage us to have conversations about her feelings when she was struggling with her addiction. I was a better mom when I engaged in "dialogue days" because I had a better relationship with my daughter and, through the trust we built, allowed me to better support her when she needed it.

LeMar points out that dialogue is often confused with other forms of interaction such as conversation, debate, or discussion. But dialogue is a special, distinct way of communication "in which we communicate to understand others that we share life with." Specifically, it is what Meredith describes as not having expectations, in contrast to a debate, which has at its goal to convince and 'beat down' the conversation partner, as dialogue expert William Isaacs puts it.

Some of the approaches below come close to what Meredith describes but none of them focus only on keeping alive the connection to the person who uses substances, without expectations of treatment or recovery.

Co-dependency — A Useful Construct?

The term 'enabling' is related to the concept of co-dependency. Many therapists and some researchers see families of people suffering from substance misuse as entangled in it. The idea is that co-dependent people let others unduly and unnecessarily influence their thoughts, feelings, and actions. This results in certain types of self-defeating and often ineffective behaviours and attitudes, such as stifling one's own and others' expression of feelings and ideas, trying to control others, and experiencing an exaggerated sense of responsibility. In terms of addiction, the family/friend is thought to be as dependent (hence, co-dependent) on this behaviour as the person with the addiction, therefore continuing — 'enabling' — the addiction with too much helping, too much control, or often both.

It is not clear how useful a construct co-dependency is. It is most often discussed in twelve-step groups such as Al-Anon, a self-help group styled along the lines of Alcoholics Anonymous, but for families and friends. In reviewing several philosophies in supporting families, social work professor Jan Ligon found no evidence that co-dependency–based approaches worked particularly well.

A Harm Reduction Approach — Community and Connection

Psychotherapist Patt Denning of the Harm Reduction Therapy Centre does not feel that the concept of co-dependency is helpful, because it does not place enough emphasis on values that are typically important for families, such as community and connection. Denning proposes an approach that relies on harm reduction principles and also on community and connection.

She recognizes the rollercoaster of families' experiences: one day, earnest promises to never touch the bottle again; the next day, yet another intoxicated phone call. Denning writes:

> Loved ones struggle with extraordinary questions about loyalty, love, support, and limits. How much help is too much? How long should you put up with it? How many times should you cover for them and pick up the pieces? The question becomes: "Should I give up hope of them ever changing?" ... Loved ones have been told to stop bailing them out, stop cleaning up the mess, and let them face the consequences ... Eventually, we're told, they will hit bottom. If they live through it, maybe then sobriety will be possible. And only with sobriety will come a life.

This is often followed by families trying to persuade their loved ones to go into treatment. Unfortunately, that does not necessarily bring about the desired results. According to one study, dropout rates for residential treatment are around 30% and the relapse rate is around 50%. Denning points out that this often turns into a cycle of hope, despair, and rage for all concerned. She offers a different perspective, honouring that "people are trying to maintain attachment, family, and/or community in the face of a disabling problem." Understandably, these attempts are difficult and far from perfect, but that is no reason to pathologize the family by labelling them co-dependent.

What Is the Specific Harm? How Can It Be Reduced?

Rather than reaching for the often-elusive goal of absolute sobriety, Denning practices harm reduction. She helps the family define what harm has been done or is still happening, and then together they choose the most urgent issues and work on reducing the harm. Denning points out there is a fine line between healthy and destructive helping, then guides families in finding where that line is for them. There are parallels between this and Meredith's 'List', the tool that helps families "figure out what's for you to do and what's for the loved one to do."

One example is where a woman had sleepless nights over her brother who was living in another part of the country, was precariously housed, and was using drugs. Denning helped the woman come to the conclusion that she would pay for her brother's move to her city and for modest accommodations for him, while at the same time making it clear that that was all the financial assistance she would give. The biggest harm to the sister was her sleeplessness over her worries; once she had her brother closer, she could sleep again, even though her brother made no attempts to reduce his drug use.

Another example of Denning's approach is when she helped a family think of ways of how to best communicate with young Alice, who was using drugs, starting by telling her they missed her and wished that they could renew their usual phone calls.

It is worth mentioning that Denning bases her approach on clinical experience and does not cite research she has conducted; however, her approach has been cited in other scholarly work.

CRAFT — Community Reinforcement and Family Training

CRAFT is a well-researched approach and probably the most well-known. It also does not use the co-dependency model and supports people who problematically use substances, as well as their families.

CRAFT, Motivational Interviewing, and the Stages of Change
CRAFT leans heavily on Motivational Interviewing, a technique that helps people change by using and enhancing their own motivations. In the example above, Denning used Motivational Interviewing to help the sister carry out the action to which she was motivated. Motivational Interviewing uses the Stages of Change that Meredith mentioned in the interview. They were developed by psychologist James Prochaska and colleagues, recognizing that most people undergoing major behaviour changes go in and out of several phases.

The first phase is Precontemplation, marked by at most a passing interest in change. This is where we find Lyle in the story. In Contemplation, the person realizes that change may be beneficial. The Preparation stage shows the person investigating ways to bring change about. In the Action stage, they are actively working on new behaviours. In the Maintenance stage, change is sustained long-term. Many people also experience a Relapse stage. More simplified, some have referred to the stages as No, Maybe, Prepare, Do, Keep Going, and Oops.

CRAFT, Motivation, and Positive Communication
Beyond Addiction is a book for families of people with addiction issues, written by psychologist and addiction researcher Jeffrey Foote and collaborators. It lays out the CRAFT system and starts by explaining what motivates people:

- feeling acknowledged, understood, and accepted as you are (independent of what you do or don't do)
- getting information without pressure
- having options
- having reasons that make sense for a particular choice
- having a sense of competence about how to change and what steps to take
- getting positive feedback for positive change.

The opposites of these — e.g., feeling misunderstood — destroy motivation. "Confrontation," says Foote, "is the biggest motivation killer." CRAFT aims to make positive change inviting and palatable to the person, to reward healthy behaviours, and to withhold reward when problematic substance use occurs. This invitation is extended with empathy, respect, hope, and the ability to see the other person's point of view. Just as important is to focus on positive communication, which is where most of the similarity with Meredith's approach comes in. An example of that is when she talks about listening and responding to her son's interest in exotic animals.

Stressed relationships make communication difficult for families. Often unspoken or unconscious, the desire is understandably not to feel that stress (similar, in fact, to what drives many people to drink or use drugs). The solution that offers itself so easily is to fix things or to demand apologies or instant change, maybe even retribution. However, that rarely works — negativity abounds, wounds deepen, connections become more and more frayed.

CRAFT's Seven Elements
CRAFT suggests a way out: positive communication. It has seven elements:

1. Be positive in word choice, tone, and framing.
2. Be brief.
3. Be specific.
4. Express and label feelings.
5. Offer understanding.
6. Accept responsibility.
7. Offer to help if that's possible.

This last one is where we find a direct similarity to the story and Meredith's interview. It's important to observe that this help is not 'fixing' anything: the mother in the story just offers something that she knows her son will like, and Meredith uses the metaphor of coming to the shore: "They can row across to us; when they get to us, we have everything they need to get better." Incidentally, in interviewing people who used substances about what family interactions they found helpful, psychologist Mya Krishnan heard that practical support was one of the positive supports. Generally, however, the literature seems to be unclear as to the helpfulness of families providing practical support.

CRAFT Research
In 2020, psychologist Marc Archer and colleagues looked at fourteen research studies and found that CRAFT was twice as effective as comparison groups. Families that took part in both individual and group sessions resulted in very high rates (roughly 80%) of substance users entering treatment, with lower rates for those attending individual sessions only, groups only, or using self-directed workbooks.

Another recent survey by psychologist Stephanie Merkouris found that CRAFT appears to be quite effective at improving families' well-being and improving marital relationships but somewhat less effective than another (similar) method, Pressures to Change, in getting substance users to treatment. In contrast, public health researcher Ruth McGovern and colleagues synthesized the evidence of fifty-eight experiments and did not find any outstanding merit of CRAFT. She lamented that none of the interventions they studied, including CRAFT, fully addressed the complex, multidimensional difficulties that families experience.

The Art of Invitation

Another approach that has similarities with Lyle's story and with Meredith's words about "the deep root to remain connected" is the Art of Invitation (AOI), a relationship-based approach that uses the U.S. Substance Abuse and Mental Health Services Administration's principles of recovery as well as Christian teachings. One of SAMHSA's principles of recovery is building and restoring relationships. As social workers Katti Sneed and Debbie Teike explain, the Art of Invitation connects the altruistic value of being 'invitational' to the desire to build and restore relationships, and helps participants develop a sense of relational 'belonging' whether an 'insider' or 'outsider' in any particular circumstance. An invitational approach strives to relate to others as equals, regardless of role or position.

Three Types of Communication: Confrontational, Presentational, and Invitational
Teike points to three types of communication:

- confrontational — correcting, confronting some views as wrong, faulty, or different
- presentational — as in a traditional teacher-learner situation
- invitational — inviting a relationship where equals choose to share information or experience.

It is this invitational style that reminds us again of Meredith's metaphor: "we show up every day, wave to them, wait for them to get in the boat." In AOI, participants learn about these styles and about other topics, such as challenges arising from conflicting values, unmet relationship needs, emotional dysregulation, barriers to the invitational approach and how to overcome them, and of course, recovery.

Addiction — A Relational Disorder?
Teike bases some of her work on the idea of addiction being a relational disorder. The person struggling with addiction focuses completely on their substance or behaviour of choice, damaging their health but also their relationships; everyone feels deceived, abandoned, and hurt. This leads to

isolation, which further entrenches the addiction. However, because humans are intensely social animals, relationships can be restored and perhaps lead out of the addiction. It is important though, according to Teike, that expectations of control be abandoned.

In this view, any motivation to change lies in the person who is using substances and no one else. This perspective is similar to Patt Denning's, who bases much of her work on self-determination theory, developed by psychologists Richard Ryan and Edward Deci. Their theory states that all humans tend towards growth, mastery, and meaning-making. These tendencies require constant nurturing and support, especially regarding the basic human needs for autonomy, competence, and relatedness. Both Teike and Denning focus heavily on building the kinds of relationships that can fulfill these needs. Like Denning's approach, it appears AOI has not (yet) been studied in comparison to other approaches.

Other Family Programs

According to a 2012 study in the UK, the vast majority of help that families receive is through written information such as pamphlets. A little over half reported receiving services via support groups or individual counselling. 30% received clinical interventions specifically targeted at families, and of those, three-quarters were co-dependency or twelve-step based.

In terms of treatment success, psychology researchers Talia Ariss and Catharine Fairbairn analyzed studies comprising over two thousand individuals enrolled in sixteen independent treatments and found that involving families and friends decreased substance-use frequency by about 6%, "the equivalent of approximately 3 fewer weeks a year of drinking/drug use."

Below are a few more examples of interventions apart from the ones already mentioned. Psychologist Robert Edgren and colleagues systematically reviewed seventeen studies about help for families of individuals with gambling problems. They found that among the nine approaches they investigated — including CRAFT, as well as the 5-Step Method described below — none was more beneficial than any of the others.

5-Step Method

The 5-Step Method intervention was developed by psychologist Jim Orford and colleagues. Living with a person with substance-use problems is stressful, typically leading to physical and psychological strain. How well family members deal with this strain depends to a significant degree on how effective their coping mechanisms are and the quality of their own social support.

The five steps consist of:

1. listening to the family's story and giving reassurance
2. providing information relevant to the particular family
3. discussing ways of coping and responding
4. exploring sources of support
5. reviewing and arranging further help if needed.

The interesting aspect of the 5-Step Method is that it focuses mostly on the experience of the family, rather than on the person using substances. There is not as much research evidence for the 5-step intervention as for CRAFT.

Network Therapy

Network Therapy engages a group of family or friends in therapy sessions with the person using substances, drawing on ties to family and friends to help follow a treatment plan. This is combined with individual therapy. Network Therapy uses some elements of CRAFT and Behavioural Marital Therapy; for example, behavioural skills training or medication monitoring by a significant other. Developed by psychiatrist Marc Galanter, Network Therapy has been shown to be useful in decreasing drug use.

ARISE (A Relational Intervention Sequence for Engagement)

ARISE® Intervention and Continuing Care has the express goal of long-term recovery and healing for all concerned. Using an interventionist model, it mobilizes a network that motivates the person using substances to enter treatment. The process is transparent to all. In contrast to other interventions, it does not suddenly surprise the person using substances. It also does not spend much time on education. ARISE begins with one person making first contact with the interventionist. Soon more people (e.g., extended family, employers) join. In meetings, family strengths are discovered and the participation of the person using substances is encouraged (but not required). Consistent approaches and messages are developed. Sometimes efforts need to escalate to a point of setting strict limits and consequences, always delivered in a loving and supportive way. Network members support each other, e.g., in implementing limits. In an aftercare phase, the interventionist supports all participants, with the goals of treatment completion, improved relationships, grief resolution, and relapse prevention. ARISE was first developed by social worker James Garrett. There has been some outcome research but comparison research was not found.

Pressures To Change

This model, developed by social work researcher James Barber, begins with assessment of the situation, including the family's response to the problematic behaviour. It includes education and teaches families/friends to encourage activities incompatible with substance use, to avoid 'enabling', and to negotiate contracts to avoid or decrease the use of substances. Similar to Network Therapy, families/friends enlist others to assist with following through.

Johnson Intervention

This method is the furthest from the route described in the "Bicycle Creatures" story and by Meredith. The Johnson Intervention helps families/friends plan and implement a confrontation with the goal of getting the person who is problematically using substances into treatment. In the planning stage, the facilitator assists families/friends in engaging others in the person's network. In two following sessions, participants are educated about the goals of the confrontation and the dangers of enabling, problem-solving strategies relating to family needs are discussed, and the confrontation is planned. The confrontation, also attended by the facilitator, happens in the final session, with the goal of getting the person into treatment. In a widely cited study, carried out by psychologist William Miller of Motivational Interviewing fame, the Johnson Intervention was compared to CRAFT and Al-Anon. CRAFT scored higher on initially engaging the person who uses substances. The Johnson Intervention scored higher on getting the person into treatment, if only in the somewhat rare cases in which the intervention was carried out from beginning to end.

In one of the studies mentioned earlier, McGovern laments that none of the approaches she surveyed address the complex, multidimensional experience of families. This chapter struggles with the same issue. There is so much more that could have been addressed: research on the multitude of consequences for the family from divorce to financial problems to physical ill health, for example. There could have been an exploration of family systems and family therapy, models of addiction, or research on support groups. All of that relates to the topic at hand. Without in any way wishing to minimize the experience of families, one can see similarities: there is only so much time, only so much space, only so much energy. Which way to turn in this jungle of hopes, information, and opinions? I am grateful for Meredith's guidance in making me stick to one topic, as difficult to research as it was, and for the guidance she has given to so many families and hopefully will for a long time to come.

BIBLIOGRAPHY: CHAPTER TEN

American Psychological Association (2011). *Johnson Intervention.* https://www.apa.org/pi/about/publications/caregivers/practice-settings/intervention/johnson-intervention

Archer, M., Harwood, H., Stevelink, S., Rafferty, L. & Greenberg, N. (2020). Community reinforcement and family training and rates of treatment entry: A systematic review. *Addiction, 115*(6), 1024–1037.

Ariss, T. & Fairbairn, C.E. (2020). The effect of significant other involvement in treatment for substance use disorders: A meta-analysis. *Journal of Consulting and Clinical Psychology, 88*, 526–540.

Barber, J. & Crisp, B. (1995). The 'pressures to change' approach to working with the partners of heavy drinkers. *Addiction, 90*, 269–276.

Bischof, A., Krüger, J., Brandt, D., Trachte, A., Rumpf, H. & Bischof, G. (2019). Wirksamkeit von Behandlungsangeboten für Partner* innen von Suchtkranken: Ergebnisse der EVIFA-Studie. *Suchttherapie, 20*(S 01), S40-03.

Cole, N. (2015). *The Effects of Family Functioning and Tangible Support on Treatment Outcomes in an Opioid Addicted Population* (Doctoral dissertation, Virginia Commonwealth University).

Daley, D., Smith, E., Balogh, D. & Toscolani, J. (2018). The impact of the opioid epidemic and other substance use disorders on families and children. *Commonwealth, 20*, 93–121.

Denning, P. (2010). Harm reduction therapy with families and friends of people with drug problems. *Journal of Clinical Psychology, 66*(2), 164–174.

Edgren, R., Pörtfors, P., Raisamo, S. & Castrén, S. (2022). Treatment for the concerned significant others of gamblers: A systematic review. *Journal of Behavioral Addictions, 11*(1), 1–25.

Edwards, M., Best, D., Irving, J. & Andersson, C. (2018). Life in recovery: A families' perspective. *Alcoholism Treatment Quarterly, 36*(4), 437–458.

Galanter, M., Dermatis, H., Glickman, L., et al. (2004). Network therapy: Decreased secondary opioid use during buprenorphine maintenance. *Journal of Substance Abuse Treatment, 26*, 313–318.

Garrett, J., Landau-Stanton, J., Stanton, M.D., Stellato-Kabat, J. & Stellato-Kabat, D. (1997). ARISE: A method for engaging reluctant alcohol- and drug-dependent individuals in treatment. *Journal of Substance Abuse Treatment, 14*(3), 235–248.

Isaacs, W. (1999). *Dialogue: The Art of Thinking Together*. Doubleday.

Landau J., Stanton, M., Brinkman-Sull, D., Ikle, D., McCormick, D., Garrett, J., Baciewicz, G., Shea, R., Browning, A. & Wamboldt, F. (2004). Outcomes with the ARISE approach to engaging reluctant drug- and alcohol-dependent individuals in treatment. *American Journal of Drug & Alcohol Abuse, 30*(4), 711–748.

Lappan, S., Brown, A. & Hendricks, P. (2020). Dropout rates of in-person psychosocial substance use disorder treatments: A systematic review and meta-analysis. *Addiction, 115*(2), 201–217.

LeMar, M.D. (2020). *Overcoming Stigma With Dialogue: My Experiences as a Parent of an Opiate Addict* (Master's thesis, Boise State University).

Ligon, J. (2019). Helping families affected by substance abuse: What works and what does not. In: J. Wodarski & L. Hopson (eds.), *Empirically Based Interventions Targeting Social Problems*. Springer.

McCance-Katz, E. (2020). The National Survey on Drug Use and Health: 2019. *Substance Abuse and Mental Health Services Administration, 8*.

McGlone, J. (1992). *An Examination of the Codependency Construct: The Effects of Labeling* (Doctoral dissertation, Ohio State University).

McGovern, R., Smart, D., Alderson, H., Araújo-Soares, V., Brown, J., Buykx, R., Evans, V., Fleming, K., Hickman, M., Macleod, J., Meier, P. & Kaner, E. (2021). Psychosocial interventions to improve psychological, social and physical wellbeing in family members affected by an adult relative's substance use: A systematic search and review of the evidence. *International Journal of Environmental Research in Public Health, 18*, 1793.

Merkouris, S., Dowling, N. & Rodda, S. (2020). Affected other treatments: Systematic review and meta-analysis across addictions. Prepared for Australia: NSW Office of Responsible Gambling.

Miller, W., Meyer, R. & Tonigan, J. (1999). Engaging the unmotivated in treatment for alcohol problems: A comparison of three intervention strategies. *Journal of Consulting and Clinical Psychology*, *67*(5), 688–697.

Pescosolido, B. & Martin, J. (2015). The stigma complex. *Annual Review of Sociology*, *41*, 87–116.

Prochaska, J., Norcross, J. & DiClemente, C. (2013). Applying the stages of change. In G.P. Koocher, J.C. Norcross & B.A. Greene (eds.), *Psychologists' Desk Reference*, 176–181. Oxford University Press.

Ryan, R. & Deci, E. (2000). Self-determination theory and the facilitation of intrinsic motivation, social development and well-being. *American Psychologist*, *55*, 68–78.

Sneed, K. & Teike, D. (2019). Restoring damaged relationships through the art of invitation: Application with addicted incarcerated women. *Social Work & Christianity*, *46*(3), 27–50.

Velleman, R. (2010). *The 5-Step Intervention as a Way of Working With the Adult Family Members of Those with AOD Problems*. Presentation. Making it Happen 2009 — Western Australian Drug and Alcohol Conference.

CHAPTER ELEVEN

"Thank You"

THE PRACTICE OF GRATITUDE

The last chapter tells a story of good mental health. The person interviewed is Kathy, a mental health worker. Choosing a poem about gratitude, she states with enthusiasm that she could add to the poem "verses and verses and lines and lines of contributions of what I'm grateful for."

Kathy talks about how much better her mental health is compared to when she was younger, when she had a diagnosis of Complex PTSD from child sexual abuse. After many years of growing and thriving, this label has become irrelevant.

The research section looks at gratitude from various angles ranging from the physical to the spiritual, shows how gratitude is not always positive, and gives some examples of gratitude practice.

THE POEM

Thank You

thank you for
water
for showers running over my arms,
for peace among my friends. for
fire
for warm socks on my feet,
for laughter. for
air
for soft winds over the mountains,
for love that heals.

for the good
earth
that feeds our herds and carries our dance.

THE INTERVIEW

Kathy

I asked you whether you wanted to participate in this project because I think of you as person with excellent mental health, more so because that was not always the case. I offered you a number of poems and you chose this one. Why was that?

It has the same form as my email gratitude practice with a friend of mine. I am so comfortable and familiar with that form that this poem resonated a lot. It felt like I could write more things to add on to it in the middle between the text and the last three lines. I could add verses and verses and lines and lines of contributions of what I'm grateful for.

Does that mean that gratitude is part of your mental well-being?

Yes.

Would I say it that way? Or would say that I have integrated gratitude practice and what I call 'wish practice' as part of my life and I don't think in terms of mental well-being and mental non-well-being for myself? Isn't that great? I'm not constantly checking — how's my mental well-being? how's my mental illness? I don't ask myself those questions. It's more — do I have time to send that gratitude email right now? If I don't have time to send one, then I will read the last one I got and just feel the gratitude for that. Gratitude is part of my life.

Was there a time in your life when you felt it useful to check in regarding your mental well-being?

Yes! The *just about to go into crisis* times and the *just gone through crisis* times, and in those two places, it was either "When is the storm going to hit?" or "Can I handle this task before the storm hits?" That one was before the crisis and I know it's coming. After the crisis, it was "Can I do this thing that's hard without going back into a crisis state?" And "maybe" was a good enough answer for me to try in either case and "no" just meant "not yet." So — yeah, there was a time. A long time ago.

Well… in my thirties, it would happen fairly often and for long enough that I couldn't maintain a consistent job because I would have had too much time off to look after myself and calm down. But for a long time now, I haven't a bad two full weeks straight of *can't manage* or *can't manage outside of basic care*. In the last five years, there have been days when sometimes I've had a bad weekend. But ordinary people sometimes have a bad weekend! And a bad weekend these days doesn't mean I have to call the crisis line. In the last fifteen, twenty years, I haven't needed to call the crisis line.

I liked the poem because I wanted to talk about the content of the poem. I thought I could talk about water and peace among my friends and fire and love that heals... that stuff is what engaged me about the poem and how much I can appreciate those things. And the pace of it. We can be kind of slow, slow with talk, slow with action, taking time to consider, figuring out what peace among friends looks like.

I also kind of wanted to brag. Because I was able to support my introvert self at a time when roommates were just not making it easy for me to figure out how to be in a pandemic.

Earlier you said that mental well-being wasn't quite the term you would use. What should we call this experience or state then?
It might be resilience, it might be adaptability. Might even be maturity, although I don't like what that word connotes sometimes, because I'm going to be sixty this year. But that really just is a number. Maybe it's steadiness. I have steadiness. But it's not a rigid steadiness.

The whole topic of steadiness... the part you're aware of and not aware of and the things that happen and how we respond builds the steadiness muscle. I think they call it resilience. But steadiness is a good placeholder word for now for what I'm experiencing.

What built your steadiness muscles?
It's been some important relationships.

At a time when I was feeling quite fragile after a medical crisis, I got a part-time job looking after someone completely confined to a wheelchair. I had that job for three years. In that job, I had to do things on somebody else's schedule, I had to be reliable, I had to put my own needs aside, and it showed me that I could do that.

It showed me what I can manage and what I want to do, and it helped me put aside the story about being physically and emotionally broken because it proved that I wasn't. That's the biggest thing that helped with that, I think. Getting work, demanding paid work once my need to be on deck as a single parent was finished, and moving forward with that and trying stuff.

Then there was a pretty radical mental health training program I took for peer support workers that switches the narrative about mental illness. The critical thing there was the People First language that is used in the world of disabilities. The problems that the person has, the 'mental illness' that the person has, is a portion of their experience and it's not that big a portion of their experience. It doesn't need to be something that people are overly focused on. The person is first, not the disability.

And then there was the fact that despite this giant brokenness in my life, I managed to raise a child, challenged the government and won, went to school, attended university and succeeded, found employment, built community. And volunteering in complex, interesting roles that have very strong requirements for sound ethical judgment and discernment and careful communication. Not sweeping-the-floor kind of volunteer jobs.

So at some point, I switched "I'm so broken, I have this big thing going on that's a mental illness, don't get near me" to "I got this big thing going on, and I'm doing this, and this and this, and I'm arguing about this other thing." Arguing about things was a big step forward for me because as a young person I 'learned' that I can't argue, because my judgment and perceptions can't be trusted because I have this mental illness thing. That is wrong!

Everything about my work has been relational. This work with the woman in the wheelchair, that was 100% relational. For example, I had to check, am I going too hard with the toothbrush? Right away I went to "I'm a klutz," but it turned out I can do it. I developed a relationship with her and I could make mistakes and she could correct me and I was allowed to make mistakes as long as she would correct me. The mistakes weren't really awful anyway. The corrections were actually smaller than I thought they would be.

I had support roles and advocacy roles and non-profit board roles. All of this is so confidential. And now my work is all relational and all confidential. Everything about my work is "I'm a whole human being" and everyone I work with is just as strong in principle, and allowed to be, and I make room for myself to be as strong as I am and I make room for wherever they are and everybody kind of moves forward.

So it's a lot of important relationships.

Other than work, are there any other milestones in your journey?
Deciding that I didn't need the safety of roommates and I could live on my own was a huge milestone. That was nine months ago. Deciding that I could do it and it wasn't going to take away from my steadiness, that it wasn't going to stop me from being good enough for my job. What actually happened — all of that stuff improved. Turns out that the ideal roommate for me is me and there aren't many of me on the planet.

I changed my environment and then I started functioning better. I changed my commute so that I felt better at work. You change anything in a system and everything else changes.

Much of what you mentioned sounds like tools you used to make your life better. Is gratitude a tool too? Are there any other tools?

There is a big list. I know that exercise is good for me, but I'm not an exercise kind of person. Knowing that, I have to walk up or down to get in and out of my building, and to go to any transit point is a minimum ten-minute walk. So I have a minimum twenty-minute walk and walking up and down the stairs. I have the minimum required exercise. I manage my environment so that I'm healthy. So much strategic stuff here.

I have phone calls on weekend mornings to change the story of "weekends are lonely" — I have four good conversations on a weekend. That's critical for my well-being.

One evening a week, I do a peer counselling trade over video chat. Also critical. At least one day during the week, I'm having a very nice conversation.

I love Lego and jigsaw puzzles. I have made it so that I have access to jigsaw puzzles or Lego that's new to me all the time.

I have a love of choose-your-own-adventure stories, and there are free games for that on the internet and I have those as options. I make sure I think about those kinds of choices.

I have a weighted blanket, which is great for anxiety. That means that sleep is easier, and I am vigilant about sleep. I do my own version of sleep hygiene.

Setting aside a day for indulgence once in a while.

Paying attention to people, whether I want to or not.

And then there's the usual stuff, like making sure I have enough water.

I don't do the sit down for fifteen minutes a day meditation. I'm doing the breathing while I walk to the bus in the morning type of meditation. I actually believe that is meditation.

I think about what I want for myself and for other people.

Staying interested in fiction, humour, current popular culture in terms of fantasy, science fiction, and young adult fiction. Writing practice that I'm allowed to do half-assed.

I just want to play all day. I care about the people I'm serving. I have a caseload of about sixty right now. When I do my work, then I can come home and play all day!

Isabella Mori

THE RESEARCH

Kathy wanted to focus on gratitude for the research section.

What Is Gratitude?

The word gratitude comes from the Latin *gratus* (pleasing, beloved, favourable) and *gratia* (thanks or grace). English words associated with the same origin are 'agree', 'congratulate', 'graceful', 'gratify', 'gratuitous', 'gratification', etc. In the most neutral definition, something happens, you have a positive reaction to it, and you express that reaction with kindness. It is the kindness that makes it different from appreciation; after all, *schadenfreude* — taking pleasure in the misfortune of others — is also a form of appreciation and far removed from gratitude. However, we shall see that the words 'appreciation' and 'gratitude' are often used interchangeably.

Opinions abound on what exactly is gratitude and to which category it belongs. Psychologist Robert Emmons, a leading expert on the topic, lists a number of categories: an emotion, a virtue (Cicero called it the mother of all virtues), a skill, an attitude, a motive, a coping mechanism, a moral sentiment. Or is it perhaps better to think of it as a tendency?

Gratitude — An Emotion

Most do see gratitude as an emotion. It's a pleasant emotion about benefits received, says Emmons, particularly when they are freely and benevolently bestowed, without having worked for them. Philosopher Robert Solomon calls gratitude a "philosophical emotion," one that goes beyond an individual's feelings about a particular thing and relates to the world as a whole, to existence, to human nature. To Solomon, gratitude is all about seeing the bigger picture.

As a neuroscientist, Hongbo Yu takes a different approach: gratitude is a feeling, yes, but it depends on a chain of thoughts, for which he finds neural representation in the brain. Contrasting that, psychologists John Elfers and Patty Hlava talk of gratitude as more than a cognitive event; rather, it is a complex network of emotions in response to receiving or experiencing something valuable. They also see emotions as pre-conscious 'first-order experiences' that happen much faster in an individual's body than any thought.

Yet another perspective — many call it 'transpersonal' — states that while gratitude is an 'other-oriented' emotion, this 'other' is often more than an individual or a group of individuals. It is fate, nature, God, etc. This is indeed what Kathy and the poem speak of.

Gratitude and Evolution

If it seems that this is all semantics and 'gratitude' is just another term that academics quibble over, it's useful to look at evolution. Neuroscientist Summer Allen, who wrote a comprehensive overview of the topic of gratitude, tells us that it, or something like it called 'reciprocal altruism', occurs not only among humans, but also among animals as diverse as birds, fish, vampire bats, and non-human primates. For example, in one study, chimpanzees shared food more often with other chimpanzees that had groomed them before and were more likely to assist another chimpanzee that had helped them previously. Says Allen, "Gratitude may have evolved as a mechanism to drive this reciprocal altruism, thereby turning strangers into friends and allies who are more likely to help one another."

Gratitude, Well-Being, and Resilience

In the beginning of Kathy's interview, I referred to the term 'well-being'. Kathy was not particularly interested in it, preferring 'resilience', or what she calls 'steadiness'. It turns out that there are interesting connections between well-being, resilience, and gratitude. (Resilience is the ability to respond successfully to adverse experience.)

Some background on gratitude and well-being: Much of the research on gratitude comes from positive psychology, a large area of research and practice pioneered by psychologist Martin Seligman. In 2011, he refined his thoughts on positive psychology and happiness, stating that the topic of positive psychology is not so much about happiness as it is about well-being. To Seligman, this consists of five elements, with the acronym PERMA:

> Positive emotion
> Engagement
> Relationships
> Meaning and/or purpose
> Accomplishment.

Gratitude clearly fits into the areas of positive emotion and relationships. When gratitude is literally a heartfelt emotion — when the heart overflows with gratitude — it can also fit into the category of engagement, which Seligman also described as 'flow'. When a person experiences 'transpersonal' gratitude (a term we will explore later on), it fits into the category of meaning.

The Connection Between Resilience and Gratitude, 'Savouring', and Optimism

Psychologist Isabel María Salces Cubero and colleagues investigated how gratitude, optimism, and 'savouring' affect well-being. The exercises for a 'savouring' group were about appreciating objects and experiences. In a group focusing on gratitude, participants were asked to think and talk about things past and present for which they were grateful and about the feelings that led them to gratitude. The optimism group learned about planning for pleasant future events and decreasing pessimistic thinking using humour, songs, jokes, etc.

The result was that gratitude and savouring increased scores in life satisfaction, positive emotions, subjective happiness, and resilience. Optimism alone did not produce a significant change in those areas. The researchers measured resilience with Wagnild's Resilience Scale. It has topics such as "I usually manage one way or another," "Keeping interested in things is important to me," "I can get through difficult times because I've experienced difficulty before," and "I feel proud that I have accomplished things in life." All of these remind one of what Kathy talked about in the interview, for example when she says that her job showed her "what I can manage and what I want to do, and it helped me put aside the story about being physically and emotionally broken because it proved that I wasn't."

Multiple Sclerosis and Breast Cancer: Quality of Life and Resilience

The connection between gratitude, well-being, and resilience was also found in other studies, including on breast cancer and multiple sclerosis (MS). Psychologist Tara Crouch and colleagues found that the higher research participants with MS scored on gratitude, the higher their quality of life was. They also suggest that an innate tendency to be grateful ('trait gratitude') could be a factor in resilience in MS.

Psychologist Joanna Sztachańska and colleagues found that women who had gotten a mastectomy for breast cancer improved through writing daily journal entries listing what they were grateful for and why. Among other things, their mood, self-esteem, and optimism increased. Earlier research had shown that highly resilient people have a tendency to 'undo' negative emotions with positive ones. Sztachańska wonders whether that was part of the mechanism that made gratitude journaling so effective.

More on Physical Health: Sleep and Heart Health

Let's explore the topic of physical health some more. Health psychologist Anna Boggiss found that in over half of the studies she surveyed, gratitude had a beneficial effect on sleep. Similarly, gratitude tends to improve heart health. For example, behavioural oncologist Lakeshia Cousin reviewed thirteen studies. Overall, there were improvements in endothelial dysfunction (a type of coronary artery disease) and inflammation related to heart disease, as well as adherence to the type of health behaviours that increase heart health.

Gratitude exercises are easy to 'prescribe' and carry out; often, they are as simple as writing down five things one is grateful for a few times a week. This simplicity makes it a useful tool for doctors, nurses, counsellors, and others to suggest to their patients.

Gratitude, Body Acceptance, and Intuitive Eating

Gratitude also factors in improved eating behaviours such as 'intuitive eating'. Intuitive eating is a promising approach to disordered eating. The person listens to internal cues such as hunger and fullness, and thus avoids eating for emotional or external reasons (including diet prescriptions). Nutritional scientist Vivienne Hazzard and colleagues followed 1,491 women and men for eight years and found that intuitive eating had a positive effect on a number of factors (e.g., extreme diet behaviours, depression) but particularly on binge eating.

Psychologists Kristin Homan and Tracy Tylka traced a connection between gratitude, body image, and intuitive eating. They discovered that gratitude directly influenced body appreciation, which then strongly influenced intuitive eating. What is more, they also detected that gratitude indirectly influenced intuitive eating. This occurred through a decrease in comparing their bodies and eating behaviours to others, as well as decreasing the importance of physical appearance and letting the approval of others dictate their self-worth. Gratitude, say Homan and Tylka, orients a person towards body appreciation. Grateful people are conscious of the good in their lives, which in turn leads them to seek out people and experiences that enhance this goodness. Indeed, some research suggests that people with a positive body image seek out others with a similar outlook, who have a broader concept of beauty than the one prescribed by mainstream media. Gratitude is also connected to self-acceptance — it implies that the person is worthy of receiving good things in their life.

Gratitude as a Physical Feeling

Let us return for a moment to the idea earlier in this chapter that emotions are the 'first-order experiences' that Elfers and Hlava speak of. Whether that is the best way to talk about emotions is a matter of debate among psychologists and philosophers, but what is true, without question, is that emotions often show up in physical feelings. Metaphors abound — the 'sinking feeling', the 'butterflies in the stomach', the 'racing heart', those 'warm fuzzy feelings' — and when we hear these metaphors, we can usually identify moments when we too had those experiences.

Elfers and Hlava were interested in the emotion of gratitude as a felt experience. They conducted in-depth interviews with fifty-one participants, asking them to recall a specific, memorable time they felt grateful and to focus on the physical experience of it. Fifty-five percent of the time, participants spoke of sensations in the chest or heart. For example:

> I noticed a fullness in my chest like my heart is bursting, and it's full. Not an uncomfortable feeling, like a warm feeling, almost like love but not as localized or something. It's less concentrated. It's just a bigger feeling.

Closely related to that were feelings of warmth, often felt in the heart or chest area but also as a flush in other parts of the body. Elfers and Hlava explain that warm and pleasant feelings in the chest are associated with the vagus nerve. This is the main nerve of the parasympathetic nervous system and, among other things, involved in regulating heart rate. The parasympathetic nervous system calms fight/flight responses.

Other sensations reported by participants were relief:

> I just feel so relieved, just like something left my body.

> It was like I had a huge weight lifted off of me.

Awakening and energy:

> Every cell of my body is just lit up, festive and celebrating, as if life is given to me once again.
> I was literally jumping up and down.

Feeling grounded:

> Yeah, I felt real grounded, and centred, and refreshed.

Smiling/joy:

> I was smiling, on top of my feeling a sense of joy in
> my face, and then a welling up in my eyes.

Spirituality and Religion

It is surprising that in the research I surveyed, the joy that was just mentioned did not come up more often. After all, both gratitude and joy are significant positive emotions. It did show up in one study by psychologist Jesus Saiz and colleagues, which looked at the connection between religion/ spirituality, gratitude, and mental illness. Joy only appeared as one item in the Daily Spiritual Experiences Scale they used, which contains statements such as:

- "I experience a connection to all of life."
- "During worship, or at other times when connecting with God, I feel joy which lifts me out of my daily concerns."
- "I ask for God's help in the midst of daily activities."
- "I am spiritually touched by the beauty of creation."
- "I feel thankful for my blessings."

Saiz and colleagues mapped feelings of gratitude onto the stages of recovery in mental illness. They are similar to the Stages of Change mentioned in the previous chapter and comprise:

1. Moratorium: denial, confusion, and hopelessness;
2. Awareness: the person feels hope and raises the possibility of recovery;
3. Preparation: work begins on recovery;
4. Reconstruction: recovery work is carried out, with the purpose of forging a positive identity
5. Growth.

The results were that gratitude correlated significantly with stages 2, 3, and 4. This raises interesting questions such as, how is gratitude connected to hope — does hopelessness also mean a lack of gratitude? Does the achievement of growth mean less need for gratitude?

Religion, Gratitude, and Socio-Economic Status

Given that there is quite a bit of research on gratitude in general, it seemed natural that some researchers would have set out to investigate the connection between socio-economic status and gratitude. However, only two articles were found that mentioned both topics. Incidentally, those articles also tie in with the topic of religiosity.

One group of research participants were elderly women living in poverty, studied by social work researcher Amanda Barusch. Barusch noted that while there was much general research on how religion and religious organizations helped people cope with life, very little research effort had gone into interviewing elders, who constitute a large percentage of churchgoers. The study was specifically about older women living in poverty. Barusch reports that gratitude was mentioned in 94% of the interviews. A few examples:

> I thank the Lord because He has given me a life that
> is so good. I couldn't ask for more.
> *(84-year-old Hispanic)*

> The Lord has been... wonderful to me... through a
> long time with the hardship... He's providin' a way.
> *(86-year-old Caucasian)*

> But I thank God for everything anyway. I'm able to
> manage and able to keep some bread to eat.
> *(69-year-old African American)*

And in a study by psychologist Tes Tuason about the experience of people in the Philippines who lived or had lived in poverty, every single one of them spoke of gratitude towards God, affirming that only God knew about their difficulties and thanking God for blessings received. That sense of gratitude also made it easier for those who had improved their finances to overcome the trauma of poverty, trauma that manifested itself in behaviours like obsessively comparing themselves with others. As an aside, both of these studies did not set out to study gratitude; it just so happened that gratitude emerged as an important theme.

Religiosity, Gratitude, and the Willingness To Intervene in Sexual Assault

College campuses are, unfortunately, a common location of rape. Encouraging bystander intervention is an element of many campus rape prevention programs. Together with colleagues, John Foubert, an education researcher and expert in sexual assault prevention for the U.S. Army, chose three characteristics known to be associated with prosocial behaviours: gratitude, empathy, and 'extrinsic religiosity'[8] and investigated whether they would make a bystander more likely to intervene. The researchers found that people scoring high on gratitude and extrinsic religiosity were more likely to intervene as bystanders. Interestingly, they did not find the same for empathy. They theorized that a part of bystander behaviour "includes a feeling that others have helped one and that intervention may be one way to pay it forward" and suggested that college campuses could introduce gratitude programs.

Generalized Gratitude: Not Easy To Articulate

Gratitude felt in a spiritual context is closely related to what some call 'generalized gratitude' (and others transpersonal, impersonal, untargeted, cosmic, or dyadic gratitude). The poem that resonated so much with Kathy starts with "thank you for / water / for showers running over my arms / for peace among my friends." Some argue that this type of gratitude simply leaves the benefactor unnamed, who really is a divine being, the universe, luck, or a similar force. In this particular case, since I am the one who wrote this poem, I can say that the 'you' I am thanking is indeed some undefined sense of universal force, but that 'you' is so vague that it feels quite different from saying, for example, "Pete, thank you for boosting my car last night." In the latter, I appreciate the human bond that led Pete to commiserate with my plight and his willingness to help. In the former, I am filled with awe and wonder — a 'philosophical feeling' that is bigger and perhaps more difficult to articulate than reactions to momentary experiences.

Benedictine monk and psychologist David Steindl-Rast, the person perhaps most widely known internationally as a proponent of gratitude, says "transpersonal gratitude belongs to our inner realm and we often find no words for it … being grateful is a state; thanking is an action." He cites Alexander Maslow, known for his hierarchy of needs. Highest on the hierarchy

8   Individuals in this category tend to use religion for basic needs such as personal comfort or socializing, with less emphasis on the faith or creed aspects of their religion.

are so-called 'peak experiences'; Maslow states that during and after these experiences, people often feel fortunate and grateful.

In one of Elfers and Hlava's studies, participants are struggling to find the right words, as demonstrated in the quotes from three participants:

> But I guess it would be some form of a spiritual connection, just a very direct, very personal connection with nature, with the ocean in particular, just being in the water. But it's more of an experience of bliss or being at peace with the environment and of just feeling full.
>
> I think when I'm in those moments [of gratitude], there's a sense of connection to something greater than me, whatever that is. I'm not even sure what that is.
>
> I just had this sort of overwhelming feeling just rising up from my feet up through my body and over my head and just this unreal sense of beauty and gratitude. I mean I was touched in a way that I'd never been touched before.

Poetry is well-suited to expressing that which is hard to articulate. Kathy said she was comfortable and familiar with the form of the poem and that she felt like she could "write more things to add on to it in the middle between the text and the last three lines. I could add verses and verses and lines and lines of contributions of what I'm grateful for." She, too, feels this generalized gratitude.

Ordinary People's Definition of Gratitude

Generalized gratitude is not nearly as much researched as 'situational gratitude' (like the example where Pete helped with the car) or in studies that don't differentiate between types of gratitude. Interested in generalized gratitude and also in finding new ways to define gratitude, psychologist Nate Lambert and colleagues set out to explore what laypersons thought of the concept (similar to what Kovács did when they explored the concept of authenticity, Chapter 4). In a series of five studies, the researchers gathered 219 attributes. Fifty-two were mentioned more than twice (God/religion was in the bottom ten of those fifty-two). Lambert and colleagues did find that a significant minority pointed to generalized gratitude, for example in this quote:

> I felt a time of gratitude this summer when my
> whole family was together. My sister lives in Texas
> and I live 6 hours away from home, so when we
> were all together it made me grateful that I have
> such a good family.

By coincidence, it so happens that one researcher who explored generalized gratitude also focused on water, like I did in the poem. In his doctoral study in psychology, Peter Kearns was interested in what increased or decreased gratitude for water. He found that pro-environment individuals increased their gratitude the more they learned about water and the more uncertain they were about the availability of water. Increased gratitude led to more interest in water conservation.

The Dark Side of Gratitude

Of course, gratitude is not the panacea for all that ails; what's more, some aspects of gratitude are not that wholesome. Psychologist Alex Wood, together with Robert Emmons and other gratitude experts, recognized this; much of the following is inspired by their 2016 article on what can go wrong with gratitude.

Individual Level: Personal Histories, Personal Dispositions
How a person was parented has an effect on how they view, feel, and behave around gratitude. Wood and colleagues point to a theory developed by schema therapists. The idea is that our upbringing moulds us into organizing what we experience into longstanding, deeply ingrained patterns (schemas). These schemas, among other things, lead us to developing styles of coping with the world. The creators of 'schema therapy' believe that most people fall into eighteen different types. Wood and colleagues think that there are certain types for whom gratitude can become problematic: the self-sacrificing type who believes they will suffer dire consequences if they do not put others' needs before their own, the subjugating type who cannot express their needs, and the dependent type who always defers to others.

Another problem on the individual level are so-called 'positive illusions': a tendency to see things in a more positive light than warranted. In 1988, psychologists Shelley Taylor and Jonathon Brown wrote a highly influential paper on the benefits of positive illusions. Over the years though, it turned out that for many people, the benefits are short-lived. An example occurs in a study by psychologists James Collard and Matthew Fuller-Tyskiewicz which suggests positive illusions could be an unhealthy defence mechanism with negative consequences for long-term mental health. It is, of course, not hard to imagine that these defence mechanisms come from the upbringing discussed in schema therapy.

Indebtedness and Transactional Gratitude

When a person feels indebted to another, gratitude can have a forced taste. 'Transactional gratitude' is similar; it's a tit-for-tat exchange. Summer Allen cites a study where people with disabilities who received care free of charge felt an uncomfortable sense of indebtedness; they generally preferred paying for services. She also mentions a study about relationships where gratitude was expected as a type of payment; things become problematic when one or both partners believe they have not received their due. Indebtedness is also a crucial element in nepotism and corruption. Most of the unhealthy forms of gratitude described below are based on indebtedness and transactional gratitude.

Abusive Relationships

"You're nothing without me," "you could not survive without me," "no one else would put up with you" are words many people — mostly women — have heard in abusive relationships. There is an expectation of gratitude in response to the abuser's supposed generosity, often gratitude even for lesser abuse ("you're lucky I only gave you a bruise"). Psychology researcher Ellen Sinclair and colleagues reviewed studies about the relationship between positive attitudes and domestic abuse. They found that while positive attitudes such as gratitude, empathy, acceptance, etc. are beneficial in healthy relationships, they can serve to prolong abusive ones and even put victims in danger. Gratitude is also problematic in other relationships of unequal power. For example, Wood asks what kind of gratitude it is when a slave is grateful to those above them for treating them with a little kindness.

Justifying Harmful Systems and the Cult of Gratitude

When Hitler came to power, he pulled Germany out of the aftermath of the Great Depression and many people out of abject poverty. The gratitude they felt for him reverberates among some Germans to this day. Social and political psychologists often see this type of gratitude as 'systems justification'. People living in these systems — from families to companies to nations — bolster, defend, and justify often unjust and harmful systems. This artificially increases satisfaction with these systems. Among other harmful effects, this can hurt those who disagree. In a series of five studies, psychologists Inna Ksenofontov and Julia Becker found that publicly expressing gratitude to someone higher in power who had treated them unfairly silenced the protest of many others who were in a position of lower power.

It is fitting that this behaviour is called 'ingratiating', which has the same root as gratitude but carries a negative connotation. Another study, by organizational behaviour researcher Ayana Younge, even used the word 'slimy'. Here, those who witnessed other students or employees express gratitude to professors or managers (i.e., those higher in status) did not judge those students or employees too kindly. However, they felt less negative about professors or managers showing gratitude to students or employees (i.e., those lower in status).

Another effect can be found in organized religion, where gratitude is often promoted as a moral obligation. This can be harmful to those injured by the church — children abused by clergy, for example — and also in situations where organized religion supports unjust regimes. Another instance of systems justification is the 'cult of gratitude' (a term coined by sociologist Melvin Tumin). According to Stijn Daenekindt and colleagues, also sociologists, faith in and gratitude for existing social orders and the forces that uphold them is expressed in "euphoric wallowing in present comforts," especially by those who are upwardly mobile. This results in decreasing healthy distrust in political systems.

Gratitude Practices

After this digression into the darker corners of gratitude, let us return to Kathy. She sees gratitude practices as one of many tools that support her mental well-being or, as she puts it, her 'steadiness'. Kathy talks about a daily gratitude exchange with a friend. Other practices in the articles surveyed were:

- gratitude journals
  - simply listing what one is grateful for, and perhaps also why
  - a structured journal, e.g., 1) Overall my day has been... 2) Today I am grateful for... 3) Did you express thanks? How? 4) Did anyone express thanks to you?
- talking about what one is grateful for
- gratitude meditation
- 'mental subtraction': imagining what life would be like if a positive event had not occurred

- gratitude letters (sending a letter to someone who has done something the person is grateful for; the more specific, the better)
- gratitude visits (same as above, but in person)
- surprisingly, reflecting on one's death: "Because our very existence is a constant benefit that we adapt to easily, this is a benefit that is easily taken for granted ... reflecting on one's own death might help individuals take stock of this benefit and consequently increase their appreciation for life."
- exercises aimed at gratitude for specific things, like Expand Your Horizon, a program that helps women appreciate their bodies more by focusing on body functionality.

Let us end with Kathy's words:

> I thought I could talk about water and peace among my friends and fire and love that heals ... that stuff is what engaged me about the poem, and how much I can appreciate those things. And the pace of it. We can be kind of slow, slow with talk, slow with action, taking time to consider, figuring out what peace among friends looks like.

BIBLIOGRAPHY: CHAPTER ELEVEN

Allen, S. (2018). *The Science of Gratitude*. John Templeton Foundation.

Boggiss, A., Consedine, B., Brenton-Peters, J., Hofman, P.L. & Serlachius, A.S. (2020). A systematic review of gratitude interventions: Effects on physical health and health behaviors. *Journal of Psychosomatic Research, 135*, 110165.

Barusch, A.S. (1999). Religion, adversity, and age: Religious experiences of low-income elderly women. *Journal of Sociology and Social Welfare, 26*, 125–142.

Bolin, K. (2005). *Grace: A Contrastive Analysis of a Biblical Semantic Field* (Master's thesis, University of Idaho).

Collard, J.J. & Fuller-Tyskiewicz, M. (2020). Positive irrational beliefs and mental health. *Journal of Rational-Emotive Cognitive-Behaviour Therapy, 39*, 335–354.

Cortini, M., Converso, D., Galanti, T., Di Fiore, T., Di Domenico, A. & Fantinelli, S. (2019). Gratitude at work works! A mixed-method study on different dimensions of gratitude, job satisfaction, and job performance. *Sustainability, 11*, 3902.

Crouch, T.A., Verdi, E.K. & Erickson, T.M. (2020). Gratitude is positively associated with quality of life in multiple sclerosis. *Rehabilitation Psychology, 65*(3), 231–238.

Daenekindt, S., Van der Waal, J. & De Koster, W. (2017). Social mobility and political distrust: Cults of gratitude and resentment? *Acta Politica, 53*, 269–282.

Epstein, M. (2014). *Philosophical Feelings*. https://philosophynow.org/issues/101/Philosophical_Feelings

Erichsen, G. (2023, April 5). *"Grace" and "Gracia" Are Derived From the Same Root*. Thought Co. https://www.thoughtco.com/gracias-and-grace-3080283

Foubert, J.D., Mwavita, M., Hunger, K., Kao, W.K. & Pittman-Adkins, P. (2022). Prediction of bystander intervention behavior in a sexual assault situation: The role of religiosity, empathy, and gratitude. *Dignity: A Journal of Analysis of Exploitation and Violence, 7*(1), 8.

Grider, H., Douglas, S. & Raynor, H. (2021). The influence of mindful eating and/or intuitive eating approaches on dietary intake: A systematic review. *Journal of the Academy of Nutrition and Dietetics, 121*(4), 709–727.

Hazzard, V.M., Telke, S.E., Simone, M., Anderson, L., Larson, N. & Neumark-Sztainer, D. (2021). Intuitive eating longitudinally predicts better psychological health and lower use of disordered eating behaviors: Findings from EAT 2010–2018. *Eat Weight Disorders, 26*, 287–294.

Homan, K. & Tylka, T. (2018). Development and exploration of the gratitude model of body appreciation in women. *Body Image, 25*, 14–22.

Kearns, P. (2020). *Feeling Grateful for the Benefits Of Life, No Matter the Source* (Doctoral thesis, Purdue University).

Ksenofontov, I. & Becker, J. (2020). The harmful side of thanks: Thankful responses to high-power group help undermine low-power groups' protest. *Personality and Social Psychology Bulletin, 46*, 794–807.

Kyeong, S., Kim, J., Kim, D., Kim, H. & Kim, J. (2017). Effects of gratitude meditation on neural network functional connectivity and brain-heart coupling. *Scientific Reports, 7*, 5058.

Lambert, N., Graham, S. & Fincham, F. (2009). A prototype analysis of gratitude: Varieties of gratitude experiences. *Personality and Social Psychology Bulletin, 35*, 1193–1207.

Salces-Cubero, I., Ramírez-Fernández, E. & Ortega-Martínez, A. (2018). Strengths in older adults: Differential effect of savoring, gratitude and optimism on well-being. *Aging & Mental Health, 23*(8), 1017–1024.

Scarantino, A. & de Sousa, R. (2018). Emotion, in E. Zalta (ed.), *The Stanford Encyclopedia of Philosophy* (Winter 2018 Edition). https://plato. stanford.edu/archives/win2018/entries/emotion/

Schema Therapy Institute (n.d.). *Schema Theory*. http://www.schematherapy.com/id30.htm

Seligman, M. (2011). *Flourish: A Visionary New Understanding of Happiness and Well-Being*. New York.

Sinclair, E., Hart, R. & Lomas, T. (2020). Can positivity be counterproductive when suffering domestic abuse? A narrative review. *International Journal of Wellbeing*, *10*(1), 26–53.

Solomon, R. (2004). *Forward*. In R. Emmons & M. McCullough (eds.), *The Psychology of Gratitude*. Oxford University Press.

Sztachańska, J., Krejtz, I. & Nezlek, J. (2019). Using a gratitude intervention to improve the lives of women with breast cancer: A daily diary study. *Frontiers in Psychology*, *10*, 1365.

Taylor, S. & Brown, J. (1988). Illusion and well-being: A social psychological perspective on mental health. *Psychological Bulletin*, *103*(2), 193–210.

Tuason, M.T. (2010). The poor in the Philippines. *Psychology & Developing Societies*, *22*(2), 299–330.

Tugade, M. & Fredrickson, B. (2004). Resilient individuals use positive emotions to bounce back from negative emotional experiences. *Journal of Personality and Social Psychology*, *86*, 320–333.

Wagnild, G. & Young, H. (1993). Development and psychometric evaluation of the resilience scale. *Journal of Nursing Measurement*, *1*, 65–78.

Wood, A., Emmons, R., Algoe, S., Froh, J., Lambert, N. & Watkins, P. (2016). A dark side of gratitude? Distinguishing between beneficial gratitude and its harmful impostors for the positive clinical psychology of gratitude and well-being. In A.M. Wood & J. Johnson (eds.), *The Wiley Handbook of Positive Clinical Psychology*, 137–152. Wiley-Blackwell.

Younge, A. (2020). *Grateful or Slimy? The Influence of Social Hierarchy on the Witness-Recipient Difference in Perceptions of Authentic Gratitude* (Doctoral thesis, University of North Carolina at Chapel Hill Graduate School).

Yu, H., Gao, X., Zhou, Y. & Zhou, X. (2018). Decomposing gratitude: Representation and integration of cognitive antecedents of gratitude in the brain. *The Journal of Neuroscience, 38*, 4886–4898.

APPENDIX

PERSONAL COMMENTS ON THE TEXTS

Chapter 1: "Believe Me"

The poem was written when I was wrestling with child abuse; Gina interpreted it quite correctly. Where is a mother situated in this complex, dense web that is about much more than one person hurting one child? How much can she hear and see when she is both victim and perpetrator in systems based on oppression? Church, patriarchy, class systems, nationalism… systems upon and within systems. My question is not an excuse, it really is a question, and I certainly don't know the answer. But in the end, we always come back to the stark reality of that one child who is hurting, right here, right now.

Chapter 2: "Noodle Oracle"

For those not used to reading poetry, here is a 'translation': Close to midnight just before the new moon, a woman is eating a bowl of alphabet noodle soup. The woman wants more warmth and softness than the soup can give her; although old enough to wear a "lady outfit," she is longing for her mother. The letters in the soup seem like an oracle. It tells her that deep in her soul, she always wants more. She doesn't know whether she likes hearing this. She does want more, though — but more of what? The oracle reveals that she can have more but it's in "other forms," hinting there is more to life than food and regressing back to a childhood with an idealized mother. The woman pretends not to understand and that it's all just about food, but she knows that one day she won't be able to stand it anymore and then she will listen to the oracle again — because she does want more than food and yearning for mother. But for now, the coat, the soup, and the bed where she will soon sleep are enough.

In some ways, this is autobiographic. I have struggled with too much interest in food most of my life. Interestingly, about ten years after writing this poem, I took the bull by the horns, and today my relationship with food is much healthier. Yearning for the mother and "more" stand for the deep and complex origins and contexts of the overly developed interest in food.

This poem was first published in *isabella mori's teatable book* (Alphaglyph Publications, 2006).

Chapter 3: "Depressed"

This is in the Japanese form of haibun — a text of lyrical prose combined with haiku. Both haibun and haiku strive to use concrete imagery without getting philosophical. The reader is invited to draw their own conclusion. This, of course, is the case with any text, especially in fiction and poetry, but haibun and haiku place a special emphasis on this open-endedness. This is illustrated in Lucinda's response to the haibun. While I wrote it with a vague sense of wanting to get at the waxing and waning that happens in depression — not every moment is equally bleak — Lucinda focused on "But you will not burst" and took it as a springboard for musing on a positive thing: what has kept her from attempting suicide.

Ironically, from my point of view, the next sentence, "Even that cannot be done," is the lowest moment of the text, pointing to the sense of abject failure that can come with depression. When a reader takes something I have written to a totally different interpretation, I feel I have succeeded — they have made it their own.

My own context for this story is that, like so many people, I have also experienced depression. I have had times where I found it extremely difficult to go through the motions of getting out of bed, have blundered through the thick fog, have wondered how I made it out the door. These are not theoretical descriptions.

Chapter 4: "Balloons"

The reader, Eva, Barbara — everybody gets to be confused here. The reader is thrown right into a sort of word salad, Eva has a hard time finding words, and Barbara is confused because of the doubt she has about herself as a therapist. Confusion has been a constant companion in my life and, particularly, albeit to a small degree, the confusion Eva experiences around language. I often have a hard time retrieving the right word. I'll have a certain feeling, image, or knowing — but where the heck have they hidden the word for that?! Then it seems like there is a slow little old gnome inside me who goes rummaging for it, finally finds it, puts it in a little bucket, and laboriously hauls it up to my mouth, where it sometimes arrives way too late for my lips to utter — the conversation has already moved on.

The question is — what to do with this confusion? Eva bears it with remarkable grace and both she and Barbara have patience with it. And I have been given the gift of using it as a springboard for creativity but also as a way to help my clients be comfortable with uncertainty. Because with that comfort also comes the kind of openness for possibility and growth that we see developing in Eva's and Barbara's newly defined relationship.

Chapter 5: "To Smile at with a Nod"

This story began with a visit to Lund, a coastal village about 180 kilometres northwest of Vancouver, British Columbia. It has the interesting distinction of being the most northerly end of the Pan-American Highway, which reaches all the way down to the tip of Chile. It is there that I sat on the patio of a restaurant that inspired Martin's window and looked down to the harbour, where earlier I had seen a starfish. A melancholic feeling of loneliness is easily evoked in that neck of the woods and it soon combined with the bafflement I often feel that comes from wondering how anyone can ever learn all the incredibly intricate rituals, rules, and dances of relationships between human beings. It felt natural that the images appeared of people I know who are not neurotypical and who are even more baffled by these rituals and rules than I.

This is how stories and poems often develop for me: one little thing pops out — the starfish, in this case — and if I am receptive, it brings with it all sorts of other associations and connections and the text naturally fills out.

Chapter 6: "The Monastery"

I am intrigued by the mystery of the mundane and by randomness and events that are not neatly tied up. In this story, the driving force behind the monk's action is boredom and, when Blair shows up, he finally finds a way to amuse himself. Blair's apparent cure is a side product. A number of people who have read this story find Brother Sean, the monk, callous and the apparent cure unlikely. However, just like my other stories and poems, I am not attempting to tell morality tales or stories that illustrate a particular point — I am writing down what my muse gives me and, in this case, a series of random events: Blair happens to end up in the monastery, the monk happens to find his stash, happens to find relief for his boredom through putting Blair through a wild goose chase, and Blair happens to run and sweat his cravings out of his system. (Whether he is 'cured', nobody knows; many people with past addictions would say they are never completely cured and can't explain why their last attempt to overcome addiction seems to have worked and not others.) It is only after the main story is long over that it slowly dawns on Brother Sean that he might just have found a way to help a few more people.

Chapter 7: "Purgatory"

This story started in a course about depth psychology, where we looked at how we experience the mythical in our present lives. I immediately had an idea: the old hospital building where I worked was connected to other parts of the hospital through a series of dark, echoing tunnels, the likes of which would have set a great scene in any horror movie. The tunnel led to the part of the hospital that housed the psychiatric unit I visited the most, but finding that unit required the skills of an echolocating bat. It was easy to think of a mythical underworld and the metaphor of the purgatory just at the gates of hell felt very apt.

This story was first written as a lyrical poem. I turned it into a story but kept the poetic rhythm as much as possible, which is why you will find phrasing such as "He came in, hand broken, bloody with glass — the window he had jumped through. The window and the void beyond? Who knows."

A version of this story was published in 2021 in *Signs of Life*, a literary anthology themed around first- and second-hand experiences of illness and caregiving.

Chapter 8: "Pink Dragon"

I wrote this poem while sitting in a Chinese restaurant on Good Friday. While I was comfortably enjoying a meal by myself, I was aware of how many people hate eating alone. Out popped the image of a pink dragon sitting at a table all by themselves, silently crying. (The image was probably related to a children's show I had watched earlier that day.) Everyone is happy all around, but the pink dragon is a lonely alien, accepted because they will bring money, but otherwise ignored. I have often felt that way — related, perhaps, to growing up in a chaotic artists' family that was very different from everyone else's family I saw around me. Maybe my comfort with sitting alone in a Chinese restaurant has something to do with that — I'm just so used to it.

Chapter 9: "When the Doorbell Rings"

Many years ago, a friend of mine rang the doorbell of a woman he knew and when her boyfriend opened the door, my friend said that if he heard one more time of any abuse, he would kill the boyfriend. It so happens that my friend (fortunately?) did not follow through on his threat. As far as I know, the couple is still together and the abuse still continues, after all these decades. This is a 'what if' story — what if my friend had been more powerful, more authoritative? Or — what if someone as imposing as Michaela Arch had followed up on this fateful visit? In the beginning, Michaela had a different name, but slowly, as I kept working on this story, she evolved into an avenging angel, a dragonslayer.

What shines through in this story is my strong commitment to nonviolence, as well as a perhaps unfortunate tendency towards saviour fantasies.

This story was first published in 2019 in *Prachya Review*.

Chapter 10: "Bicycle Creatures"

"Bicycle Creatures" is a multi-layered story of magical realism (my favourite genre). Is it about Jules, half-bicycle, half-human? Is it about a magical melody that guides Jules to the person they are trying to find? Is it about the squalor of substance use, a mother's suffering, is it about hope? Something else entirely? As with all my stories and poems, I'm not interested in forcing the reader to follow my direction to a theme, moral, or conclusion. It makes me happy when it takes them to a place I had not thought of.

This story was first published in *English Bay Review* in 2020.

Chapter 11: Thank You: The Practice of Gratitude

This simple little poem expresses gratitude for water, fire, air, and earth — the four elements. Each element is connected to concrete experiences in my life: showers, laughter, wind, nurturing…

I consider myself very lucky to be someone for whom gratitude comes easily and plentiful. As the research shows, that is not the case for everyone and gratitude is not always positive. I definitely also have experience with that: I was one of those women whose abusive partner always wanted to be thanked. For some reason, neither that nor my German-Russian grandmother's admonition to compare my life to those of "the poor soldiers in Siberia" when I felt I was hard done by kept me from enjoying gratitude. Something to be thankful for!

ABOUT THE AUTHOR

Isabella Mori, M.Ed, writes novels, short fiction, poetry, and nonfiction, and is the author of three books of and about poetry, including *A bagful of haiku — 87 imperfections*. Poetry and short fiction have appeared in publications such as *Kingfisher*, *Signs of Life*, and *The Group of Seven Reimagined*. They also hold a bachelor's degree in psychology from Simon Fraser University.

An alum of SFU's The Writers Studio, Mori is the founder of Muriel's Journey Poetry Prize which celebrates socially engaged poetry. They were a writer-in-residence at the Historic Joy Kogawa House.

Isabella looks back on a thirty-year career as a counsellor. During this time, they wrote for and co-edited *Family Connections*, a newsletter for people touched by mental health and addiction.

They live on the unceded traditional and ancestral lands of the Musqueam, Squamish, and Tsleil-Watuth nations, aka Vancouver, BC.

www.ingramcontent.com/pod-product-compliance
Lightning Source LLC
Chambersburg PA
CBHW070101030426
42335CB00016B/1964